And Here the World Ends

And Here the World Ends

THE LIFE OF AN ARGENTINE VILLAGE

Kristin Hoffman Ruggiero

STANFORD UNIVERSITY PRESS
STANFORD, CALIFORNIA
1988

Stanford University Press
Stanford, California
© 1988 by the Board of Trustees of the
Leland Stanford Junior University
Printed in the United States of America

CIP data appear at the end of the book

Published with the assistance
of the Andrew W. Mellon Foundation

For Guido

Acknowledgments

Contemplating this book's history brings to mind the many friends I have made through its writing—people from two continents where the book was researched and a third where it was written.

I want first to thank the subjects of the book, the people of San Sebastiano and La Paz. Having concealed their identities in the text, I cannot reveal them here, but each name in the Glossary of Names represents someone who has had a very special place in the making of this book. Few people can have been so warm and helpful to an outsider; they are a testimony to what is good in Argentina and the Argentines. And in Italy, in the Waldensian Valleys, people were also interested in my work, and provided me with the background for understanding Italian emigration to Argentina.

At the various research facilities I used—in La Paz, Paraná, and Buenos Aires in Argentina, and in Torre Pellice and Pinerolo in Italy—the patience of many archivists, librarians, and public officials was tried, and triumphed. I thank them all.

John V. Lombardi has been a constant source of encouragement and a perceptive reader of the manuscript from its beginning. I regret that James R. Scobie could not have read this final product of my adoption into a country he loved; I think he would have liked the human perspective of the result. In addition to colleagues at Indiana University, the Institute for Advanced Study in Princeton, the University of Tennessee, the University of Cincinnati, St. Lawrence University, and Syracuse University in Florence, who have assisted me along the way, I especially thank Samuel L. Baily for his thoughtful reading of the manuscript and his suggestions. Norris Pope at Stanford University Press has, throughout, been a most enthusiastic and sensitive friend and reader.

Grants from the Organization of American States provided the means for my two stays in Argentina in 1976–77 and 1981. Thanks are also due to the *Journal of Interamerican Studies and World Affairs* for permission to quote from "Gringo and Creole: Foreign and Native Values in a Rural Argentine Community." All translations (unless otherwise noted) and errors are my own; any similarity to names of actual persons and places is coincidental.

Finally, it has all been made possible and worthwhile by the person to whom this book is dedicated.

K.H.R.

Contents

Foreword

I arrived in Argentina in September of 1976, as winter reluctantly gave way to spring and as the military junta that had recently overthrown Isabel Perón tightened its repressive grip. One of the western hemisphere's potentially richest and most important countries, Argentina has become part of daily parlance through strangely fragmented and contradictory glimpses provided by the musical *Evita*, the Malvinas (Falklands) conflict, and reports on its foreign debt or the fate of the "disappeared." I headed north from Buenos Aires to the town of La Paz, in the province of Entre Ríos. It had been a difficult trip because well-meaning people along the way had been sure that I really meant to go to La Paz, Bolivia. No one, least of all a foreigner, went to La Paz in Entre Ríos. And that was not my final destination. I was headed for one of the colonies surrounding La Paz. Colonia San Sebastiano is an agricultural complex of village and farms, at once a part of the prairie environs of La Paz and yet separate from it. Its approximately one thousand inhabitants call both the farms, in distinction from the village, and the total complex "colony," a term reflecting the community's early days as a new settlement. My purpose was to write a history of the colony and its environs, which are peopled with descendants of nineteenth- and early-twentieth-century Spanish, French, British, and German immigrants, as well as a sizable group of "native" Argentines or creoles, that is, people of very old Argentine stock. The dominant group, socially and economically, are the descendants of Italian immigrants, especially a little-known Protestant sect called the Waldenses.

Before my arrival in Argentina, I had spent several months in the Italian heartland of the Waldensian religion, in Torre Pellice in the province of Turin. Waldenses emigrated from Italy chiefly to Argen-

tina and Uruguay, but Waldensian communities are also found elsewhere in North and South America. Indeed, my connection with
the Waldenses had begun in a North American town, Valdese,
North Carolina, in the foothills of the Smoky Mountains, an area
reminiscent of the Italian-French Alps where Waldenses have lived,
originally as a heretical group, since the twelfth century. The friendships I made with Waldenses in Valdese and in Italy gave me the first
of those family connections that were to prove so useful in Argentina. While in Italy I wrote to several Waldensian pastors in Argentina (and in Uruguay, since I could not be assured at that time of
being allowed into Argentina), asking them for assistance and suggestions. One reply stood out from the rest: the pastor of La Paz
and San Sebastiano was clearly interested in my project. These Waldenses were the first to receive me into the community—to house
me, to introduce me to others, and to "make known" to me, as they
put it, their world.

What ultimately led me to Colonia San Sebastiano was my historian's interest in a community that had immigrated to South America more or less as a group, but I quickly found that very little written history was left in the colony. At first this caused frustration.
Slowly, though, I came to realize that the most important record of
the period of immigration and colonization still remained, namely,
the area's inhabitants. As I worked through the materials available
in La Paz, and later through those in the provincial and national
archives and public offices of Paraná and Buenos Aires, I realized
just how valuable my time spent in the colony had been. What the
inhabitants had identified as important in their colony's history
made only an occasional, implicit appearance in the surviving historical records.

People in the colony and La Paz were not themselves too concerned about the lack of documentation for their history. After all,
they were used to the fact that, because public offices were often in
private homes, old records had to be tossed out every so often to
make space for a new child or an ailing grandmother. But they sym-
pathized with my dilemma and, perhaps because of this, tried to
draw my attention to their more contemporary history.

By the end of my first stay in Argentina, I realized that the contemporary history of the colony and town would make a good
book, and after a second trip in 1981 I hoped that I could write it.
A town unknown even to most Argentines, and an even more ob-

scure colony, located in one of Argentina's less progressive provinces, a province only marginally part of the famous pampas (Argentina's grain and cattle-raising region), far from the awesome Andes and austere Patagonia—why did I think they would interest English-speaking readers? It seemed to me that in this small, isolated community much of the history and present-day tensions, conflicts, and successes of rural Argentina came together on a direct and human level. It did not matter that this community was not the most typical one in Argentina or indeed that Argentina is not wholly typical of Latin America. What mattered was that this community allowed me to present a people's vision of themselves and of their country, and to re-create life as it is being lived in contemporary Argentina.

Because one of my goals was to let the community speak for itself, I have tried to keep myself out of the text. Of course, it would be misleading and absurd to claim that the book was written without me, but perhaps a word is in order on my position in the book, as author and recorder and as a visitor to the community.

I have mentioned that I originally went to La Paz and Colonia San Sebastiano for reasons other than those that eventually led me to write this book—as a historian of the past. But to the Waldenses I was an acquaintance (and sometimes a friend) of relatives in North America and Italy. By the community at large I was considered to suffer from the same malady as the newspaper reporter cum local historian of La Paz—a penchant for history and old documents. People did not consider me a scientist involved in a quest for interviews. I did ask many questions, and people volunteered information to me, but we related more as friends than as investigator and subject; I was not thought to be trying to elicit responses. Actually, I did not have to try. Information came my way quite naturally through my position as participant-observer—to use the methodological term that most closely describes my position in the community. My follow-up questions to people's remarks seemed natural reactions rather than probings. Whatever this approach may have lost in its lack of order, I think it gained back in the rapport established with the people involved. When I returned to the community in 1981, I had no trouble asking direct questions about contemporary society. My wanting to know the community better was taken as a compliment by everyone, except, that is, the ever-suspicious police, who "invited" me in for questioning and, finding me interested only in a small rural community in a way that seemed insignificant to them, released me.

To protect villagers and townspeople, I have had to fictionalize the names of people and places and have occasionally had to fashion composite characters, but the conversations and scenes in this book are records of what was actually said and actually occurred, rather than of the merely probable. (A few names have changed in archival and bibliographical references as well; I will be glad to provide the actual names to researchers.) I have not hesitated to put quotation marks around people's words, which I heard and recorded in journals. Though I have sometimes condensed the results of several conversations into single discussions, I have preserved the words and speech patterns of my informants. The important point is that none of the book is fabricated.

If my early association with the Waldenses was ever a factor in my relationship with non-Waldenses, it did not remain one. My contacts came to extend far beyond the Waldenses during both my visits. As the reader will discover, several people spoke critically in my presence about the Waldenses, and Waldenses frankly criticized each other. The Glossary of Names at the end of the book is not therefore a "Who's Who" of Waldenses or of important people, but rather it represents all the variety of the region—in religion, in socioeconomic class, in gender and age, and in ethnic background. There is political variety too, but it is much more difficult to report, since people could not voice their politics openly at the time. In any case, politics in an area so far removed from the national and even from the provincial political scene has a different quality from that in cities.

In the lives of these people, as in all people's lives, there is both good and bad, hope and sadness. I try to present both. Lest the result somehow be misinterpreted as a defense of human misery, underdevelopment, or the former military government, let me explain that, as much as I like Argentina, Argentines, and Entrerrianos, my visits to the Republic included many moments of depression and despair: it was an often brutal and black period of military dictatorship. Yet there were other factors too—a family's closeness, one person's humor, another's goodwill and strength—and it is this particular mix that I hope to convey in my book.

And Here the World Ends, as a title, reflects the rich ambiguity of Colonia San Sebastiano's place in the world as perceived by its people. I first noted it as a passing remark in a conversation with a well-educated and fairly prosperous descendant of European immigrants. In this context, it seemed an explanation for why this man, with so many other possibilities and a full and frank awareness of San Sebastiano and La Paz's isolation and limits, had decided to live his life there. He seemed to be saying that for him as a member of this community, the world really ended at its boundaries. I thought it might indicate a defensiveness, but with time I came to realize the richness of the vision: the sense of a community that stressed building and supporting within itself and took the relationships found there as an end in themselves. Even as I began to understand the remark in its positive aspects, I became aware also of a negative side. For there was no denying that this community was virtually a forgotten one at the edge of the Western world. Newspapers, television, radio, government, and the whole apparatus of Western culture informed these people that they were politically, economically, culturally, and physically at the end of the world. Thus, "end" as self-contained community and "end" as isolated and marginal one co-existed in people's self-perception. As such, this phrase, neither so innocent nor so simple as it at first sounded, seemed a particularly evocative title.

The question then arises, Are we to regard this community as an anomaly? I think not. While it may not be typical of Argentina, it does exemplify an important type of community in the countryside of the Republic. Rural Argentina is dotted with such towns, villages, and colonies of nineteenth-century vintage that either flourished as expansions of already-established towns or sprang into being during the Republic's mass immigration and colonization movements. Moreover, anyone familiar with the legacies of this period in the other areas of the Southern Cone, namely, Uruguay, southern Brazil, and Chile, will recognize in La Paz and San Sebastiano the traits of rural immigrant settlements elsewhere.

Furthermore, in depicting the character of this community, I hope to show something of what it has meant to be Argentine in recent decades. The inhabitants of this community reflect the ethnic and religious diversity of Argentina in general. Nearly one-third of Argentina's population is either Italian or of Italian descent; people of German, British, and Spanish backgrounds are also important, Protestant and Catholic alike. La Paz and Colonia San Sebastiano affirm this diversity. Yet even in their isolation the people here share popular national concerns such as the sovereignty of the Malvinas Islands. Although townspeople and villagers are content to remain near their birthplace, they have a broader perspective and speak about their individual socioeconomic positions being affected by Ronald Reagan, John D. Rockefeller, and Milton Friedman. They try to manipulate their bank accounts to obtain the best interest rate just like the *porteños*, the inhabitants of Buenos Aires, but continue to keep a secondary savings account in a shoebox at home. While many are descendants of Europeans, and some still speak their family's native tongue after four generations, they share with natives an enjoyment of horseracing in the countryside, drinking the strong tea called maté, and participating in contemporary "gaucho" life.

The distance of La Paz from major cities did not protect its inhabitants from the heavy hand of the military government in the 1970's and early 1980's or from a paranoia perhaps even greater than was felt by porteños: in a small community people felt more exposed. Still, isolation and size had their effect on the community. In Colonia San Sebastiano, for example, the head of the local junta was affectionately nicknamed "the father of the village." But while La Paz and Colonia San Sebastiano are interesting for their unique features—insofar as they are a little less progressive than some communities, and a little more isolated, Italian, and Protestant than others—they are also interesting for what they reveal about the general Argentine situation. I hope they will interest specialists, both Latin Americanists and Europeanists, concerned with the structures underlying life at the village and family levels, with the relationship between local and national society, and with the place of a small community within the larger world picture.

And Here the World Ends is also written for those with little or no knowledge of Latin America, those who know nothing of how people in contemporary rural Latin America live or of what they think and say. With those readers in mind, I have fashioned the book as a kind of narrative, and I have tried to write prose that is free of jargon, eschewing paradigms such as "modernization" that do not fit the situation. Using everyday language, I hope to give life to small town and village society and to allow the community to speak to the reader directly. The notes that accompany the text are intended to provide a fuller historical context, further information, and a degree of interpretation, but the text (and La Paz and Colonia

San Sebastiano) can to a large extent be enjoyed and understood without them. I have tried to present a background and to let the people present their society to the reader as they presented it to me. In turn, I hope the reader will find the people and society as rich, complex, and interesting as I did.

And Here the World Ends

Introduction:
The Land and Its People

THE MORNING SUNLIGHT spreads over the land from the east, giving substance to the shapes of the prairie. It brings the small village of San Sebastiano into view over one of the many undulations of surrounding land. It flits among the tree branches overhanging the Posadas River, intermittently lighting up patches of dark water. It casts shadows along the road into the village, dallying at the Baridon dispensary, and slides up on Miguel Moreno's old dog rounding the far side of a hut, a *rancho*. It strays in and out of the corners of courtyards. Suddenly it etches in its slanting rays a woman carrying a large tin; it is Teresa de González on her way to the well. Resting for a moment on the wet pasture, it notes with satisfaction the first stirrings of day.

It could be any day in 1981. Since the coup of March 1976 the military's campaign against the Left and attempts to stabilize the country have only plunged Argentina deeper into political chaos and economic and moral depression. There is a new president this year, Roberto Eduardo Viola, and a new one in the United States, Ronald Reagan, who will ease the pressure on Argentina to improve its human rights record. In Buenos Aires the Mothers of the Plaza de Mayo keep up their vigil for the 20,000 to 30,000 people who "disappeared," victims of the post-coup anti-Left campaign: but economic concerns have eclipsed political ones. Inflation that will eventually reach 800 percent, the highest in the world, has brought about the collapse of many businesses and has increased unemployment. Many of the external pressures placed on the country as a result of its foreign debt, the third-largest per capita in the world, have led to a depression of wages, a limiting of job opportunities, and a general impoverishment of life for the poor.

Until the 1930's Argentina was a dynamic country, equal to Canada in its economic and cultural development. The splendid architectural style of Buenos Aires' buildings, the city's broad boulevards, its cultural life, earned it comparison with Paris. But today the streets are crowded with homicidal bus drivers whose need to garner additional fares overrides any concern for pedestrians, with people demanding news of political prisoners, with lines of panicked investors at banks. A sleepy pajama-clad boy is bustled into a car at seven in the morning to spend the day in his parents' office because there is no money for child-care. His sister comes home at noon to make her own lunch because there is no money for her to eat at school. Their parents get by with loans from friends. They have been living this way for some years. Now, though they are middle class, they may have to join the poor in raiding the municipal waste cans for food. The question of what has gone wrong in Argentina overwhelms all others. The soot that has hung heavy over Buenos Aires for years, an annoyance but a symbol of the city's place in the modern world, now seems merely to echo the current bleakness and confusion. Yet the thought of revolution has somehow passed Argentines by: they are beyond it, ready for a return to normalcy. It is the beginning of the decade in which the junta has promised to hold elections, and it is hoped that the economy has reached its nadir.

If people could have looked ahead, though, they would have seen the economic crisis worsening and, in March 1982, their country entering a war with Great Britain over the Malvinas Islands. Argentine sovereignty over the islands had long been a unifying, patriotic issue, and analysts speculated that the war was designed as a distraction from the economy. But Argentina lost the war. In October 1983 the military at last permitted a general election, and a civilian government was elected, headed by Raúl Alfonsín, the Radical Party candidate. This would perhaps mark a real change in Argentina, since it would be the first time in forty years that the Peronists had lost an election, and the first time since 1930 that the Radicals, a conservative, middle-class party, had won. But this change lies in the future.

*

Teresa de González of San Sebastiano has not escaped the human tragedy of the 1970's, the stagnation and even elimination of life, but she goes on. This makes us curious about her world. What reason does she have for going on? What is the basis for her hope? Or is it the inertia of frustrated hopes? Her world begins in the province of Entre Ríos, a very different place from downtown Buenos Aires—from the windows of Harrods department store, from the crowds of stylishly dressed office workers at the fast food shops on Florida Street, from the lines of taxis taking important people to the government offices flanking the Plaza de Mayo. Entre Ríos lies north of the province of Buenos Aires and east of Santa Fe, and has a population of about 900,000. This northeast section of the country, which also includes the provinces of Corrientes and Misiones, has a reputation for being more isolated and backward than Buenos Aires or Santa Fe.

It is easy to perceive Entre Ríos this way because the province is located, as its name states, between two rivers, the Uruguay and the Paraná. The Uruguay River separates Uruguay and Argentina, with only two bridges crossing it from Entre Ríos. The Paraná, one of the main arteries of southern South America, was "bridged" only in the early 1970's, by an underwater tunnel linking Paraná, the capital city of Entre Ríos, to Santa Fe. The engineering of the tunnel was difficult, since the Paraná is impressively wide—in places a person standing on its banks can barely discern the islands in the middle where cattle graze, much less the opposite shore. Before the tunnel was built, the rivers enveloping this mesopotamia served more to obstruct than to aid contact with other regions. Car ferries had crossed the river since the 1930's, replacing the old steamboats and barges, but there were too few of them, and trucks often waited in line for days to cross the river, causing long delays in deliveries to the towns of the province. Teresa has seen the Paraná but has never crossed it.

At one point in Entre Ríos' history, its isolation became an advantage, when Paraná served as the hub of a renegade national government in the 1850's and 1860's, challenging Buenos Aires' domination of the Republic. As recently as the 1930's it was home to further protests against centralized government, by local strongmen, or *caudillos*. On the other hand, much of Entre Ríos is prime agricultural land and it attracted a good deal of the immigration and colonization movement of the nineteenth century, the western part of the province in particular. This area is on the edge of the Argentine pampas, the country's fertile grain and cattle region, but its land is more rolling, humid, and florid than the heart of the pampas.

The place Teresa knows best in this province is San Sebastiano with its thousand inhabitants, a community settled during the immigration and colonization period when Europeans came to Argentina in large numbers to become farmers and landowners in the new agricultural colonies. From the paved road a mile to the west, San Sebastiano would be unseen by a rapid passerby. If he were to catch a glimpse of the village, it would be of short *ñandubay* trees, tall grasses, and low buildings, all at a uniform height as if in a conscious design to harmonize man and nature. There would be no reason for him to stop there. Nothing beckons—no gas stations, no signs advertising restaurants or stores, almost no one to ask directions from. The road into the colony might well be flooded anyway, which is enough to turn away even some trucks. Besides, a passerby would know that La Paz is just down the road.

La Paz, the nearest town to San Sebastiano, is the department (county) seat; with a population of about 19,000, it qualifies as a city. In fact, almost 70 percent of the department's total population of 58,000 in 1980 was considered urban. Besides La Paz, the department includes Santa Elena, with 15,600 inhabitants, and Bovril, with 5,000. The department is essentially rural, however, and though La Paz may qualify as a city, it is of another order than, for example, Buenos Aires, which has more in common in many ways with New York City.

The dawn in La Paz rolls back the formless cover of night clouds to reveal a sky more vast than the land in which even a town of 19,000 is lost on the horizon. As the passerby is admitted beyond the police barrier, the sun lights up this once-thriving port town, now waking to the Coca Cola truck's clatter, a horse's steady clip-clop, the shouts of children on their way to school. There is a new eight-story apartment building, with shops underneath, facing the central square, several paved streets, some hotels and cafés. Down by the river are tourist cabins for fishermen and a park with a museum. But the way of life and the values in La Paz are linked to its surrounding countryside, that is, the *campo* of San Sebastiano, and much of the two communities' population overlaps.

The road takes our passerby on to Paraná, the provincial capital, three hours to the south. There is nothing along the road except a few low buildings, one gas station–café, and prairie. Paraná, with its 200,000 inhabitants, is noticeably different from what has gone before. Its center bustles with activity, a Cathedral looks out on the main square, a luxury hotel (built to capitalize on tourist traffic brought by the new tunnel) overlooks the river, restaurants offer the *asado* of roasted beef and the *dorado* fish, a fancy store carries imported fashions. There is another side to Paraná, however. Much of the population dines out at modest eating clubs and lives in simple homes; the city's paved streets turn quickly to dirt roads outside the center; and the downtown is silent and dark by nine at night. Ten more hours and the passerby can be in Buenos Aires.

For Teresa, however, all of this matters little. She seldom goes to La Paz, and has never been to Paraná or Buenos Aires, even though it no longer takes days to get to these places. The world in some senses is only potentially more accessible for Teresa. But San Sebastiano offers her a sense of belonging to a wider world, without the loss of customs and a familiar lifestyle. People say their world ends at the edge of their yards, yet their world includes elements from a wider one.

If the passerby had stopped in San Sebastiano, what would he have learned? He would have found that the people there embody what is right and wrong with Argentina, good and bad, happy and sad. They are vulnerable to political and economic crises, aware of their inability to change anything, and yet resilient and interesting. They make us want to understand this aspect of their lives—how their crises have not totally quashed their humanity, how the influence of the Western, industrialized world has left what is special about their lives unchanged. As members of the "modern" world, we are well known to them. They know about our comforts and gadgetry, but do not have them or necessarily even want them. They know about our Western democracy, but have lived in a military state for eight years and have even learned to joke about it. They know about the organization of our society, but ingeniously cope with its absence in their own. They know the same things we do, yet they are different. Though one cannot claim that they are typical of all of rural Argentina, the inhabitants of San Sebastiano do live a life common to the people who reside outside the major cities.

*

There was hardly anyone abroad in the village when Teresa was setting off to the well. When she awoke, her children were still asleep and her husband was away working at Baltasar Koenig's ranch, his *estancia*. She awoke, rather, with the chickens, which moved with ease between the yard and the rancho. The earth served the house for a floor and the yard served as a kitchen, so that the family and the chickens held these spaces in common. Except for the animal sounds it was quiet. On the road to the well Teresa heard a truck go by on the highway, and someone's radio. It was so still that the suddenness with which Miguel Moreno on his horse rounded his rancho and the speed at which Eduardo Howard drove his Citroën through the village were noticeable for their abrupt intrusion into this world of slower motions. The tempo of the village must not lull one into thinking that little is happening, however, or that emotions do not run strong. Teresa is quietly involved, with the land, with her family, with her friends, and with all that these mean. Like her village, she seems understated, by nature fading into her environment. One might therefore suppose that she is difficult to know. It is true that San Sebastiano and its people do not lend themselves to casual observation from afar. On the other hand, the life of the community seems more vivid for its rural setting; there is time to observe more because life passes by more slowly and in more discrete units.

Small though San Sebastiano is, it has two parts: a village and a colony. There is a certain unity between the two. The colony contains the farms of San Sebastiano, about thirty of them, and the village is the commercial and service center of the colony, though when Teresa stands in the middle of the village she is in a cow pasture. Looking north, she sees the Cerutti general store and bar on her right and the hospital—really a home for the elderly—on her left; to the south, the police station and the now unused Waldensian church. Immediately to the right of the cow pasture are the school and the town hall; to the left, the Catholic church and the Gilly general store. Almost out of sight are several more stores and a couple of bars, but Teresa has no trouble distinguishing these buildings from the tall grasses and scrub trees because she knows they are there. If she had been standing in this spot eighty years ago, her view would also have taken in a flour mill, the sumptuous two-story chalet of the administrator of the colony, and a hotel and restaurant. Teresa does not know that the cow pasture was to have been the central plaza; that in San Sebastiano's urban plan the dirt roads criss-crossing the village have names like Bunge Avenue and Schiele Avenue; that the fields apparently challenging the space of the village's few buildings were to have been city-like blocks full of houses, thirteen by ten blocks in all. But the colony and the village never reached this level of distinctiveness.

San Sebastiano did not get off to a good start. Within a few years of its founding in 1888, its first colonists, from Baradero in the province of Buenos Aires, began to desert it. For others, though, the landscape of fields and ranchos had become home, and they stayed on. They tended to be mainly native or creole people, and their descendants still distinguish themselves from the immigrants or gringos. Soon after San Sebastiano's abortive beginning, other groups of immigrants picked up where those from Baradero had left off. Among them were French, Germans, Russians, Italian Catholics, and the group that was to become dominant in San Sebastiano and make it a success, Italian Protestants of the Waldensian sect. But it might seem a limited success.

San Sebastiano had been founded with its destiny planned. Like other agricultural colonies established during and since Argentina's immigration and colonization period, from the last quarter of the nineteenth century to the years preceding World War I, the village of San Sebastiano was to have expanded, filled out its allotted space, and prospered. The villages of this epoch developed in various ways. Some now resemble abandoned movie sets through which the world passed only briefly. San Sebastiano is one of these, a relic of a more prosperous time when Bunge and Born, its founding company, still orchestrated the burgeoning colony, when the mill flourished, the hotel was full, and commercial and building activity was intense. Between 1894 and 1900 drought and locusts, the scourges of the pampas farmers, attacked the infant colony. Later the mill closed, and Bunge and Born, today an international corporation with offices in Buenos Aires, New York City, and Antwerp, eventually pulled out.

Teresa knows of these historical landmarks: the failure of the mill, the selling out of Bunge and Born, the removal of the railroad. But the more important events in her vision of the past were those of the 1970's: the coming of electricity, though her rancho does not have it; the building of more wells in the village; the linking of San Sebastiano to La Paz by bus; the transfer of the La Paz hospital out toward San Sebastiano. She sees not what the village might have been, but what it is. She has a home near her parental family; her husband has work; her children are getting an education; and she is learning to sew at Iolanda Avondet de Gilly's house.* It is a pleasant village where people share much the same kind of life regardless of class, ethnic background, and values, where social relationships are, at least on the surface, amicable and life has a social evenness. She is pleased to see laborers and landowners get along so well most of the time. There is Iolanda's husband Tullio Gilly, for example, the secretary of the government junta, a gringo—they call him "the father of the village" because he takes care of everything. He's always working down in drainage ditches or up on rooftops. Then there's Miriam de Barea, that shrewd toothy old creole woman, so sharp she's a match even for Tullio. She embarrasses him when she won't let him go on about how poor he is—Tullio in his comfortable new house and she in her rancho! Or Don Eduardo—bless him!—son of the British estanciero and now in his eighties, still making the village laugh as he races his car down San Sebastiano's two and a half miles of asphalt.

In a word, San Sebastiano is a place that seems, even in its uniqueness—its people, particular setting, and history—representative of rural Argentina and, to a lesser extent, of rural Latin America in general. The goal of this book is to examine the form taken by familiar themes, values, and institutions in an environment small enough to make them discernible in their human context. There is no Middletown in Latin America, but a Latin American visitor to San Sebastiano would find much that is familiar there. He would recognize the relentlessly demanding immediacy of the rural environment, the animal sounds and smells, the pace of life—much of it still not very different from the early days of the colony described by the old-timers in Chapter 1. If the visitor were from the Southern Cone of Latin America or another area shaped by European immigration, he would also find familiar the European origins of much of the population and a past colored by the nineteenth-century immigration and colonization movements. He would recognize the agri-

---

* I have rendered the surnames of married women in two ways: the husband's surname preceded by "de" and the woman's maiden name (Iolanda Avondet de Gilly), or the husband's surname preceded by "de" alone (Teresa de González). I have not included maiden names for all the women in the book. Women do sometimes use their husband's surname without "de," but I have avoided this usage for clarity's sake: a woman identified in the text by a surname without "de" is unmarried.

cultural basis of the community discussed in Chapter 2, empathizing with its problems and perhaps finding himself struck by the particular relationship between San Sebastiano and its nearest urban neighbor, La Paz. Though in many ways particular to the area, the strategies for surviving the current economic crisis of Argentina would also strike a familiar chord, if only in terms of people's surprising adaptability in times of hardship. At first the mixture of society, presented in Chapter 3, might seem strange—creoles, gringos, and outsiders, landowners and peons, Catholics and non-Catholics, country and town people—but the integration of these disparate elements through a commitment to public honor and social place would seem quite natural. In the same way, although the particular institutions of government, health, education, and the media, discussed in Chapter 4, might seem an anomalous miscellany, our hypothetical Latin American visitor would recognize the personalized world behind the institutions of San Sebastiano. Finally, he would be accustomed to the particular relationship between family and community discussed in Chapter 5, though again, he might find many of its details strange and even alien.

Although at first distracted by the uniqueness of San Sebastiano, this visitor would in time recognize the people and the broad themes and conflicts of their lives. Explaining San Sebastiano to a European or North American, he would want to convey the satisfaction of that existence without allowing a romantic conception of rural life to circumscribe and idealize lives that are much more complex. He would want to explain how these people, seemingly so willing to embrace the urban Western world, are actually willing to do so only on their own terms. And although he might sometimes be able to view these people in terms of some formal theory or model, he would want to stress the rich complexity of their lives; for they deserve the dignity of their individuality. In sum, an observer who stopped to examine the apparently uninteresting rural landscape and discover its people would find that they in their individual lives and vision give a personal context to broader themes of life in Argentina, and indeed in the great part of the world at the edge of Western civilization.

Their story is bittersweet. Sewage and sanitation conditions are poor, education is minimal, economic opportunity is limited, even for the hardest-working, and infant and child mortality is high. Much has been said about these aspects of Latin American life, and this book does not neglect them. The "sweet" of the story, however, will perhaps force us to consider more closely how success and failure, the bitter and the sweet, are judged in modern times. This should not be read as an explanation or apology for what is wrong in Argentina. The world of the people of San Sebastiano lies where the larger world ends; this book attempts to examine that world on its own terms and, by extension, to discern some of the themes of rural life in Latin America writ small.

ONE

━━━━━━◆◆◆━━━━━━

The Beginnings of the "End"

THE MORNING was getting warmer. Cumulus clouds were piling up on the horizon. Toni (Antonio) Howard turned across a field, zig-zagging over a ridge of rocks and dodging low branches. The horse stumbled and Toni had to shift his weight quickly to avoid the nasty thorns of the *palo borracho* tree. Straight ahead, the land dipped down to a stream bed in a ravine. Riding up the other side, he crested a knoll and looked down on the tiny dot in the distance that was the main shed of his paternal estancia. "When my parents sent me to an English school in Buenos Aires, I missed this place," he recalled. "I lived with relatives, but it wasn't the same. One of my best friends lived over that way; his father worked for us for many years. I had almost no contact with anyone except my family and the people who worked on our estancia. My family meant home and community to me—the world ended at the border of my fa-ther's estancia." Toni sat looking for a while, then turned around and headed back. The picnic would be starting soon.

It was October; the first quickening of spring had touched the campo, and with it came the annual Waldensian spring picnic. The Waldenses, Protestant immigrants from Italy, have become the most successful members of San Sebastiano. Toni, though a Lutheran, at-tends their activities regularly, partly as a fellow Protestant without a local church, partly as a scion of one of the most important fami-lies in the community. The picnic always attracts a large crowd. All the Waldenses turn out, including many from nearby La Paz, along with many family friends and a large number of children from the community as a whole. It is more than just a picnic. Like many such annual events, it is a time for the major figures of the community to come together and quietly celebrate their successes, restating their shared values and visions. Much of this aspect of the picnic is dominated by the old-timers of the community and their remembrances of times past—remembrances that, accurate or not, still in many ways shape the present of San Sebastiano.[1]

Toni rode back to his father's ranch to exchange his horse for the car and drive his parents, Eduardo Howard and Lora Muir de Howard, to the picnic. Their memories focused on the good fortune and hard work that had earned them a place among the "aristocracy" of San Sebastiano. Eduardo's father, of Scottish origin, was a landowner, colony official, and physician in the early days of San Sebastiano. Fortune played a role in the beginning. After encountering difficulties in Uruguay, his original destination, the elder Howard took a boat to Argentina, where he had decided to buy land. This was in the late 1880's. One of his fellow passengers happened to be Eduardo Schiele, the administrator of San Sebastiano, and the two got to talking. It turned out that the elder Howard knew more about farming than Schiele did, so Schiele offered him the job of secretary of San Sebastiano. When the crops failed and prices dropped in the 1890's, Schiele sold off a good amount of land and the elder Howard bought some of it. Since Howard had studied medicine at Edinburgh, he automatically became the colony's unofficial physician and dentist.

Throughout San Sebastiano and La Paz the promise of the picnic gathering had animated the Waldensian community. Even at Carlos Baridon-Charbonier's house in La Paz, preparations were coming to a head. He was ninety and had to be helped to the car. As an old-timer, he would not miss this day in his campo, the chance to see again how the fields looked and the opportunity to reminisce about the difficulties of the good old days. Lidia, his sixty-year-old daughter, returned to the house to find her father a wool shawl. He had been unwell the past few years; otherwise he would never have moved to La Paz. Indeed, he did not move all the way into the center of town, but bought a home on the outskirts—one of those houses built for the railroad workers in the presidency of Juan Perón in the 1940's and 1950's. Carlos was a key figure for the Waldensian community in San Sebastiano, his father having been the first Waldensian colonist. People like the Howards, and even the Bunges, who were San Sebastiano's colonization company, were sympathetic to the Waldenses.

Toni's grandfather had heard about the Waldenses when he was still in Europe; they had appealed to other Protestants for help from time to time. They were an old sect, and had been persecuted as heretics since the twelfth century for lay preaching and for rejecting orthodox doctrines. After the Reformation they associated themselves with the Protestant movement. It was not until 1848 that, by decree of King Charles Albert, they were granted religious and civil freedom. Even that made little difference for them economically and socially, since they were confined by custom and social pressure to the poorest farming land in their Waldensian Valleys—the Pellice, Germanasca, and Chisone—which lie about fifty miles southwest of Turin in the French-Italian Alps. Then the crops were bad, too, and when news began to circulate about South America, Waldenses began emigrating to Argentina and Uruguay.[2]

Carlos's father, Enrique Baridon, was the first Waldense to come to San Sebastiano. He came in 1888 from Villar Pellice, spent a year or so in La Plata, returned to Villar to marry Inés Charbonier, then re-emigrated, taking Inés and three of his brothers with him. They began as farmers, in Rosario; when there were strikes, they went to La Paz; and then in 1891 they moved to San Sebastiano to do carpentry work in the new colony. Others followed Enrique's example, and they continued to immigrate until the early twentieth century. They tended to intermarry and to have large families (Carlos Baridon-Charbonier had fifteen children) with the result that there are now some three hundred Baridons in San Sebastiano. There are almost as many Prochets, and a substantial number of Gillys—all Waldenses. In fact, the Waldensian population has risen since 1900 from 13 percent to about 75 percent of the colony's total population. They dominate the village, too, though not numerically, and are very important in La Paz.[3]

In San Sebastiano, Italo Gilly and his wife Inés had risen early so that Inés could prepare a chicken for their picnic lunch. It was a special day, after all, so why not have something besides beef for a change? Beef is such a staple of the average diet that Waldenses, like other Argentines, often suffer from protein-related heart disease—victims, in a sense, of the wealth of the land. Italo had his maté, and then went into his store in the front of the house to select a new cravat.[4] He wanted to look especially good because he was hosting the picnic on his land. Inés needed some lard and asked him to go to his sister Fita's dispensary to get it. Fita was busy getting the children ready, so he went over to his brother Tullio's house. The three families live within a few blocks of each other. Tullio's lot, because it is the family's original property, reflects the interests and development of the Waldensian landowners in San Sebastiano, and reveals much of the essence of the colony's hundred-year history. The paternal family's spacious two-story home with its delicate latticework is still standing. Most of it is abandoned and empty, though, and one entire room has been carefully dismantled, its building materials destined to be used one day by Tullio's informally adopted son, who is away on military service. What was once the enormous living room has been cleared of debris and is used by Tullio's wife Iolanda for her sewing class. Around in back is a rancho for a former peon. In a nearby field is a zinc-covered lean-to for some cows now sold, as well as a corral, a chicken coop, and an outhouse. The building materials saved for their son lie in several piles. A new and smaller house for the Gillys is fitted in between the paternal house and the road. Between the two houses is a brick courtyard with a water tank two stories high. Vines from a trellis grow up its legs. Iolanda had risen early to garden and had repotted some of the plants from the washtub into old cans that once held *dulce-de-membrillo*, a popular jelly-like sweet made of quinces.[5] Before leaving for the picnic, she spread some thumb-size coconuts on a screen to dry, watched by her Pekinese who, as usual, was flopped down on her belly in the grass. Iolanda put the dog in the house before she left for the picnic.

In La Paz, Ernestina and Liliana Prochet finished washing up after their "tea" the day before. Their discovery of toasted bread has prompted them to have more teas than they used to. They got their ailing brother Italo in the car with some difficulty, and drove out to the paternal estancia to pick up another brother, Esteban. They found him sitting on the edge of the well in the yard in front of the house—the same observation point once used by their father for gazing out at the fields. Esteban was swatting flies, and watching the cows and chickens feed in the yard and try to work out a satisfactory division of their territory. He climbed into the car beside his brother, and Ernestina drove off, honking at Esteban's old farm dog and nudging him out of the road.

As they turned from the dirt road onto the paved road, a green pickup truck sailed by. "Isn't that Elsa and Aldo (Prochet)?" asked

Ernestina. "But then who's that other boy with them next to Antonio? It can't be Miguel, can it, back from school?" They are already busy sorting the important elements of their world, in this case into its identifying genealogical compartments.

At the Micols' house in La Paz, Oscar was getting impatient. As the Waldensian pastor, he really should have been at the picnic already. "Come on, Dora," he called to his wife. "You can tie Vera's shoe in the car! Be quiet, Tango, why do you always have to bark when I yell!" The six Micols arrived in the campo not too long after the others. As they drove into the field where the picnic would be held, they were greeted by Toni Howard and his wife Marina Merati de Howard. Marina and the children had come to the picnic after Toni with some friends. Marina and Dora went off one way, the children went another, and Oscar began his rounds greeting people. Toni stood smoking a cigarette and looking around the field. His parents were sitting on camp stools by the car, the old farm dog between them. "Eduardo, the dog's starting to smell again—get him out of here," said Lora, trying to move the dog away.

As the picnic gets under way, many of the old-timers quickly find each other. Eduardo Howard is telling the group about some gypsies. "I met some gypsies the other day and they tried to tell my fortune, but I told them theirs instead." He winks. "Do you know, they're into the used car business now? Times sure have changed."

From his shawl, Carlos Baridon-Charbonier concurred. "I remember how hard my parents worked. It's not like that now; it's not as hard and we have our comforts. There weren't any myths about Argentina's wealth. They didn't come to live the easy life. They worked hard the whole year just to live, nothing more. If they weren't planting and harvesting, they were making charcoal." Work was divided along lines of origin, and although some Waldenses made charcoal, it was usually the Tuscans, Catholic Italians, who were the *carboneros.* They were already in San Sebastiano when the Waldenses began to arrive. They sold the charcoal in La Paz and did not make much money. The Italian storekeepers, also Catholics, did better. They got along well with the Waldenses and reportedly were willing to advance them credit of seeds and supplies in hard years. Some Italian families, also Catholic, became wealthy landowners, like the Martinellis. Russian, German, British, and French colonists and their descendants also became part of the San Sebastiano area.[6] Relations between these groups and the Waldenses are cordial, but only a few non-Waldenses would be coming to the picnic.

Carlos continued with his family's trials. Once he begins, he can go on for some time. "They said you needed two hands when the locusts were around—one to protect your food and one to shoo them away. The government tried to help us, but the commissioners they sent up north to the Chaco to study the locusts just spent the government's money and lived well. Their attitude was, 'If you've got a problem, take it to God!' But my family got ahead. Here in Argentina it wasn't hard to eat. Everything was at our fingertips. Argentina was a rich land.'"

Bruno Bouissa, a fellow old-timer, offered Carlos the maté gourd. "That's not what my grandfather said. He said it was so bad here that if he'd had the money, he would have gone back to Italy immediately. All he had was a wooden plow—no seeds. He lived by making charcoal, and he hired himself out as a peon too. The only reason he came in the first place was that his brother told him lies about the place. Of course, here *I* am," he laughed. The same brother had lured Bruno to San Sebastiano. He was already an adult when the boat brought him up the Paraná to La Paz in 1925. The river was memorably red at the time, dense with the clay soil washed down from the Chaco. "My great-uncle wrote that there was everything here, a hotel and all. But what did I see of it? Within two days I was off cutting wood. My hands got full of calluses. I worked like an ass cutting those trees. Of course, I worked like this in Italy too, but I never got anyplace; I worked in the mines in Pomaretto." Every year—this was after he had his own land—Bruno swore at his great-uncle as he watched his fields play host to a new menace. "The first year I had no harvest at all: the locusts ate 130 sacks of grain. The second year lightning struck the stack of grain and my harvest was reduced to almost nothing. The third year the harvest seemed like it was going to be good, but God punished me for killing the locusts—he sent me the caterpillar!" Bruno and the others have warmed to their subject.

Old-timers are important in an immigrant community because they are both a link to the Old World and the shapers of the New. Indeed, the respect and affection with which the word "old-timer" (*viejo* or, often, *viejito*) is used implies their special historical relationship to the colony. They not only knew the old times, they directed them, that is, they have lived the community's history. They have the longest memories in the community, and some of them know even "more than the devil," as the local saying goes. Their accounts of the early days provide a chronological perspective on the community and a justification of values found in contemporary society, such as hard work and progress.[7] A certain ambiguity arises, though, when one sees more village land dedicated to unsown cow pasture than to elegant houses like the old Gilly paternal home. In part this is because the idea of progress remained linked to nineteenth-century needs and did not develop beyond the idea of personal progress, or even beyond the idea of advancing individual farming interests. The Waldenses were an economic success in San Sebastiano; most became landowners after renting their concessions for only six years.[8] Though some of the farms' profits could have been used to meet household and familial needs after the initial years of colonization, and though community progress might have been a reasonable goal, the concept of success remained narrowly defined as the amount of land a person owned and the income derived from it. While agricultural profits increased, then, little evidence of this prosperity surfaced in the cultural and material life of home and community. The economic crises have not helped, and in any case the values of hard work and progress have become tempered by concern for family and community harmony.

Many of the women of the church are seated in a group, peeling potatoes for the salad. Some long wooden boards have been set up on sawhorses for them. Elsa Martínez de Prochet, along with other women, is tearing up lettuce and throwing it into a large washtub. Her son Antonio is hanging around nearby. Ernestina and Liliana Prochet are there, too. "Was that Miguel we saw with you in the truck, Elsa?" Elsa tells them that, yes, Miguel is home on vacation from the university in Rosario. Ernestina and Liliana are now satisfied; they like to keep informed about people's comings and goings.

Elsa has been looking forward to the picnic because, like others who live either part-time or full-time in La Paz, she misses the campo. An understanding of the campo, and an ability to survive there, is important to the community, women and men alike, and serves as a bond not only between San Sebastiano residents but between the populations of San Sebastiano and La Paz. Elsa explained that nature was her distraction when she was young and lived full-time in the campo. "I can still remember the birds I used to see in the fields. Until I was seven we lived in the campo in a little rancho. I remember moving to my grandparents' house after that. We were excited because it was a bigger house and had two *galpones* (large sheds). It was ten miles from the village. I lived there till I was twenty-two. My sister and I used to take food to the men working in the fields—slung over a horse in a big sack. They didn't want to stop working because midday is the best time for harvesting: it's the driest. Later we took them the *merienda* (afternoon snack)—a liter each of maté *cocido* (maté cooked in a pan rather than made in a gourd), and bread. We fed the calves when their mothers were too thin to feed them, and when animals got stuck in the muddy ponds, we'd help pull them out."

Aldo Prochet, Elsa's husband, was standing by the caldrons of maté cocido, one with sugar and one without, sharing a gourd of maté with some other men while watching over the fire under the caldrons. They turned as a horn blasted behind them: it was Italo Gilly and Oscar Micol with the children. Every year the Waldenses take Italo's big cattle truck and go to the poor barrios in the nearby area and pick up the creole children who want to come to the picnic. The practice was begun at Oscar's suggestion.

Oscar sees a problem in the way society has developed. The Waldenses and the other immigrants in Argentina have benefited socially and economically from a hierarchy that has favored them ever since the nineteenth century, when the government first encouraged Europeans to settle in Argentina and work the land. The government also hoped that the newcomers would bring "civilization" to the nation's creole population, which it saw as holding back progress.[9] Argentina was there almost for the immigrants' taking, more a territory than a nation, with a numerically insignificant native population and an ineffective government. It was a place, some Italians thought, better suited to becoming an Italian colony than a sovereign nation. In San Sebastiano, there was little surrounding society to challenge the immigrants, so the colony became rather self-contained. Little of the outside world passed through San Sebastiano: occasionally a new immigrant from Europe, a migrant laborer from Corrientes, an itinerant preacher, every six months a caravan of traveling merchants. People's outings were also limited: infrequent trips to the village of San Sebastiano for the family, and biyearly trips to the Bola de Oro general store in La Paz for the men.

The provinces were neglected and even scorned by the porteños of Buenos Aires. Transportation and communication were inadequate. Given the official attitude toward creoles, the lack of social institutions, and the indifference to the campo, it was not hard for immigrants in such a community to become isolated from creoles. Even geography divided and continues to divide the groups. Immigrants live, quite naturally, on the original land concessions that were rented and sold by the colonization company. The few creoles who own land in the general area of San Sebastiano have long been important landowners, distinct from the lower-class creoles who became the farmhands of the immigrants. The latter group tends to live in the village section of San Sebastiano. Even within the colony itself, the landowners live on the rises of land, and their creole peons in the lower areas. It is not difficult to explain gringos' feelings of superiority to creoles. They feel that everyone started on an equal footing, but that creoles were too naive and uncaring to take advantage of the land and get ahead. Gringos got ahead, on the other hand, because they valued hard work and parsimony, and because they were able farmers and businessmen. Oscar Micol and a few others, however, feel that there is a negative moral dimension to the immigrants' economic success. Inviting the creole children to the annual picnic is one attempt to make gringos aware of what Oscar sees as their at least partial responsibility.

Carlos Baridon-Charbonier and the other old-timers were still sitting off at the edge of the circle of cars, drinking maté. They too heard the horn, and Carlos, who was facing the center of the circle, announced the newcomers. "It's *los chicos* (the kids)!" Everyone turned at the noise of fifty or so children shouting and jumping from the truck on all sides. Italo and Oscar rushed to unlatch the truck's gate and tried to get the children off in a safe, orderly fashion, but it was wasted effort. The women hurried over to divide the children into groups and begin some games. Some children were compliant, but others had their own plans for the day. It was not long before the older boys began throwing stones at birds' nests. Some of the women noticed and hurried over to cajole the boys into stopping, but as soon as the women left, the boys started again.

Carlos had been watching the scene. "I remember when creoles and gringos ate together. In the beginning our people saw no difference. But at a certain point a difference in morality developed. It turned out that the creoles didn't feel right eating with us gringos, and then we had to put them outside or in another room. There were two types of creoles: the timid ones who were ashamed, and those who were brazenly unashamed and did impermissible things. The creoles had to be put in their place. They considered us 'gringos.' It's a word that's a little disrespectful."

"The creoles did nothing," added Esteban. "They only cared that their bellies were full. It was the Italians who began the dairy business and making charcoal here; the creoles never would have."

"Have you heard the story about the creole and the gringo?" Carlos chuckled. "Well, one day in the Chaco a gringo moved into an estancia next door to a creole. Next day the gringo went to introduce himself. The creole asked him what he was going to do there, and he replied that he was going to grow wheat. The creole declared that nothing would come of it. The gringo couldn't understand this because an agronomist had assured him that wheat would grow there, so he said, 'Oh well, I'll grow corn.' 'Corn doesn't grow here either,' said the creole. 'Well, I'll grow cotton then,' replied the gringo, undaunted. 'Cotton doesn't grow here either,' said the creole. Exasperated, the gringo despaired, 'But I was told if I planted—' 'Oh,' said the creole with sudden understanding, 'if you're going to *plant!*'" Most of the men had heard the joke before, but they laughed anyway.

"Well, the peons in my house ate with the gringos," said Bruno Bouissa. Bruno had actually been a peon himself for a while, so he looked at the situation a little differently. He had not been exactly like a creole peon—after all, he was a European and a Waldense and related to the important Gilly family—but he had shared the peon milieu for a time, living in a kind of middle ground between his immigrant relatives and his creole co-workers. Though he had long been a part of the established citizenry, he could be more critical of the gringos and more sympathetic to the creoles—sometimes. "You know, the problem was, they were innocent. They always said, 'Gringo here, gringo there. The gringos came to take away our land.' It's true. Old Costantino did this when creoles couldn't pay for their drinks at his store. They'd ask for a peso's worth of *caña* (rum) and he'd give them two pesos' worth. Then when the creoles couldn't pay, Costantino would take their land as payment and act as if he was doing them a favor. The creoles didn't understand they were being taken advantage of. The only thing they cared about was drinking rum, and when they finished they found they had no land. They threw everything away and still expected to do well. When I was a peon there was another peon who had the same salary I did. At the end of the month the creole was always left with nothing and in debt. But I was never in debt. Later, when I became a landowner, the same creole peon came to me because he didn't have a place to live. I gave him a house on some land, a sack of food, permission to milk the cows that were there—I said he could take what he needed for his family—and permission to work the land. But the creole took all the milk he could get and sold it or gave it away to other people. Then he left and took all the farm tools with him. See, even with all this help he couldn't progress."

"Yep," said Carlos, "creoles weren't worried about anything. They worked for *yerba* (the herb from which maté is made) and clothes, nothing more, day to day. They never worried about tomorrow. Some days our peons came to work, other days they never showed up at all."

The old-timers are watching the boys try to hit the birds' nests. "Creole mothers didn't know how to raise children," says Carlos Baridon. "Who knows if old Luigi Baridon would ever have . . . " His voice trails away. Someone else concurs knowingly, "Yeah." They are thinking that Luigi, a fellow Waldense who married a creole in 1930, might have done better to marry a gringo. His fortunes have confirmed the community's dire predictions about intermarriage. Luigi has not had the usual Waldensian economic success, and for a long time his was the only Waldensian family that did not own land. Even his grandsons are seen as not having done well: one has an unprofitable position as a pastor, showing no entrepreneurial spirit, and the other owns one of the less prosperous stores in San Sebastiano. People say the family lacks the spirit to work hard, sacrifice, and save—gringo values, which they believe, a creole woman can't be expected to encourage in her husband and children. Intermarriages are perceived as successful, however, if the creole member of the couple does demonstrate gringo values. Elsa de Prochet's parents' marriage is a case in point. Her mother was a gringa and her father a creole, a peon laborer for his future bride's family, the Gillys. He impressed them with his hard work and thus was able to win the hand of one of their daughters.

Waldenses and others in the San Sebastiano community are not alone in their evaluation of creoles. The stereotypes that emerged from the nineteenth century are still commonplace throughout the country, and one often hears that if the Argentines would only work as hard as the Italians (the group most commonly cited), Argentina would get ahead.[10]

The men around the fire began to serve the asado. People were looking forward to the calm they hoped would come when the children had eaten and were feeling drowsy for the siesta. Most of the Waldensian families took their food to their cars to eat. The Micols were sitting in their Citroën. "I wonder if Aldo Prochet will ever get rid of that old pickup he's had, since before Claudia was born, as I recall. You know he could afford a new one." Oscar pounded his elbow on the dashboard. "Stingy, that's what he is; he prays to the virgin of the *codito* (the elbow)!"

Thrift, though, has been an important value since the early days of the colony. Old-timer Bruno Bouissa, sitting on a campstool nearby, said that in the beginning all he had to eat was corn pudding (*masamorra*), no meat. "My aunt was half stingy—she didn't want to give me what I needed. After a long day's work all she fed me was pumpkin and milk for supper, nothing else. The Waldenses worked hard and made their children finish everything at dinner, even spoiled bread, before they'd give them anything more to eat. They ate only what they could get from the campo—they never bought anything at a store. They didn't have wine either; this is still true in the colony. They only serve wine when the pastor comes and on Sundays—not for moral reasons, mind you, but because they don't want to spend the money." Bruno pounded his elbow on the table, then pulled on it. "People are stingy. See what I mean? Look at that kid over there trying to eat that stale bread. He'll break his teeth!"

The notion of thrift, so important in the life of the colony, ran directly counter to the creole free-handedness Bruno observed and disapproved of in the peon he had tried to help. Like free-handedness, however, excessive thrift is also disapproved of. People call it stinginess. The distinction between thrift and stinginess is not always easily made, but the Waldenses, and gringos in general, tend to talk of "thrift" when they are driving a bargain, making a purchase, or deciding what to have for dinner; of "stinginess" when they are talking about someone else's thrift or at least thrift taken too far. The dangerous way that "thrift" can slide into "stinginess" concerns people. As a result, villagers and townspeople spend a great deal of time trying to sort out such value judgments.

Viewing each family in its own separate vehicle eating its asado or chicken and discussing the others, one might think that a community picnic has broken down in a very modern way—into family units isolated by their means of transportation. But that would be too easy an interpretation. The values of hard work and personal progress, a tradition of individual struggle and family survival in the campo, and the concentration on thrift play a larger role than the automobile in pushing these people apart. Such values, considered together, imply an individualistic society intent on winning out against nature, a culture that measures accomplishment in economic terms, and a people who will sacrifice even the most basic comforts to get ahead. But the breakdown is only a momentary surfacing of these strong familial and individualistic elements in what is consciously a communal event. And in fact, life in San Sebastiano and La Paz is full of events and traditions that promote community values and community rapport. The old-timers like to reminisce about how in the early colony people helped each other— by sharing oxen and farm tools, for example, or lending seeds and supplies—in the interests of economic progress.[11] In contemporary San Sebastiano they helped each other in the interests of community "harmony," a concept of the villagers. One of the working principles of society is to avoid confrontation.

The day before the picnic, Oscar Micol had forgotten his keys and left them hanging in the door. "I came back fifteen minutes later and they were gone! So I called the police and they told me to hold. Meanwhile, I asked the girl in the stationery shop across the street if she'd noticed anything, and she said she'd seen a small boy who begs around here on the front steps. My daughter (informally adopted Mirta) recognized the boy from the stationer's description and said he came from her barrio.[12] She described the house and family to me and then I went down and found the place. There was a woman there, and I told her I was looking for a family with three boys. She said she had only one boy—which of course I already knew. She wanted to know why I was looking for this family, and I said it was because I was trying to find something. I hadn't been home an hour when the woman brought me back my keys—she said her son had found them on the ground. Of course, I knew it would all happen this way. Then I tried to call the police back and tell them there was no theft, but they didn't answer—I still couldn't get them this morning!"

The principle of harmony is reflected in everyday phrases. "Qué sé yo?" (What do I know? or, Don't think that I have the last word, but I would say that . . .), a popular phrase preceding or following a statement of one's views, should not be interpreted as a lack of interest or strong opinion or as fatalism, but rather as a mode of promoting harmony. "Qué vas a hacer?" (What are you going to do?) certainly sounds like a shoulder-shrugging expression of fatalism, but in everyday usage it reflects more of a desire not to rock the boat. "Es costumbre, nada más" (It's just custom) is a frequently heard explanation and justification for almost any belief or activity. Respect for tradition helps preserve harmony, whereas change can cause disruption.

Harmony, though, is an operating principle, not an achieved fact of life in San Sebastiano and La Paz. Every generation, from the old-timers on, has had to deal with a potentially volatile society composed of creoles impoverished by a new economic situation and of newcomers (non-Spanish speakers, non-Catholics, non-campo people) with different values. The society is by no means lacking in tensions, but people's sense of public honor and social place, and of a shared living and working environment, engenders a kind of homogeneity and altruism, a consensus that harmony is one of the most important values.

"Ah, there you are at last! Fernando's been begging me for a Coke-cito. Should he have it, do you think?" asks Toni Howard. Marina, Toni's wife and Fernando's mother, answers no, and Toni is left with a screaming Fernando while Marina takes the film out of her camera. She and Dora de Micol have been walking in the campo, taking photos for Dora's grade school class on local flora and fauna. Meanwhile the picnickers have begun to disperse. The creole children have been taken back to their homes. Cars are beginning to leave and departing wishes of "Que le vaya bien" (Take care) are heard. "Marina, you know we should probably be leaving too, because I have to do that radio program tonight," Toni reminds her.

Toni, Marina, their two legally adopted sons, and Toni's parents and their dog crowded into Toni's Dodge Colt. After a stop at Eduardo and Lora's estancia, the two families continued on in separate cars, following each other back to La Paz—where Eduardo and

Lora actually have their home, a block away from Toni and Marina. They stopped at a kiosk to get Fernando a Coke and some soda crackers. Shortly after they entered La Paz, Toni turned onto Jujuy Street and Eduardo onto Pilar; they called to each other, "See you later." They waved as they traveled up the parallel streets. As Eduardo and Lora pulled up in front of their town house, they saw that some of their chickens had gotten loose. Lora stepped out of the car and chased them back to their pen while Eduardo tried to wake up the dog in the back seat.

A block away, Marina began preparing supper. "Would some croquettes taste good, Toni?" Suddenly the lights went out. "Must be storms in Santa Fe again. It's been some week, hasn't it? The electricity's been off more than it's been on." They ate by candlelight. As they were finishing up, Lora walked in. Though she had lived in La Paz for twenty years, she had never gotten used to the city life of separate houses. In San Sebastiano, she had had all her family under the same roof and when she looked out the door, only *her* world greeted her. On the rare occasions when a few days go by and she does not see her children, she is sad.

Toni left for the radio station, three blocks away. He is a lawyer, and he and a local doctor were going to speak on abortion. Toni feels strongly that it should not be a legislated decision; Marina is understandably reluctant to discuss the issue, since she herself is unable to have children. The radio announcer, Diego Montañes, greeted Toni as he drove up and assured him that the lights would go on soon. But they did not, so Diego, Toni, and the doctor, Laura De Pereda, sat around drinking whiskey and discussing the issue off the air. The lights finally came on and the program began. At home a few hours later, Toni, Marina, Eduardo, and Lora shared maté; the children had gone to bed. Toni's brother, who is a doctor, and his uncle, who is in forensic medicine, dropped in for maté and they discussed the radio program.

The closeness of the Howard family is typical of San Sebastiano and La Paz. Thanks to extensive intermarriage, and the prevalence of extended families and households containing non-related community members like the Gillys' "adopted" son and the Micols' Mirta, and the communal features of society like the sharing of maté, community and family have over the years become intertwined. It is not surprising that for Toni and the others, the world ends and also begins in San Sebastiano.

TWO

The Economics of Survival

UMBERTO ECKSTEIN, his wife, their two daughters, and two grand-children sat in the Fiat drinking maté, eating soda crackers, and watching the driverless, remote-controlled tractor go around in a circle. It was the evening of the first day of the annual Farmers' Day festival and the tractor was the central attraction. The Ecksteins faced the windshield with a Teutonic stolidness. Every now and then one of them made a remark, but mainly they watched the tractor. The car windows began to steam over, and the children drew pictures on them with their fingers. Their mother refastened the barrettes in their long blond hair. Several military personnel with machine guns, young boys looking lost in helmets too large for them, patrolled the fair. Crowds always had to be patrolled, and anyway the port authority's office and warehouse were nearby. A few children in their white school smocks were still milling around after the afternoon's activities. The sixth grade had performed ground exercises on the wharf as a complement to the aerial ma-neuvers of the military planes.

After some time Umberto got out of the car and began walking up the line of exhibits. He examined the displays of new farm equip-ment, but not for long. The floats from the parade caught his atten-tion. He was pleased to see that Colonia San Sebastiano's entry, with its miniature farms and mechanical animals, had the largest crowd around it. Umberto shuffled past the booths selling artisans' leather goods and stopped to talk to a friend drinking rum and eat-ing a chorizo sausage at the beverage tent. It was cold and the women had remained in the car eating crackers, their attention fixed on the tractor's course. The tractor was as routine, familiar, and complete as agricultural life itself. Its pace was heavy and slow, like Umberto's movements, and its motor was as constant as his voice. The fair went on for a week; it marked the beginning of spring, a time for hope and growth. It did not offer people much except hope: they could not afford the new machinery, and had few plans. Like the tractor going nowhere in its endless circle, their hope was largely futile. This was September 1976; in 1981 the Ecksteins did not attend the fair, since it was not held in La Paz. Agriculture, like other sectors of the economy, had failed, and no one felt like celebrating.[1]

The Agricultural Basis of San Sebastiano

One morning in the spring of 1981, Umberto started off to spend the day with his son, who administers the family ranch in San Sebastiano. The Ecksteins are of German Lutheran stock. They have 200 acres in San Sebastiano; this supports four people, and goes a long way toward supporting two peon families who live in the village. As Umberto drove further out into the country, the grass got longer and the land wetter. There was a carcass by the roadside, a cow that had gotten through an unmended fence and been hit by a car. The air around it was bad and Umberto rolled up the car window. He turned off the state route onto a dirt road leading to the ranch; he saw a truck coming toward him in the distance and backed out onto the pavement again so that it could pass. The truck stopped and two of Umberto's peons got out to talk to him. They were on their way to clear land—to cut *montes* (groves of trees), they said—on the Eckstein property on the other side of the state route. One of the men had bloodshot eyes and a knife gash on his right cheek. "Must have been some race yesterday, huh, Guillermo?" kidded Umberto. When the truck had left, Umberto turned his car onto the dirt road again and continued on to the ranch. He and his son sat around for the better part of the morning, drinking maté and discussing the farm.

They find it a sad commentary that Farmers' Day activities have been suspended in an area where land has played such an important role. The demise of agriculture has lowered their income and weakened the Argentine economy, but they hope it will not disrupt their way of life. After all, no one would deny that agriculture has long been the basis of the economy and society in Argentina. It is enough to look at how developed its immigration and colonization programs were and how well-known its beef and grain became. By

1930 Argentina was the world's largest corn and beef exporter and was second or third in wheat exports.[2] When colonization programs were first initiated, the Argentine interior was unsettled and uncultivated. In the early stages of the government's programs, in 1875, the province of Entre Ríos had only three colonies, but by 1895 it had 204.[3]

The province grew during this time from a mere 134,000 inhabitants according to the first census in 1869 to 292,000 in 1895 at the time of the second census. The Eckstein family and San Sebastiano were part of this boom. San Sebastiano was a private colony sponsored by the exporting company Bunge and Born, a branch of an important export firm based in Antwerp. This company became one of Argentina's major grain dealers; it is also important in the paint and food industries, and people call it the "octopus" for its far-ranging activities.[4]

The government continued the institution of the colony as a tool for populating the countryside and developing agriculture. Between the 1930's and 1960's it established several new colonies in the San Sebastiano area, mainly by buying and dividing up some of the land owned by the largest ranchers, like the Sánchez family and Señora Von Ruden. Many of these colonies were specifically designed to settle native Argentines rather than foreigners on the land, although a group of Algerians was brought into the department of La Paz in the late 1950's to colonize San Carlos and Saucesito. There is no restriction on established farmers' buying concessions, and San Sebastiano farmers have used the new colonies to expand their holdings. Entre Ríos has twenty-five colonies sponsored by the provincial government, and ten national ones, sponsored by the National Agrarian Council (Consejo Agrario Nacional). San Sebastiano, however, is no longer run like a colony. It is independent of any company or agency and has not had an administrator for at least fifty years.[5]

Categories like "farmer" and "non-farmer" are artificial in an area like San Sebastiano and La Paz, since the land is part of every person's background. Even if a person is not a farmer by profession and even if he resides in the town, his life is apt to be linked in some way to the land and his family history is often linked to it directly. If he is descended from an immigrant, he can probably point to the land as the reason for his ancestors' coming to Argentina. If he is a native Argentine, his ties to the land go back even further. The land has played an important role in the country's history. Designations like "people of the campo" (*gente de campo*) and "he who has land" (*el que tiene tierra*) indicate a respect for the land and (usually) for the people close to it. Creoles, though, have a different relationship to land than gringos. Both have exploited it, but with different means and goals and in differing degrees of intensity.[6]

Farming involves the majority of the population in one way or another—as full-time landowners or day laborers; as members of a landowning patriarchal family who share the profit from land being worked by another family member; as part-time landowners and shopkeepers or office workers. Though many people spend little or no time in the countryside, they remain part of a farm household. The farm household is the main form of social organization in the campo. It organizes families in the sense that it incorporates their various branches and different generations. With the lack of other social units, the farm household is the main way of facing the isolation of the rural environment. Even when festivals like the national Farmers' Day are abandoned, the really important ones, those of the life cycles of the farming household, continue to bring people together.

In early May the Antoninis, one of the better-off farming families in San Sebastiano, were planning a birthday party for a member of their youngest generation, two-year-old Michela. The Antoninis form a tightly-knit economic unit several generations strong: there are the grandparents and their children, then the grandsons, thirty-year-old Domenico and his brother, and finally Domenico's children. Their farms are spaced far apart, but they are linked by dirt roads and by a private telephone. The grandparents are quite old and have moved to town to be closer to doctors.[7] The Antoninis own about 5,000 acres, 1,700 head of cattle, and the latest farm machinery. Their farms support eleven people, not counting the five peon families who work for them and live on their land. "Domenico has a rich father," people say, rubbing their thumb and forefinger together to indicate wealth.

Five years ago Lucia, daughter of Aldo and Elsa Prochet, married Domenico. Lucia's background is middle-class and Waldensian; she married into a higher class and into an Italian Catholic family, originally immigrants to Concepción del Uruguay in the eastern part of the province. Like many young couples, Domenico and Lucia began their life together at his parents' house, residing there a year while they renovated one of the old estancias on the property for themselves. This was an important test period for the future of the Antonini farming enterprise. Differences in economic class—especially since Lucia's maternal grandfather was a creole and a peon—and in religion might have been a problem, but the success of the marriage attests to the couple's good nature and enthusiasm for shared goals. In addition, Lucia has proved quite able to handle her end of the farm work. She often cooks for the peons when every hand is needed in the fields, and makes chorizo sausages and tends to the household's vegetable garden and fruit orchard.

The goodwill Lucia has earned by her hard work does not mean that she can afford to be impolitic where her in-laws are concerned. As she struggled over Michela's three-layer birthday cake, her husband's grandmother observed that she, for one, would never waste time on making such an extravagant cake. This could well have been meant as a slight to Lucia's family—suggesting that they are not as well off as the Antoninis because they did not use their time wisely—but Lucia pretended it was just an old woman's comment on the soft life of the younger generation. Later on, when Michela's presents had been opened and it was discovered that the Antoninis had given her a new store-bought outfit (an expensive item in Argentina), Lucia immediately dressed Michela in it. The outfit that Elsa, Lucia's mother, had made for Michela, out of an old pair of slacks that Lucia's brother Antonio had outgrown, was left lying on the chair, the many hours of work and love that had gone into it seemingly forgotten. Elsa noticed, but tried to share in everyone's interest in the manufactured clothes. For her part, Lucia was not being unappreciative so much as diplomatic, although it was possible that she felt a bit ashamed of her family's well-known thrift.

An important part of any event in the campo is the adventure of getting there. Battling the elements is one of the things that bind campo people and families together and test their prowess. The Friday night before the birthday party, Elsa had worked late at home in La Paz to finish her granddaughter's present, though the early winter rains made it uncertain that the Prochets would even go. The Antoninis' ranch was twenty-five miles away, the last fifteen of them along a dirt road. At about ten on Saturday morning, Aldo concluded his silent debate and he, Elsa, and their son Antonio set out in the old green pickup truck with its gears wrenching and its springs straining over the bumps.

Domenico was out getting wood for the cooking fire when the Prochets arrived about eleven. A big burly man, Domenico greeted his father-in-law enthusiastically with a solid thump on the back. Aldo joked with Domenico about the heavy rains that had almost kept them from coming; he was confident now, after all his misgivings, because the dirt road had not been slippery as he had feared. After the usual tour of the yard, the group moved into the house. They entered through a large back room, dodging the winter supply of chorizo sausages and aging raw meat that were hanging from the ceiling, and squeezed past the electric freezer into the kitchen. They felt a gust of intense heat as they passed the roaring fire prepared for the asado: the beef, already roasting in the large open waist-high fireplace in a narrow passageway between the back room and the kitchen, would be ready for eating in about two hours. Lucia's husband threw more wood on the fire and turned the meat. People congregated in the kitchen and Lucia began the party by handing the maté gourd and teakettle of hot water to her father. The maté was left to Aldo since the host Domenico was in charge of the roasting beef and Lucia and her mother Elsa were busy with the rest of the meal. Aldo, his son Antonio, and Domenico pulled chairs into the center of the kitchen, joining Domenico's grandparents, whom he had fetched the day before from La Paz. They sat waiting for the maté to be passed. Lucia and her mother worked at the stove and the children played on the tile floor. Lucia's live-in maid, or *chica*, occasionally peeked at the guests as she moved along the courtyard from room to room, making the beds. Domenico's frequent trips out back to get wood let in a pungent odor of raw meat that mixed with the smell of the roasting asado inside. Lucia caught her husband on one of his trips through the kitchen: "Your mother just called to say that your family will be ready to have you pick them up at the stream in fifteen minutes."

Domenico grabbed the keys to his truck and invited Aldo and young Antonio to join him on the ride to get his family. For Aldo it meant a chance to see what his hosts were doing on their land and to compare this with work on his own ranch, where he lives during the week. For Antonio it meant possible adventure, even though he was reluctant to leave the bustle of the kitchen. "So this is your new truck, Domenico. Nice," said Aldo, thinking of the years he must keep his own pickup running. On the other hand, he mused aloud on his way home later, it runs well, so why should he spend the money for a new one? And a new level of satisfaction in his thrift took over his thoughts.

Domenico's parents, his brother and his brother's wife, and his sister and her boyfriend were already waiting on the other side of the Arroyo Jacinto, having arrived there by truck from the family ranch. The swollen river had washed out the road; it does this every year, and a rowboat is kept along the bank for crossings. No one seemed particularly to be dressed for the conditions, and for the women, with loafers on their feet and hair curlers under their scarves, this might almost have been an ordinary outing to town. No sooner were they in the boat than the current momentarily whipped them downstream, provoking screams of surprise. Pulling forcefully on the oars, Stefano Gilly, the boyfriend of Domenico's sister, gained control of the boat and pulled it up safely along the opposite bank.

The spectacle of the whirlwind ride down the stream was only a brief interruption of the ride to and from the river in the truck. The three women crowded into the cab with Domenico, and the men climbed in the back. Most of the men sat on the floor of the truck; even there it was a challenge to avoid being flung over the side as the truck bounced along the deep muddy ruts. Old hands, Lucia's father and Domenico's father sat on the edge of the truck, gripping its sides in an unprofessed contest of wills. As the ruts knocked them into each other, they discussed the crops they were planting and when they would harvest, with Domenico's father dominating the conversation.

The party descended laughing on Lucia's kitchen with stories of the wild journey by boat and truck. Domenico's father got the tea-kettle from its permanent place on the back stove burner, and the rounds of maté began again. He emptied the gourd of its old maté leaves, put in some fresh yerba, stuck in the straw (the *bombilla*), added the hot water, and handed the gourd across the circle to *abuela*, Domenico's grandmother. She drank to the bottom, making a sucking noise as she finished, and handed the gourd back to her son. The gourd was offered next to the grandfather and then proceeded on through the generations, two and three times, reaching Aldo and Domenico's father yet a fourth time. Elsa and Lucia had to be reminded to take their turns occasionally; they were too busy with the dinner to sit down. Antonio, being the youngest, is always the last to drink. He normally refuses maté, but this day he accepted, to be more a part of the group and more adult. Like all rural children, he had drunk boiled maté and milk, as well as coffee, since he was a young child; recently, however, he had lost the taste for maté. Domenico interrupted a discussion of the economy (the men were exchanging figures in American dollars) to suggest that they watch an important auto race on the television in the living room. Stefano and Antonio joined him, and the living room, normally unused and kept dark behind heavy curtains, came to life with the sound of a sports announcer's voice. Aldo and Domenico's father continued talking in the kitchen about the Minister of Economy.

Michela's birthday dinner was to take place in the courtyard. On one side of the courtyard are the bedrooms; off the other are two bathrooms (identical down to their partial disrepair and seatless toilets), a pair of washtubs, and the maid's tiny windowless room, perhaps once a storage room. Her living quarters are actually an improvement over those in her family's rancho, and her position with a landowner like Domenico is a good one. Lucia is displeased with her, however, and may let her go. "It's very hard to find good peons and chicas nowadays and to keep them. They're unsteady and just don't stay very long in one place. And now I've discovered our chica writing to her boyfriend. She sends him notes through her sister and I've intercepted them. Can you imagine, they talk about wanting to sleep together! There's a lot of problems when these young girls mix with peons. It's dangerous. They get all kinds of ideas."

The guests had finally been summoned to the tables and were anticipating the meat that was producing such good smells. The asado always consists of the same food, but it is a treat all the same. The group arranged themselves at the table by family and generation and began helping themselves to the wine and Coke. Domenico ferried in the various meat courses in big baking pans: first the *empañadas* (pockets of dough stuffed with a mixture of meat, olives, and raisins) and pork cheese, then the spicy chorizo sausages, then the tough roasted beef. "A meal without meat isn't a meal," Domenico announced as he put several large chunks of fat-laden beef on his plate. The meal was informal and knives dipped in from all sides noisily spearing pieces of meat and bread. At one point, in a confusion of reaching hands and the filling of glasses, one of the large bottles of Coke was overturned, wetting the tablecloth and a couple of the guests, but it did not disrupt the meal. The meat was eaten quickly, accompanied by a salad of lettuce and potatoes. Then Lucia opened the courtyard refrigerator to reveal the birthday cake. The chica, who had been sitting beside Michela during the meal helping her eat, tried to get her to blow out the candles, but Michela's sister was too quick and did it for her.

After the asado everyone was glad to take a walk. Domenico showed his father-in-law around his two enormous barns full of farm machinery—he has the latest money can buy in Argentina. After doing the dishes, the women went out to look at the household orchard and garden. Stefano and Domenico's sister, Irene, went off by themselves, openly affectionate now, but they took care not to leave the sight of the rest of the company. The grandparents had gone to the veranda, which surrounds the house on two sides, and were drinking maté. Little by little the others joined them.

Aldo was once again apprehensive about the roads. Each of the three generations of farmers who were present had their own weather prediction. The rain, which had held off all day, started to fall lightly. At the first sign of it, Aldo quietly consulted with Elsa, anxious to be off. Not quite so anxious herself, and reluctant to leave her daughter Lucia, Elsa delayed a bit, and by the time the old green pickup swung onto the road, it had been raining for twenty minutes, long enough for the clay mud to have formed a slick, ice-like surface. It was an effort to stay on the road, and Aldo swerved perilously close to the soft shoulders with each turn of the steering wheel. Occasionally the odor of decaying animal carcasses drifted up to the cab's passengers, but Aldo was too preoccupied to close his window. Even on the asphalt road he did not alter his slow pace, since much of the road was already flooded. The pedestrian traffic beside the pavement moved along as usual in spite of the weather and the wash from passing vehicles. Easing back in his chair at the La Paz house that night, Aldo sipped his maté and returned to his normal measured response to life. He considered the Antoninis' prosperity and told Elsa that he was happy for his daughter.

The Unprofitableness of Farming

When Aldo looked at the books for his estancia, he found too many expenditures and too few entries on the credit side. The agricultural year of 1981 finished badly for most farmers; even the Antoninis did not do as well as usual. Many problems of agriculture in general had been getting worse. Small farms of 150 to 225 acres were becoming more common, though less than 500 acres was often said to be unprofitable. Some people had left San Sebastiano over the years, but many more had stayed and the land had been continuously subdivided to accommodate them all. The same families had been on the same land for generations; they felt ties to the original land and they tended to stay in San Sebastiano and marry within the local population.

The inheritance laws have furthered this tendency. Domenico's father could not exclude certain members of his family from his will even if he wanted to, except by a court procedure. The civil code requires specific bequests for family members broadly defined. For example, if legitimate children survive, they must receive at least four-fifths of the estate. If only natural (i.e., illegitimate) children survive, they are guaranteed one-half of the estate. Other combinations are also considered, securing the rights of the wife (guaranteeing her a maximum of one-half the estate if no other heirs survive) and of surviving parents. These laws protect the interests of Domenico and his brother and sister and facilitate the distribution of land among a greater number of people, an important objective of the original laws. The result, though, is the creation of properties too small to be farmed economically. Some people, like the Antoninis, form family-based companies, pool their properties, and then divide up the work and the profits. Some of these companies are informally constituted partnerships, or *sociedades de hecho*, and others are formal stock companies, *sociedades anónimas*. Sometimes one of the heirs to an estate takes over its entire administration for his siblings or his parents while they do some other kind of work or retire and take their share of the profit in cash or kind.

Whatever the uncertainties of the economy, the farmers of the area seemed at least to be in no immediate danger of losing their land, though some had been selling out. The great attraction of Argentina for the ancestors of San Sebastiano farmers was the opportunity to own land, and to some extent the promise has been fulfilled. Entre Ríos has a large number of small- and medium-sized farms, but it is well acquainted with the universal Latin American problem of land concentrated in too few hands. Only 2 percent of the province's population controls 39 percent of the land; 29 percent owns 50 percent of the land; and 68 percent of the population owns only 10 percent.[8]

Most farms are small, then, like Aldo's, which has about 200 acres, and most farmers are *colonos* or *agricultores* (these words are used interchangeably in Entre Ríos; a colono can thus mean a "colonist" or renter as well as a landowner). The small farms are suited to dairy farming, cotton growing, and some cattle raising. Five hundred acres seems to be the minimun size for an economically prosperous farm—Aldo gets by because his unmarried brother and sister each have 200 acres, which helps them all out—but according to the La Paz branch of the National Institute of Agricultural Technology (Instituto Nacional de Tecnología Agropecuaria, or INTA), even farms of 1,500 acres count as small farms. A farmer with this acreage would be likely to plant half his land with crops and reserve the other half for cattle raising, tending to avoid the tedious daily routine of dairy farming. A truly large farm has between 1,500 and 2,500 acres; it also combines crop cultivation and cattle raising. Anything larger is considered to be an estancia.

The Antoninis, with their 5,000 acres, are estancieros. Their farm is primarily a ranch, where cattle and sheep graze on natural pasture, and there is little crop cultivation. A typical estanciero with 5,000 acres might have 600 head of cattle, 400 calves, 30 bulls, 20 horses, and 600 sheep. His land would probably be 50 percent montes, or small groves of trees, 40 percent cleared, unplanted land, and 10 percent sown pasture or land planted with a crop such as sorghum or flax, depending on whether the price is higher for grain or for meat. The largest estancia in the department of La Paz is 60,000 acres. It belongs to Cesare Martinelli, a third-generation Lombard Italian who is a lawyer and politician in La Paz. The Canciano estancia of 150,000 acres, north of La Paz in Concordia, is considered to be the largest in Entre Ríos.[9] Generally, the estancias in the San Sebastiano and La Paz area are a far cry from the elegant estancias of the province of Buenos Aires, where large staffs of servants look after multiple sets of china and silver and keep the marble floors polished year-round, waiting for the occasional visit of the owner from Buenos Aires, Paris, or Rome. The Canciano and Martinelli estates are nevertheless a class apart from the typical estancias of the campo with their unused, newspaper-coated kitchens and their rickety outhouses in the back yard.

In San Sebastiano and the surrounding area, where small farms are the norm, the Antoninis are considered upper-class estancieros, and even Aldo Prochet is considered an upper-middle-class estanciero because of the total size of his family's property. Besides, he owns two houses (his house in town and his farmhouse) and he has a son in college. "Aldo does all right," says a neighbor, pounding his elbow on the table to indicate tight-fistedness. "He has land, a tractor, a truck, two houses, a son at a university, and animals that cost him almost nothing to keep, and his expenses are small for everything else. But he's still careful with money. His family eats mainly leftovers and pasta."

Aldo makes a living, but it is good that his eldest son is studying engineering, because the Prochet property would surely be too small to support both his sons. His second son, Antonio, who is studying business in high school, could probably also follow a different profession, but he intends to take over the farm. He prefers the campo to the town and is learning everything he can from his father about farming. Aldo is a true "man of the campo," a man of few words who enjoys his work and the singular pleasure of drinking maté. The even cadence of his voice conveys the relentless rhythm of rural life, its inevitability, and the satisfaction it offers. He is not an entrepreneur like the Antoninis; all he asks from farming is that it continue to allow him to work and live in his customary way.

Aldo does not normally initiate conversations, but the Sunday morning after Michela's birthday party and his successful drive in the rain, he was encouraged to reminisce by the expansive feeling survival brings and some prodding by a curious Antonio. Enjoying his maté, Aldo chuckled as the sight of the water dripping through the leaks in the roof of the living room and running under the door from the courtyard reminded him of his days in the army. The Prochets had enclosed the living room, once part of the courtyard, when they bought the house. A not-very-watertight green plastic material served as roofing, and every hard rain found the same holes. "I did a year of military service on horseback in Corrientes," Aldo told his son. "I was too dry half the time and too wet the other half. We slept on triple bunk beds and we didn't always eat. 'Have some bread?' they'd offer us for dessert—when that's what we'd already had for the meal!"

For twenty years Aldo was a dairy farmer, a *tambero*. "Remember how early we used to get up, Elsa, when we had the dairy farm?" He, Elsa, and their older son used to get up early and milk their thirty cows by hand. Then Aldo delivered the milk locally in a horse cart. Finally, nine of the tamberos got together and bought a truck so that they could take the milk to the central market in La Paz. That was before the San Sebastiano Dairy Cooperative was formed, Aldo explained. "We had chickens, too, then; from August to March they laid and then they rested. Yep, even the chickens have their history." Later, when he had more land, Aldo began raising beef cattle.

Still sipping maté, Aldo discussed with Elsa which cattle he was going to sell at the upcoming auction. Meanwhile, Elsa was busy taking apart a sweater that Antonio had outgrown; she would use the wool to make something for her granddaughters. "If I can get the cattle bathed for ticks next week, I can get Rafael to come on Friday and certify them for the sale.[10] Then when I come into La Paz on Saturday I can get the other papers at the Animal Health office. I think I'll sell twenty of our calves and ten cows, and Amalia's got thirteen cows to sell, and Attilio's got seventeen. I want to get rid of them—they're skinny and need fattening—but if I can't get a good price I won't sell." Thinking of business matters, Aldo wrote Elsa a check for the week and, while rummaging in his "purse," recalled that he had brought something to show her from the ranch. "Remember I said I was going to clean up those boxes in the back room last week? Well, I did, and look what I found, a map of San Sebastiano. Must be from Miguel's old school stuff. I haven't really had a chance to look at it yet. Let's see. Where's the river? Um, then we have to turn the map this way. Ah, yes. Let's see now. Here's our ranch and this must be Don Eduardo's land. No, wait, that can't be. Boy, I'd better not give the wrong names or the owners will hear and come after me!" he chuckled. "My goodness a lot's changed. When was this map made? 1974? Look at this plot: it's all divided up now!" Once Aldo found his own estancia, Las Flores, he tested his memory, locating everyone else's property in San Sebastiano and listing the number of acres and livestock they own.

They were still poring over the map when a car pulled up in front of the open street door of the house. Elsa guessed from the sound that it was Oscar Micol's car. Antonio cocked his head and started to challenge her, but Oscar was already halfway through the door, clapping his hands to announce his arrival. "Buenos, pastor. Have some maté?" asked Aldo, offering him the gourd. Oscar sat down for a couple of rounds, waiting while the maté passed to Aldo and

Elsa and back to him. He had come to remind them about a church function, and mentioned again the weekly youth-group meetings that Antonio was invited to attend. He has never understood how a teenage boy can bear to stay so cooped up, as he says. Aldo was uncomfortable—he rarely goes to church, with the farm and all, as he says. Oscar was restless as usual and had much to do, so he was soon off again.

Elsa suggested that she start dinner. "What would you like, Aldo? I have some rice left over from the girls last week. And I could open a can of mackerel and make a sauce for it." "Anything is fine with me," answered Aldo, and Antonio, who cares mainly about quantity, concurred. At about one they sat down to dinner, and Aldo said grace, a custom the Prochets always observe: "Thank you, God, for this food, and help us with our work and help others with their work."

After dinner, and the washing and sweeping up, it was time for the siesta. Antonio rested awhile, then went out to ride his bike. Elsa rested about an hour, but then got back to her sewing. Aldo climbed into bed with the portable radio. Propping it on his stomach, he listened to its sputterings, adjusting the dial until Radio La Paz came in. After the news, a farm report, and a program on rural folklore, Aldo turned off the radio and committed himself fully to the siesta. About 5 o'clock his bed creaked and there was mumbling as he searched for his shoes in the dark bedroom. The green French doors resisted as he tried to open them—they were swollen from the humidity—but then with a yank Aldo emerged from the bedroom. Elsa heated some water and they drank maté, talking and drinking into the early evening, when Elsa warmed up more leftovers for their supper. Their boarder Emilia arrived while they were eating, but assured them she was not hungry and hurried off to a girlfriend's to watch a movie on television. The Prochets do not have a TV. Dusk had been settling in for some time before they flipped the switch for the overhead light, but the electric lines must have been down again because nothing happened. La Paz depends on Santa Fe for its electricity, so when there is a storm in Santa Fe the lights go out in La Paz. In 1971 the department of La Paz made a contract with the national electric company to receive a fixed amount of electricity. At night this is sufficient for the department's needs, but during the day La Paz's obsolete and worn-out equipment must be used to supplement the national supply.[11]

"The lights are out all over the town," Antonio reported from the street. Satisfied that he was done studying for the night, he went outside and sat on a window ledge, resting his back against the tall iron bars outside the window of his room. Soon Elsa and Aldo joined him, and the three of them sat there enjoying the darkness. Someone drove by in a yellow Peugeot. "Who's that?" asked Aldo. "Oh, you know," said Elsa, "it's Daniele Baridon, the son of Roberto who's my mother's first cousin. He has one of those places over in the new barrio by the river now, but he used to live with my mother's cousin in the next block. He's probably been over there visiting." They sat there until late evening, enjoying the quiet street life of the town under the unmarred darkness of a country sky.

On Monday Aldo dressed in his ranch gear—a checked shirt and cravat, *bombachas* trousers (baggy pleated gaucho trousers with gathered legs, worn in the campo), and a hat. After visiting the store around the block for some meat and bread to take to the campo, he kissed Elsa and Antonio goodbye for the week and headed off to San Sebastiano. At the ranch he found Attilio sitting by an open fire with his leg propped up. His horse had stumbled and half-fallen on him the day before. "This weather, it's made a mess of the fields for everything," said Aldo. Aldo and his brother and sister, Attilio and Amalia, live together, and their lands are contiguous. They wanted to call their estancia the "Triple A," but thought better of it: the Triple A was a terrorist group, the Argentine Anticommunist Alliance. It was founded in 1973 under the last elected Peronist government by the social welfare minister, José López Rega, to combat Leftist terrorism. Its members, mainly retired military and police officers, became infamous for robberies, kidnappings, and assassinations.[12] On reflection, the Prochets decided to go with the safer, inoffensive name "Las Flores." The three Prochets cooperate in certain aspects of ranch work—Aldo would be taking Attilio's and Amalia's cattle as well as his own to the auction—but for the most part Aldo prefers to work his land alone. He sums up his position with a bit of word play: "I don't like to work with other people (*en sociedad*), to go halves (*medias*). There's an old saying, 'I don't like socks (again, *medias*, which can also mean a pair of socks), not even for putting on my feet.'" In fact, Aldo usually does go sockless, too.

Aldo prepared some maté for Attilio, who likes it with a little sugar, and sat down to talk awhile. "Boy, if it weren't for the rains, I'd be out there planting my flax and wheat right now." Depending on the rains, planting for the La Paz zone follows this schedule: in March, farmers sow oats; in June and July, flax and wheat; in August and September, corn and sorghum; in October, cotton and sorghum; in November, beans. Farmers usually plant flax for three years, and for the next seven or eight years they rotate corn, sorghum, and wheat, not necessarily in that order.[13] "But it's the cattle I'm really worried about," Aldo continued. "If it rains so much that I can't plant fodder, the cattle won't have enough food again for the winter. I don't want to have to buy alfalfa and that powdered corn—the cattle just don't fatten up eating that powdered stuff. I'm afraid they'll get sick too, standing around in the mud so long." A streak of yellow sun cut a warm line across the floor; Attilio's dog moved instinctively to it and attracted Aldo's attention to the weather outside. "Well, it looks clear today, so maybe I can take them through the tick bath this week. They're overdue, but the bath has been too muddy. Guess I'll go into the village later today and see if I can line up some peons—maybe get old José to do the cooking, and a couple of his grandsons for the cattle, and maybe Julio. And I'll get the wine and beef for the asado. Qué sé yo? Maybe I'm the only one around who still gives the peons wine and pays them 20,000 pesos or $6 a day too.* Right now, though, I'm going to see if I can't get that tractor running." Aldo went out to the shed.

Later in the day Aldo ran into Pierre Benabou in the village. Pierre is in charge of the La Paz branch of the National Institute of Agricultural Technology. INTA is charged with agricultural research and development and employs about 4,000 workers nationwide, half of them agricultural workers, and others scientists and administrators. The agency maintains a number of experimental stations on plant and animal diseases, soil, agricultural techniques, and so on; it is funded by a tax on agricultural exports, by fines, and by revenue from some of its services. Pierre's office is one of 180 local centers that organize information services, social services, and young farmers' clubs. Pierre had been out in San Sebastiano giving advice to a farmer about digging a well, and had stayed the whole afternoon helping a neighbor interpret the directions he had given him for building and using an outhouse.

---

*All peso amounts are given in the currency used in 1981, new pesos. I have used U.S. $1 = 3,000 Argentine new pesos as an approximate valuation since equivalency rates were changing daily.

Aldo sometimes goes to Pierre for advice, and then usually does what he planned to do in the beginning. "Poor Benabou," he remarks. "He's only 29. He was brought up in Paraná and trained at the university in Santa Fe. He knows a lot and he works hard. I heard they were even going to send him to Australia or the United States next year to study sheep farming. But what he can accomplish here, I don't know. We've tried pretty much everything and know what works best. He says we should plant different crops and all, but I think that Argentina's problem is that it has only a few people and lots of land. There aren't enough people to clear the land, although there used to be a lot more montes than there are now. Montes are a real problem—everyone wants land that's been cleared. That's one of the problems of the New World." For his part, Pierre thinks Aldo is unnecessarily hampered by the small size of his property. "He could do a lot more to get ahead with the land he has, but he needs to change his mentality. These gringos think they're so progressive, but it's not true any more. They're not that much more forward-thinking than creoles. They won't change the kind of crops they've always planted. They won't fatten their cattle themselves; instead they sell them off to ranchers in the south of the province to fatten. They refuse to go into dairy farming. If I had Aldo's property, I'd go into the dairy business. Take Stringat—now he's different."

Hugo Stringat is an enterprising local farmer, the administrator of the San Sebastiano dairy cooperative, the Cooperativa Tamberos, established in the 1960's. He is not a native of the area, however, and he and Pierre are still considered outsiders because their attitudes are different from those of people with deeper roots in San Sebastiano. Hugo has been trying unsuccessfully to interest farmers in expanding the operations of the cooperative. On his way to the village, Pierre stopped in at Hugo's office to pay his bill. Hugo was at his desk, oblivious of the stiff winter wind that nervously whipped at the door and blew around the loose papers in front of him. Pierre entered and kidded him about his inattentiveness, then closed the door, only to have it blow open immediately. "Oh, I see," laughed Pierre. Bending over the hot plate, they warmed their hands over the steam from the teakettle and shared maté. When Pierre announced that he should be going, Hugo fumbled through the bills stashed in a drawer and finally found Pierre's accounts for the past month, making a little pile of them. Pierre paid his usual 30,000 pesos ($10) on his bill, charged another plastic bucket of milk pudding (dulce de leche) to his account, and returned the maté gourd to Hugo.

In back of Hugo's office is the cooperative—merely an empty building with a refrigerator, no more than a brief stopping point in the chain of collection and distribution of milk from about fifty farms. The cooperative itself owns no equipment: the province owns the refrigerator, and the large cooperative in Paraná that buys San Sebastiano's milk owns the truck that picks it up and takes it to Paraná. San Sebastiano makes no milk by-products, such as cheese, butter, or dulce de leche. Hugo has them in stock only because he has bought them from the Paraná cooperative.

Pierre finds frequent indications of the difference between Hugo and the other gringos in San Sebastiano, who are mainly Waldenses. Pierre is a gringo himself, but is of Catholic French and Italian background. "You'd think the farmers in San Sebastiano would cooperate with a fellow Waldense like Hugo, but they don't," he said one day after a particularly frustrating meeting he'd held in the campo. He is asked most often to speak on the kind of forage to plant. "Farmers here could do a lot more to improve their living conditions. Not just in the sense of fixing up their homes either, though there's certainly room for that. There's hardly any difference between creole and Waldensian houses—the people who do fix up their houses have usually been to the city or abroad. But they could also improve their methods of farming. Waldenses in Belgrano (in the province of Santa Fe), where Hugo comes from, live better than Waldenses here, partly because they have better roads but also because they're more progressive." [14]

San Sebastiano is an inbred community both in blood lines and in ideas, and Pierre is not surprised, only frustrated, that people do not heed his suggestions. But at least he doesn't have to try and enforce laws like his friend Juan Coisson. Juan has worked for the Animal Health (Sanidad Animal) office for fifteen years, always in the area of San Sebastiano, and is a Waldense, but like Pierre he is an outsider. He is in charge of seeing that farmers bathe their cattle every twenty-one days for ticks (the *garrapata*). "The farmers are dragging their heels again," he says, "especially those who have only a few head of cattle. I can't seem to convince some of them that they need to keep to the bathing schedule. You know, I started out as a teacher and then I decided I didn't like 'mental work,' but I don't know, sometimes the farmers give me a lot of trouble. People here are so rooted and backward—it's because of the particular class of people who live here. Lots of farmers here don't bother to sow crops anymore: it's a lot of expense for very little profit. I don't know how, but in other provinces with fewer resources the people seem to be able to do more for themselves."

The people that Benabou, Stringat, and Coisson are talking about are descendants of immigrants, themselves once considered progressive outsiders. A new group of outsiders sees itself as having replaced them in this role. The more entrenched gringos with deep roots in San Sebastiano now echo the old creole plea—to let their world remain the same so that they can continue their way of life.

People's reluctance to change the traditional way they have lived and farmed has certainly been a factor in reducing agriculture's profitableness. But if we are to explain these people's complex vision, it is not enough to refer simply to "tradition." We must also look to some of the other features of San Sebastiano and La Paz life, and the general economic situation in Argentina. San Sebastiano lacks basic man-made improvements like good roads, and is also lacking in some of the natural ingredients, like good soil. Pierre complains that La Paz's heavy black clay soil is one of the worst in the province. "It's hard to work when it's dry and it's sticky when it's wet and it doesn't yield much; it's really better for cattle raising. Southern Entre Ríos really has much better soil," and he spouts off comparative production figures from memory.[15]

"I can help farmers cope with the soil, but I can't do anything about the economy. There's a sense of resignation brought on by the economic situation. People can't make investments now and can't take the risks that change involves. The peso is worth nothing; there's high inflation (which reached 800 percent in 1983); and Argentina's debt is one of the three largest in the world. There's high unemployment. For all intents and purposes the automotive industry in Córdoba, for example, has folded. Farmers have to sell cheap because prices for farm products are low, and go into debt to buy machinery, fuel, and seeds that are expensive. This affects the way they farm, of course. To use a simplified example—since no one talks in just hundreds of pesos anymore—if a farmer spends 100 pesos to sow two and a half acres of flax and sells his harvest six months later, he gets 130 pesos. But if he has to get a loan of 100 pesos to plant the two and a half acres of flax, in six months he will owe 180 pesos! On the other hand, if he puts 100 pesos in the bank for six months he will earn 160 pesos! So what's he going to do? Put his money in the bank, of course, not plant flax. Who knows what's going to happen to agriculture if this trend keeps up. Farmers are in a cruel bind: they need to earn more money, but they can't afford to farm more land. It's no wonder they've been letting some of their cleared land go back to montes."

With the economy in trouble, the basic structures that farmers depend on are threatened. About an hour away in Santa Elena the meat-processing plant is about to go bankrupt. Exports are down, so the plant has to sell its products very cheaply. This means that it has been falling behind in its payments. Like the rest of Argentine business and industry, it has its credit in dollars. A 10,000-peso note that used to be worth ten dollars is now worth three, so the plant can never get ahead to repay its loans. It has become so heavily indebted to the Bank of Entre Ríos (the provincial bank) that ownership has passed to the provincial government. People hope the plant will not fail, because if it does, the bank will go under too.

One day when the sun was shining strong enough to cut through the winter cold, Oscar Baridon was sitting in the doorway of his shop, as he liked to do. He owns the Girasol ("Sunflower") appliance store in La Paz. As the farmers get poorer, so does he. He was talking to his sister, who was dusting the records, televisions, and refrigerators behind him. "It's no wonder I'm not selling any TVs. Who can afford these imports? Anyway, we're only a ten-hour bus ride from Brazil here. All anyone has to do is go over there and he can buy a TV for half the price I can sell it for! I've had this store ever since we moved in from San Sebastiano, and I've never seen business so bad. A small town is at a disadvantage in this economy because there aren't enough people to absorb the goods when inflation hits. I heard that some farmers in Colonia Número 13 are selling off their land—but it would be too hard for me to move now, what with our store and land and all. I remember the early 1970's— they were good years—and even during the inflationary years between 1973 and 1975 business was stable. I sold maybe ten TVs a month then. In 1976 when the real recession set in, I was still selling maybe seven a month. Now I'm lucky if I sell three. So I'm stuck with these sets and paying interest on them and I'm bound to come out way behind.

"It's real bad now, but the other day I was talking to a landowner and he said the economy hasn't reached the bottom yet. Martínez de Hoz made this mess.[16] Now we've got Roberto Alemann and he's no better. Before Martínez de Hoz left office he said that no one sector of the economy was doing better than any other. What he meant was that the whole country was badly off, but he didn't want to put it in such a negative way!" Oscar laughed as he brushed the flat outstretched back of his hand against his chin: "Qué sé yo? We always survive."

Over on Federal Street the lawyer Toni Howard has the unpleasant job of taking care of people who might not survive. More loan default cases have been piling up on his desk than ever before. He is the Paraná Bank's lawyer and one of its twelve board members. "Well, what this means is that I must appear at the bank once or twice in the morning, or if I can't go I must call them and say why, and then they may tell me to come anyway! All they want me to do really is answer legal questions and go over the list of people who are ten days late in their loan payments to the bank. I can let a person renew his loan for up to thirty-six months, but if he doesn't pay then, I have to initiate a lawsuit against him on behalf of the bank. I'm handling eighteen cases for them now—some for lots of money. Most are under 30 million pesos ($10,000), but I have one for 140 million pesos ($40,000).

"The only reason people take out loans now is to pay off debts. All the stores here, for example, owe money to the banks because sales are down and the price of the goods they buy is up. They just can't make a profit anymore. Let's say they bought something for 30,000 pesos ($10) last month and sold it this month for 60,000 pesos ($20): they should make a profit of 30,000 pesos ($10). But it now costs them 90,000 pesos ($30) to replace that object on their shelves. So they don't make any money. Plus, they're not selling half as much as they were a year ago. There are two stores that are doing especially badly in La Paz. One sells at wholesale prices; it used to have about 10,000 different items in stock. It was doing well until a year ago, but now it's in real bad shape. And the big clothing store over on Goya Street is heavily in debt. If these stores were to ask for loans today, they would have to pay 127 percent interest a year. If they paid the interest ahead of time, which they could do, it would mean they'd really be getting no money at all from the bank—in fact, they'd owe the bank money! It's crazy!

"Everything's fantastically expensive in Argentina. Do you know what I paid for my car? Fourteen thousand dollars with the taxes, and it's one of the cheaper cars—a Dodge Colt. We'd like to get a photocopier for the office, but the simplest model costs $3,000. I bought my house in November 1979, the same one we'd been renting for years. It cost $20,000, then worth 30 million pesos. I got a twenty-month loan on it, paid $1,000 down plus 1 percent interest a month. The reason I got such a low rate was that I was paying in dollars." Like many people who are well-off, Toni sometimes pays for larger purchases in U.S. dollars. "Now, that $20,000 is equal to 70 million pesos! My partner, Rodolfo Guzmán, has a twenty-five-year loan for his house. Under his credit system, the interest rate changes monthly depending on the level of the average salary, one of the official indices." The expenses of daily life are pegged to seven indices established monthly: the cost of living, wholesale prices, wholesale agricultural products, wages and federal capital, construction costs, the cost of money (an average of interest rates), and the price of the U.S. dollar. Without knowing what these indices are, people do not know how much money they will have for the next month. Their rent may go up, for example, or the interest rate on a bank loan. "We aren't in Buenos Aires," said Toni Howard, "and can't go to the Ministry of Economy to get these indices, so we have to wait until they come out in the paper. Then Rodolfo finds out the bad news—that the interest rate on his mortgage has gone up! Of course, these indices aren't always very accurate. For example, the index of the percentage increase for consumer products is based on a package of items that includes things no longer in common use, like block ice! It's been a long time since people have had iceboxes. Lots of people have lost their homes because instead of making mortgage payments equal to a third of their salary, now they'd have to pay three times their salary. Loans are always keyed to an index, but salaries and pensions aren't." Salaries and pensions have increased, but not nearly as much as the rate of inflation: in 1976 people considered 12 million pesos ($4,000) to be an average annual middle-class income for a family of five in San Sebastiano and La Paz; in 1981 an income of 36 million pesos ($12,000) was barely enough to make ends meet.

Aldo Prochet was considering buying a new tractor, but returned home from Toni's bank disappointed: "No new tractor this year. I can't afford to ask for credit anymore—no one can. We'll just keep the old one running, isn't that right, Attilio? Or plant less land. What do I know? This indexed credit system. First I have to try and get the bank to base my interest rate for a loan on the agricultural products index, but they won't necessarily do this. But say I get them to do it and I get a loan for a new tractor at 10 percent interest. If the cost of that tractor goes up the next year and I still owe money on it, my interest rate goes up. So who can get ahead? If I plant less, I need fewer peons to help me, so then there's not enough work for them. Farming sure was different eight or nine years ago. No wonder they didn't hold Farmers' Day this year!"

It is common to hear people like Aldo attribute at least part of their problem to the "Chicago boys," as they are popularly called in Argentina—to distant Milton Friedman and the Chicago School of economic thought based on free-market theory. The "Chicago boys" became the mentors of recent Argentine economics ministers, especially José Martínez de Hoz, minister from 1976 to 1981. The result has been high inflation, the bankruptcy of many businesses both large and small, and high unemployment. "Argentina can import easily under this free-market policy," says Pierre Benabou, "but we can't export—why, we're even importing beef now and the government is telling restaurants in Buenos Aires that they can sell beef only on certain days! Five years ago Argentina hardly imported anything—it was all local production. Now everything is imported. Argentine industry can't compete."

The current economic crisis reflects the deeper Latin American problem of the unequal development of city and countryside, and the concentration on industrial development to the neglect of agriculture. About 40 percent of Argentina's population lives in Buenos Aires. Once outside the nation's capital, a person is in a different world. Even the next-largest cities, Rosario and Córdoba, are substantially different, and the contrast between Buenos Aires and the countryside is more striking still. Railroad construction in the nineteenth century reflects the overdevelopment of Buenos Aires and the coast, and the situation has not changed today. Even air traffic is funneled back to Buenos Aires instead of linking up the interior. Between the world wars there was a drive to industrialize, which many people feel damaged the country during the Peronist years of the 1940's and 1950's. Ernestina Prochet has a photo of her family's wheat threshing machine, which they had bought in 1928, on the buffet. "We sold it after Perón had been in power for a while. He was busy supporting the workers and industry and we didn't know when the government would change." Agriculture did not, in fact, fare well under the Peronists and has never realized the potential profits the 1930's seemed to promise.[17]

At an asado at the Micols' house one night, Umberto Eckstein was worrying about the countryside. "If the land was like it used to be and if the poor could work a little land, plant some vegetables for themselves and all, things would be all right now. But no, the nation's forgotten the campo. I saw a cartoon in *Clarín* the other day about President Viola's visit to the Chaco. Two men were talking and one said, 'I read that the president is going to the Chaco.' The other said, 'That's good. It seems to me that the interior should be remembered.' Then the first said, 'If I could, I'd also go visit a whole lot of provinces.' 'Yeah,' agreed the second, 'before they disappear!'"[18]

The response of people in San Sebastiano and La Paz to their economic situation provides a good measure of their values. The large multi-generational farming household, with its shared goals and its support system, is a way of life in the campo that is not easily given up, even though there are now problems with agriculture as an economic activity. Economists may feel confident in defining the parameters of the problem, but rural people are by no means in agreement about why farming has become unprofitable. The attitude of the outsiders in San Sebastiano reaffirms the old immigrant emphasis on a hard-working and progressive-thinking population. The outsiders' perception, that the descendants of immigrants have abandoned those values and adopted a different mentality, explains, for them, why San Sebastiano farmers have been unable to do more with their economic situation. They suggest change—but for the typical farmer like Aldo Prochet a new crop would involve more than just a change in the seeds he plants, and going back into dairy farming would involve more than just buying dairy cows; it would require a change in his living pattern and attitude. Aldo's "Even the chickens have their history" means that chickens, like people, have their routine, and that routine is basic to their history. He cannot change one without risk to the other.

The question of values aside, no group denies the effect of the economic crisis. Whereas once terrorism and repression were uppermost in people's minds, now it is the economy that occupies their thoughts. In the early 1980's Argentines were anxiously wondering what the outcome of the crisis would be. In an especially apt newspaper cartoon, one man says to another, "I read a discouraging article the other day about the future of our economy." The other replies, "It must not have been very discouraging if it mentioned a future!" [19]

The Relationship Between San Sebastiano and La Paz

In a configuration like San Sebastiano and La Paz, that is, a village with its farmland and a nearby town, and especially in current economic circumstances, one might suppose that San Sebastiano would be swallowed up by La Paz, losing population and economic viability. There is, however, a special relationship between San Sebastiano and La Paz that is not explained by the dichotomies of rural and urban or countryside and magnet town. Each is seen as having its own particular virtues, and together they are seen as making a whole.

Like a typical magnet town, La Paz provides the credit, business, and cultural infrastructure for the countryside. La Paz has, after all, well over a thousand commercial and industrial establishments, as well as secondary schools, a library, and a museum, whereas San Sebastiano has only a handful of stores and businesses. People from San Sebastiano go to La Paz to use the four banks, the twenty-four lawyers, the twenty doctors, the public hospital, the pharmacies, the veterinarians. They go to town for the governmental offices of the department, for the municipal offices of La Paz, for national agency offices like INTA, and for the utility offices. They can find farm machinery, televisions, kitchen appliances, and many smaller items in La Paz. If they want their children to attend high school, they must send them to La Paz. The traffic along the road from San Sebastiano to La Paz is not heavy, but it is steady.

One Saturday (an official business day like Monday through Friday), Aldo Prochet drove into town to get the papers he needed from the Animal Health office to sell some of his cattle. He also paid a rare visit to the Federación Agraria, a national agricultural union that represents small farmers, agricultores, and colonos. Its headquarters are in Rosario, where his son Miguel attends the university. Miguel had sent the Prochets a package through one of the union officials. Down the street from the Federación is the office of another major national agricultural union, the powerful Sociedad Rural, a conservative association of large ranchers that has its main office on the elegant Calle Florida in Buenos Aires. Aldo noticed the big rancher Martinelli pumping someone's hand in the Sociedad Rural's doorway; its members have money and political connections. On Sunday Aldo and Elsa decided to stay in La Paz rather than go out to their ranch in San Sebastiano. The town is peaceful over the weekend, but the pace accelerates on Monday.

Monday is the busiest day in La Paz; along with Friday, it is commonly a "town" day for campo people. Lawyers Howard and Guzmán were particularly busy because many of their clients are elderly people who have put in for a pension; they know that the lawyers go to Paraná on Friday and they come to town on Monday expecting news about their cases. This particular Monday morning it was late and Toni had just left home. He drove the three blocks to his office in a great rush, greeted Diego Montañes, the radio announcer, who was propped leisurely in the station's doorway, and as he bounded up the stairs, called a greeting back down to the Coke distributor, who had just emerged from his office. He nodded at his clients in the waiting room and greeted them with a long drawn-out "Buenos," hurrying by too quickly to follow it with "días." Bidding hello to his secretaries at their maté, he skipped up the last step to his office and tossed his briefcase onto his desk. Down the hall, on the rooftop patio, he found his partner Rodolfo, sprawled over the dismantled parts of the office toilet's flush mechanism. The toilet would have to be fixed later, Toni said; the waiting room had filled up, so it was time they got to work and attended to their clients.

The traffic to La Paz continues throughout the week. On Tuesday one might encounter Teresa de González on the bus in from San Sebastiano. Her daughter has bronchitis, and she is on her way to the public hospital to pick up some medicine. All her kids are sick actually, she explains to the nurse; it's been so wet, their rancho hasn't had a chance to dry out. On Wednesday, Domenico Antonini comes in to invest $500 in a short-term, fifteen-day account at the bank. Thursday, Tullio Gilly, a member of the governing junta in San Sebastiano, delivers some paperwork to the electric company office in La Paz. He has just finished his rounds of the seventy-eight buildings of San Sebastiano that have electricity, reading the meters and entering the figures into a log. On Friday, Stefano Gilly comes into town to visit his mother, Inés, who is recovering from cancer surgery and is living in La Paz to be close to her sisters and a doctor. Afterward, Stefano buys a record at the Girasol.

A casual observer would conclude, with some justification, that La Paz functions as a magnet town. But the relationship between town and countryside is more complex than this. Our observer might begin by watching the reverse traffic from La Paz to San Sebastiano. Monday morning, Aldo Prochet returns to live in the campo for the week. Elsa lives in town, but Aldo sometimes takes her out to San Sebastiano on Saturday to spend the weekend on their ranch. One of the Prochets' high school boarders, who takes only the midday meal at Elsa's, returns to San Sebastiano at night, and the other boarder returns to her home in nearby Massimo Castro on weekends. Umberto Eckstein drives out to the dairy cooperative to buy some dulce de leche and stops at his farm, which his son runs, to get some vegetables and some blood sausages. Eduardo Howard lives in La Paz but drives to San Sebastiano daily to work his ranch. María Carmen García's father, over in the poor Barrio La Costa area of La Paz, is a peon and like his neighbors gets most of his work in the campo.

The relationship between La Paz and the campo is not one-sided, then. Nor is it all-embracing. Many people in San Sebastiano do not use La Paz's institutions and businesses. They are more likely, for example, to use informal credit systems than to take out a loan from a bank. La Paz has only basic health facilities at the public hospital, and if people can afford it, they go elsewhere, like Inés de Gilly, to special private clinics in other towns, to Paraná, and even to Buenos Aires. La Paz does not have a full complement of government offices, which is why lawyers like Howard and Guzmán have to go to Paraná each week as part of their job. People do not necessarily depend on La Paz for manufactured goods. They buy very few consumer items, furnishing their homes sparsely, making do with what they already have. They avoid buying goods like clothing that they can make at home. For expensive items like televisions and calculators, they try to go to Brazil. They seldom have any reason to go to the utility offices in La Paz since only a few of them have phones or electricity.

Looking further at the relationship from the San Sebastiano side, we find that certain institutions in La Paz are actually dependent on San Sebastiano. INTA, the Animal Health office, the agricultural unions, the veterinarians, the seed and fertilizer stores, and the agricultural tools, machinery, and repair shops would not exist if it were not for San Sebastiano. Another level of dependence is exemplified by the banks. The La Paz banks need to know the news from San Sebastiano as well as from La Paz before undertaking loans. They are tied into the networks in both places. As Toni Howard explains, "We have the gossip system of credit here! If someone applies to the bank for a loan and I know that they've had trouble paying off a loan before or that they're unreliable in some other way, they won't get the loan. It's my job to gather information through gossip in order to analyze the reasons people give for not repaying their loans. There's also an interbank information system between the four banks in La Paz—they exchange information about a person's resources. This personal system can work for you too, of course."

La Paz has twenty times as many inhabitants as San Sebastiano, and like a magnet town it provides some of the market for the countryside's farm products. San Sebastiano sells fruit and vegetables to stores in town, but it is only a small producer of these foodstuffs. Its grain, beef, and dairy products are much more important. There are five mills in La Paz, and the Agricultural Cooperative buys grain from its San Sebastiano members. But farm products typically don't go directly to La Paz. San Sebastiano milk, for example, is bought by a cooperative in Paraná, and its beef is bought by the plant in Santa Elena. Rice, too, an important product in the San Sebastiano area, is processed and packaged elsewhere. Thus the major products of the colony find their way back to La Paz only after passing through the hands of middlemen in other cities.

The marketing of the colony's products via outside middlemen is a constant source of complaint in La Paz, as is the government intervention that has contributed to the problem. The enforcement of milk pasteurization is a case in point. The San Sebastiano cooperative pays farmers ten cents per liter of milk, but by the time the milk is taken to Paraná and pasteurized and shipped back to La Paz and San Sebastiano, it costs eighty cents. Milk may be safer to drink, but it is also priced beyond the reach of the very poor who have no land or cow. People who do, continue to drink raw milk. Another health regulation, passed recently, prohibits the butchering and selling of cattle in the campo. The law not only has increased the price of meat but has created difficulties for farmers, who are required to take their cattle to a processing plant; the nearest plants to San Sebastiano are at least an hour away in Santa Elena, or a half day's drive away in Paraná and Santa Fe. An exception is made only for farmers who sell to butchers located more than ten miles from an asphalt road where delivery trucks from the processing plants some-times cannot get through. A further problem is that the processed meat is preserved by refrigeration rather than salting. Refrigerated meat does not last as long as fresh meat that has been salted, so that when the electricity goes off for long periods—power outages can last three or four days in the campo—the refrigerated meat spoils. It can be an expensive risk, then, to buy processed meat. Besides, its taste does not appeal to people used to salted meat. Nothing can be done about taste, except to add great quantities of salt—which people do—but there is room for improvement in the infrastructure within which the regulation on meat operates.

San Sebastiano does have one way of retaining control of its prod-ucts: they are brought directly to La Paz tables by families and friends. People use farm products every day as payment in kind—some beef for fixing a television, for example, or for feeding a high school boarder in town, or as part of a peon's wages, or as the por-tion of the family farm's produce due to a relative in La Paz.

La Paz, then, does not really provide a commercial and communi-cation link for San Sebastiano like a true magnet town, since many of San Sebastiano's products are sent elsewhere. La Paz does have a port, but it has not been very active for some time. Goods are trans-ported mainly by truck. The paved road from Paraná goes through La Paz, but it also passes by San Sebastiano, making the village al-most as accessible as the town. The only difference is that people in La Paz are twenty miles closer to Paraná, the common destination, and that the smaller road into San Sebastiano can be flooded during the rainy season where it crosses the Jacinto River.

San Sebastiano and La Paz are better explained as a single unit than as a dichotomy, and an important factor in their operation as a unit is the overlap in their populations. This is not a case of migration to town leaving village and countryside depopulated and impover-ished. The people of San Sebastiano have not exchanged campo for town, one life-style and one economic activity for another. Rather, they have incorporated the town into their lives; they live and work in both town and colony.[20]

If Toni Howard makes an early start, he can catch a ride to San Sebastiano with his octogenarian father, Eduardo. Eduardo Howard moved to town twenty years ago, but he drives out daily to his es-tancia in San Sebastiano. He still has about 2,500 acres. After Toni and Eduardo pass through the outskirts of La Paz—an area of sandy ravines and low hills with one-story houses, really garden-farms—the grass starts taking over and becomes as tall as mature corn plants. After they turn off the main road into San Sebastiano, Eduardo accelerates through the village on its short stretch of asphalt—just two and a half miles long—scattering chickens and dogs and imperiously honking at people on foot and horseback, making the villagers turn in their tracks and chuckle, "There goes Don Eduardo." Of course people always stop in their path to see who is going by—it is something one does in San Sebastiano. But Eduardo, lean, straight, and energetic, inspires a feeling of proprietary affection among the villagers. Many immigrant colonies must have produced people like him: curious, dual-culture beings, oases of antiquated British customs and speech patterns on the edge of the frontier. No one in San Sebastiano chides him for his imprudent driving—pedestrians and animals are expected to look out for themselves—but they do worry for his safety.

When the car came along, Don Eduardo adapted but held to the techniques he uses with his horse, as though horse and car had the same nature. He rides his Citroën the way he rides his horse: furiously depressing the accelerator to the floor spurring it on, ignoring its bucking protests; increasing speed till the last minute, impatiently jerking it to a quick stop. Every now and then he fails to rein in the car properly, and he has had one near-fatal collision with a horse that has become part of village lore. When they found him, he was a mess of broken bones, and was not even conscious that the horse's head lay severed in his lap. But neither the memory of a mere accident nor the fact that he is now 81 ever keeps Eduardo from the daily jaunt to his farm.

Through people like Eduardo, who live in both San Sebastiano and La Paz, the economies of town and countryside necessarily overlap. Some of the San Sebastiano schoolteachers live in La Paz. The San Sebastiano telephone operator lives in San Sebastiano, but her husband, because of his work, lives in La Paz. A San Sebastiano woman who works as a maid in La Paz returns home to her husband and children on weekends. High school students live in both places. This overlapping population almost always spends money and uses services in town and village, and very often owns property in both. Eduardo has land and houses in both, does his shopping in both, and donates money to help support the school in the village of

San Sebastiano and a church in La Paz. Many shopkeepers, public employees, and professionals in La Paz own land in or near San Sebastiano, and some member of their family usually takes charge of running the farm. It is not uncommon for people to have homes in both places, like Aldo and Elsa Prochet who bought a house in La Paz when their children began high school, or Ernestina Prochet who bought a house in town so that her family could be closer to doctors.

In important ways, then, San Sebastiano and La Paz are to be seen as a unit, where neither is stifling the other's economy or absorbing the other's population. Such problems as develop are typically problems arising, not from any separation of town and campo, but from the unequal development of the porteño-centered coast and the interior, and from conditions in the national economy. Indeed, the special relationship between San Sebastiano and La Paz helps people weather those problems.

Strategies of Economic Survival

One strategy of economic survival in San Sebastiano and La Paz centers on personalized relationships that help to ameliorate the often harsh economic realities of life in the two communities. Such personalization, to a degree, now characterizes the way people live all over Argentina, even in the capital. Dora de Micol's sister Eside lives in Buenos Aires, where she and her husband, Adolfo Bounous, own a small advertising firm that employs two other people part-time. A middle-class couple with two children, Eside and Adolfo are able to buy food, pay their bills, and make their loan payments only by borrowing from their friends, a little here, a little there. When Adolfo is paid for a job, his friends in turn borrow from him. No one gets ahead; the object is just to plug the holes in the weakening dam. "It's really a lot worse now than it's ever been—we had to move to this building last year because it's cheaper," says Eside, standing on the balcony of their apartment. "I see fighting in the streets now. Look at that man down there. He's like us, not a vagrant, and he's going through the garbage. Lots of middle-class men, even, have lost their jobs now and can't find work; their wives have to go out and do domestic work. The teachers at my daughter's school tell me some of the students have trouble concentrating in class and they think it's because the children have gone without dinner the night before. And the taxi and bus drivers have gone crazy. Everything's so bad, they don't care how fast they drive."

In order to cope with the economic situation, people like Eside and Adolfo must understand a surprising amount about the functioning of the economy. Eside always knows when the new month's economic indices will be available: she watches for the sign to go up outside the Ministry of Economy. As soon as it does, she goes to the Ministry, surrenders her purse and parcels, signs a log and gets a badge, and waits in line along with hundreds of other people to get the indices.

The indices are equally important in San Sebastiano. "We're all linked to the national and international money picture, even here," says Toni Howard. "The government has been telling us since the 1950's not to speculate, but we really have to. The farmers don't have the means to be big speculators, but they do hold off selling their cattle till the price goes up—things like that. And we all have to manipulate our money in and out of savings accounts all the time. It's best to put your money into the short-term accounts, fifteen or at the most sixty days, because the interest paid there is higher than the inflation rates of the indices. We have to do something to earn a little money! I earn much less now in terms of buying power, plus I can't count on my clients to pay me these days. Same with Pellegrino and Sons. I'm handling ten cases of theirs against people who owe them money—sometimes a lot."

The personalized nature of life in San Sebastiano and La Paz makes it possible for people to live almost wholly on credit, although sometimes it does not work out, as with Pellegrino's clients. Extension of credit is a personal arrangement between shopkeeper and customer, rather than one based on credit cards or on credit programs offered by stores. It allows people to charge their daily purchases, particularly food, and pay on their accounts whenever they have some extra cash. Although shopkeepers are caught by outstanding debts themselves, they need to retain people's patronage by extending them credit. Toni and Rodolfo's secretaries make several trips a day to the stationery store on the corner for photocopies and paper. The storeowner records their purchases in a notebook kept, not by him, but by the lawyers. It hangs in the kitchen of their suite of offices, on the wall next to the hotplate. The storeowner does not enter the price of the goods until the end of the month, when Toni goes to pay the bill. This way they avoid getting tangled up by any devaluations that may have occurred during the month.

In 1976, when schoolteacher Dora de Micol's salary had not been paid by the government for nearly half a year in the confusion following the military takeover, she was able to continue buying groceries at her usual store on credit. Every week or so she would try to pay something on her outstanding bill. She finally began to receive a paycheck again, but the economy got worse and she has never really been able to catch up.

It was ten-thirty on a Saturday morning and Dora had recently come back from charging a mid-morning breakfast at the bread store across the street. Oscar had just returned on the overnight bus from his monthly Waldensian meeting in Uruguay. They were animatedly making their way through numerous matés and a pound of hard biscuits, in a slow crescendo that would peak at the midday meal, when Umberto Eckstein, stooped and red-faced, shuffled his bulky frame into the kitchen. "Have some maté?" asked Oscar, thrusting the gourd in Umberto's direction. "It's from Uruguay— packaged in Brazil, sold in Uruguay, and drunk in Argentina!" After an exchange of news about relatives and friends in Uruguay, the conversation turned to the economy. "I read yesterday," Umberto began, "about a family in the Chaco that has twenty-two children. The father earns 600,000 pesos ($200) a month in salary and 2,400,000 pesos ($800) a month in family subsidies!" Family subsidies differ depending on which union a person belongs to. "Sure makes it hard to believe what the government claims, that Argentina's economic problems are due to underpopulation!" laughed Oscar. "There used to be a saying that every child comes into the world with a loaf of bread under his arm. People think that family subsidies, and the money their kids can make, can help them, but it sure can't make up for inflation. I think we should change that saying now to, Every child comes into the world with a list of debts!"

Children are considered to have economic worth at an early age. Most lower-class families in San Sebastiano and La Paz try to keep their children in school through the third grade, but many have to withdraw them at this point, both because they cannot afford the school supplies and uniforms and because they cannot afford to keep their children out of the workforce. Working children under the age of fourteen can make an important difference in a family's income. The middle and upper classes, however, both realize the value of an education and have the luxury of being able to carry this through. They want their children to have a choice of career rather than depend on agriculture, and they are no longer reluctant to send their children to La Paz for secondary school as they were before the late 1960's when they still feared the corrupting influence of the town.

The middle and upper classes also have the means to make the best of the economic situation. They can afford to take bus trips to Brazil, where prices are lower. They have the means to earn "egg money" as they call it. Aldo and Elsa Prochet bought their house in La Paz when Miguel, their oldest son, began high school in town. Living in town has also been an advantage to their daughter, Lucia, and now their last child, Antonio. When Lucia left home, Elsa used the spare bedroom to earn extra money and began taking in boarders—high-school-age children who want to continue school and therefore must live in town. Ernestina and Liliana Prochet, well-to-do spinster sisters in their fifties, have also taken in boarders, and Ernestina earns extra money as a seamstress and sewing teacher. Their house is small, but until their brothers became ill and moved in with them, they rented a room in back to a woman and her son and took in three high school girls as well. Two slept in a narrow room curtained off from the kitchen, just large enough for two twin beds placed end-to-end. The third and youngest made up her bed on the sewing table at night when Ernestina finished working.

This type of thrift has so extended the range of what people consider to be non-essential that it has become a style of life rather than merely an economic measure—but a style of life that is nonetheless useful in straitened times. People like Ernestina and Elsa who respect the old immigrant ideal of thrift—originally the only way for their ancestor-renters to get ahead and buy their land—have certainly been able to use it to their economic advantage. Their scrimping and saving goes beyond thrift to become an almost completely utilitarian attitude toward living. To Ernestina, luxuries are occasional five-and-dime additions to her motley collection of cracked and chipped teacups, or material for a new dress. Moreover, she would not consider buying these items unless they could be paid for with her "egg money." Certain features of her house seem more appropriate to a poor barrio than a well-heeled neighborhood. Her house has glass windows and the typical rancho in a poor barrio does not, but since some of Ernestina's windows are broken, the effect is the same: neither puts up any defense against insects. A pane of glass in a kitchen window is missing, and ants have established a right of passage across the counter to the sink and out again through a break under the sill of the other window. An occasional cloud of insect spray from Ernestina's aerosol throws confusion into their ranks, but only for a moment. The Prochets eat indoors, but their eating arrangements do not differ markedly from a rancho family's. Across the kitchen from the windows, people eat in shifts for lack of enough glasses, plates, and utensils to go around. Home repairs and table service are considered unnecessary expenses. To the Prochets, this is a value-based style of life; to peons in a rancho barrio, it is necessity-based; to oldtimer Bruno Bouissa, it is stinginess. Whatever label it wears, it is a style of life that appears repeatedly. The leftovers of meals are always used up completely before any new food is cooked. Houses contain the bare minimum of furniture and decoration. The necessities of the middle and upper classes in the cities—comforts such as indoor plumbing and hot water—are here considered luxuries. Thrift may have lost the original purpose assigned it by the early colonists, but it has gained renewed importance thanks to the failing economy.

"Egg money" and thrift are as much a part of the personalized and cooperative nature of economic strategies as are devices like informal credit systems, employing children, and knowing how to manipulate, or at least be informed about, the economy. People make money by taking in high school boarders, but they also provide a service that saves people the expense and inconvenience of buying a house in La Paz or taking their children daily to and from a school miles from their home. The practice of thrift saves money that people are willing to use to help others, because, as we will see later, existing alongside thrift is a widespread generosity.

The personalized aspects of economic strategies have enabled San Sebastiano to do at least as well as La Paz, in spite of the difference in their resources. San Sebastiano cannot hope to develop as complex an economy as La Paz—it lacks a large and wealthy enough population—but neither are its services and businesses going under. It is successful, not because of formal structures and institutions, but because it operates on an even more personal level than La Paz does. Many professions are not formally represented in San Sebastiano—there are no lawyers and no doctors—but informally, Tullio Gilly gives legal advice and midwives and local healers take care of people's medical problems. There is little chance of becoming indebted to these people, since their advice and care is offered free or for an exchange in kind. There is no national phone service. A rural one exists, but only a handful of people are hooked into it and most people have rigged up their own phones to neighboring farms. San Sebastiano stores fare better than La Paz stores in certain ways. They may not have the opportunity to amass the same kind of wealth, but on the other hand they are not overinvested. Over the years, shopkeepers in San Sebastiano have come to know the needs of their customers and the folly of buying novelties, that is, anything in excess of those needs. Economic interdependence among villagers is the key to the working economy in San Sebastiano. To a large extent people can live on the fringes of the cash economy, engaging in a barter economy independent of the fragile national one. It is customary, especially among family and friends, to exchange advice or health care for some beef or maté, a car repair for the loan of a tractor, and so on. Families are often large and thus have a foothold in many areas of expertise, which benefits not only the immediate family but more distant relatives and friends as well. Carlos Baridon-Charbonier's family includes an electrician, a lawyer, a doctor, a teacher, and several farmers. In addition to the cooperative economy of family and friends, there is a certain consciousness of the interdependence of all groups belonging to the community. In a village like San Sebastiano one would rarely be allowed to go homeless or hungry. People have shown their generosity, even before the times of economic strain, by raising other people's children, by taking in adults, and by caring for entire families.

In the early days of the colony, there was a myth that Argentine wealth was there for the taking. In the present economic situation this myth seems very distant, and people have found that, if anything, they have fallen far behind. San Sebastiano farmers have weathered difficult times since the colony's founding. Their ancestors immigrated to a new land, and sacrificed to gain financial security, and now it seems they might lose what their families have gained over a century. It worries them, as a people who value profit and success, that their families' efforts may in the long run have been wasted. But at the same time they recognize that they have been able to maintain and deepen their human relationships, reinforcing the public and personalized nature of San Sebastiano society.

THREE

The Social Texture

THOUGH THE CHILL in the air hinted at the approaching winter, the men working the cattle at the Olivera Cooperative's auction sat drenched in perspiration astride their horses. One of the sellers, Señora Von Ruden, was sitting near the top of the bleachers. She was dressed like any other woman of the campo, in a nondescript skirt with a 1950's cut and length, an inexpensive sweater, and loafers; she was knitting as she listened to the auctioneer and watched the peons work. There were fifteen of them, hired the day before to set up the pens and get the cattle into them. As the auction proceeded, they drove each seller's cattle into the field in front of the stands and then back to their pens. Aldo Prochet was in the stands too. About sixty head of cattle belonging to Aldo and his brother and sister had been rounded up and brought in for auctioning. He was talking to the head of the cooperative when Pierre Benabou of the National Institute of Agricultural Technology office noticed him. Pierre had not really planned to go to the auction, but he had had some business to attend to in the campo and had thus been passing by and been drawn by the crowd sitting out in the sun.

The peons had worked hard for two days now and they were tired. Their wage was small but would last them a few days until the next job came along—and enable them to enjoy themselves a bit in the meantime. That night the cooperative would put them up in a large open shed, a *galpón*, and feed them again. The first men to finish their work started riding back to the shed about 7 o'clock— it was only a couple minutes from the cattle pens and auction ground—to get the fire going for supper. As each man arrived at the shed, he dismounted with relief and threw his saddle gear, mainly blankets, onto the dirt floor of the shed for his bed later on. When the fire was reduced to coals, the men prepared their food. They sat around the fire in front of the shed, protected from possible rain by a tin sheet awning propped up by sticks. They spoke little as they squatted on logs, drinking maté and leaning over the fire to slice pieces of meat from the carcass roasting on the spit. They ate the beef with their work knives. After they finished, they leaned back on the logs, stretching out their aching legs. By now it was dark. They filled their maté gourds with water many times, the green liquid foaming at the top. As they toyed with the bombilla and sucked at the bitter drink, they grew more talkative and began contemplating a trip to Cerutti's bar the next evening, after they had been paid. One of them bet his neighbor that his horse was faster, and a race began to take shape for Sunday.

At his estancia, Aldo reported to Attilio that the prices were too low and that he'd decided to bide his time and not sell yet. But he would sell soon, he said, because he was certainly not going to try and fatten those scrawny beasts himself. Well, the peons he'd hired had gone home happy. They'd gotten twice the work and pay they'd planned on, since they'd had to drive the cattle back to the ranch again.

Back in his office, Pierre was talking about the auction with his colleague Luis Pujol, who does a radio program the Prochets like, "El Campo Tiene la Palabra" (The Countryside Speaks). Pierre sighed and told Luis about the ranchers from the south of Entre Ríos who had come to buy up La Paz cattle to fatten, and the La Paz ranchers like Aldo who were eager to sell, except that the prices were too low. Pierre had advised the farmers all year that it would not be profitable to sell their cattle this way. Aldo and the others always thought they knew what was best, but now Pierre had been proven right.

The peon workers, Aldo, and Pierre were all pleased with themselves, though not necessarily with the results of the auction. Each was satisfied that his vision was the right one, that his goals were good ones, and that he had acted in accord with these goals.

Creoles, Gringos, and Outsiders

The residents of San Sebastiano and La Paz place people in one of three categories. No one escapes this classification: the peon crew, Aldo, and Pierre represent, respectively, creoles, gringos, and outsiders. The categories are determined by chronological, ethnic, and socioeconomic factors. The creoles were the original population of San Sebastiano. Then came the large mass of immigrants, or gringos, in the nineteenth century, who were themselves considered outsiders at this point.[1] After the original gringo families had been in the area for a few generations, they began to view gringo newcomers as outsiders, as different. It does not matter that many of these "newcomers" have been in the area fifteen years and more; they are still considered outsiders. Creoles, like gringos, have a European background. They are the old Argentine stock, often (but not necessarily) of mixed Spanish and Indian background. They are regarded, not as descendants of Europeans, however, but rather as "natives." The term has a pejorative sense, denoting people who have lived in Argentina so long that they have become as barbarian and wild as the country itself. "Native" has come to be used synonymously with "creole." Gringos, both the insiders and the outsiders, are the descendants of European immigrants, mostly Italians, who are the main immigrant group in Argentina, but also French, Germans, and British. Economically and socially, people in each of these groups could conceivably belong to any class, but the majority of creoles are poor peons who have long been the main manual labor force. Thus "creole" and "peon" are often equated. Gringo insiders have done fairly well and, along with the gringo outsiders, are middle and upper class and usually landowners. A person's socioeconomic status therefore depends on two main factors: whether he has a gringo or a creole background, and whether he owns land.

Any of these distinctions—date of arrival in the area, ethnic background, and socioeconomic status—may be intended by someone using the labels creole, gringo, and outsider. But what makes the distinctions operative on a daily basis is that people associate a particular mentality with each of the three groups. Moreover, someone may be a gringo in chronological, ethnic, and socioeconomic terms and yet be labeled creole-like or not quite a gringo on account of his outlook or disposition. Used in this way, the label may have either negative or positive connotations. The word "creole" may be used approvingly to describe a gringo who is a fine horseman, for example, or to denote the ruggedness of a gringo who eats with his work knife in the field. On the other hand, Pierre Benabou uses the word in a negative sense when he attributes a creole mentality to gringo insiders, like Aldo Prochet; he is complaining of their reluctance to better their economic and living situations. Creoles can also be said to be gringo-like. The midwife Juana Inés Vilas is strictly creole and considers herself creole in most things, but she jokingly calls herself half gringa because she likes vegetables; since gringos are more likely to have vegetable gardens, a taste for vegetables is sometimes considered a gringo trait. It is precisely this kind of emphasis on a person's "mentality" that causes outsiders to remain outsiders, in their own view and in the eyes of others, long after they have established themselves in the area.

The particular mentality of a creole, a gringo, and an outsider hinges on his attitude toward his own and his community's progress. The oft-repeated comments of the gringo old-timers attest to the importance of the notion of progress in the early days of the colony. "The creoles never worked." "They only wanted to drink rum." "They could have progressed like we did; they had all the same chances." "But we worked hard, isn't that so? That's why we got ahead." And so on. It is with explanations like these that gringos account for the gulf that has traditionally separated creoles and gringos in San Sebastiano. Geographically, gringos became concentrated in the colony section, the farming area, of San Sebastiano, and creoles in the village. Further separation occurred when gringos built their houses on hilltops and left the less desirable low areas for creoles, so that every rise of land came to have a symbolic meaning. Economically, gringos prospered and the mass of creoles did not. Socially, the colony as a whole came to be so dominated by gringos that creoles have had to redefine their position in terms of values foreign to them. They have been put on the defensive about their supposed lack of interest in progress, laziness, and unproductiveness. Pierre Benabou's evaluation of the creole mentality is typical of the opinion of gringo insiders and outsiders. He cites their drunkenness, their reluctance to try the routinized work of dairy farming, and their refusal to take their sick animals to a vet—as well as their refusal to take their children to a doctor when they have diarrhea, the most common cause of death among children in the area. "Creoles are very isolated and individualistic. For example, we've been trying to lay an asphalt road in San Sebastiano, but the villagers (the majority of whom are creole) can't agree on where it should go so the idea has been scrapped. The creole's heritage is different from the gringo's. There are almost no vegetable gardens in San Sebastiano; no matter how rich or poor someone is, he will almost never plant a garden. He eats mainly potatoes and onions because this is what he can buy at the store." The key word in what Pierre is saying is "plant." Like old-timer Carlos Baridon-Charbonier with his story about the creole's insistence that nothing grew in the area, Pierre is expressing the common view that creoles do not like to involve themselves in cultivating the land.

In the face of all this criticism, creoles continue to view their more immediate approach to life as preferable to the gringos' struggle for future wealth, at least as long as they have all they need to live in the present. Considering Argentina's economic plight in the 1980's, they might well ask of gringos, "Where has all the struggle gotten you, anyway?" Creoles dislike gringos' denigration of the creole life-style and their desire to change it. Old-timer Carlos Baridon-Charbonier points out that the word "gringo" was historically a little disrespectful. It is enough to stand along the sidelines of a soccer game in San Sebastiano and hear taunts of "Stupid gringos" hurled at one of the teams to know that this is still true.

Gringos, for their part, have usually seen themselves as hardworking, interested in progress, and future-oriented. Old-timers say they realized early on that gringos' superior morality made it important to keep the groups separate, at least at mealtimes and when gringo women were around, and to avoid intermarriage with creole women, who were unable or unwilling to teach their children the value of progress. Nevertheless, gringos have adopted aspects of creole culture, Pierre Benabou points out. "Gringos have adopted the creole food, the horse, the way they raise cattle and dress. They like their beef fatty and highly salted—and lots of it, like creoles. But," he adds, "gringos and creoles here still don't intermarry much, and when they do there are often problems, not so much because of a difference in religion but because of a difference in culture."

Nowadays people are trying to make gringos reexamine their attitudes. Oscar Micol, for example, emphasizes the creoles' generosity and willingness to do hard manual labor that gringos refuse to do, and the injustice of gringo feelings of superiority. Then there is Toni Howard. Perhaps because he and his wife have officially adopted two creole children and because his law partner is creole, Toni sees the distinction between creole and gringo as diminishing. Other gringos, however, hearing the creole taunts at soccer games, readily respond with shouts of "worthless Indians," and even educated people frequently refer to "that gringo" and "that creole."

Differences between the two groups usually center on attitudes toward progress. Olga de Weber, a museum employee in Paraná, expresses the common sentiment: "Argentines don't want to work. They should work like the Italian immigrants and then they'd be rich, too."

Sometimes the descendants of Spanish immigrants who came to Argentina in the second half of the nineteenth century encounter the same prejudice as creoles, and the same criticisms. They are considered non-gringos by gringos and are often referred to as creoles or as "gallegos" because many came from the province of Galicia in northwest Spain. Luigi Baridon's marriage to the daughter of a Spaniard was considered a marriage outside his group. She was called a creole, and her background was thought responsible for Luigi's lack of economic success. Some people, like the wealthy Cesare Martinelli, say that the area has not developed more because it has too many Spaniards and not enough Italians. Gringos have gallego jokes, which usually impugn Spanish intelligence. "How does a gallego sign his name?" one goes. "With two thumb prints," is the reply, a reference to the Spanish use of two last names, the mother's and the father's. Another joke tells of four men in an airplane: a Brazilian, an Argentinian, a Uruguayan, and a gallego. In mid-flight the engines fail and the men find that the plane has only three parachutes. While they are arguing about who is going to get the parachutes, the gallego jumps. "We can stop arguing," says the Uruguayan; "he jumped with my backpack."

Gringo outsiders are the third main social group in San Sebastiano and La Paz. They are not primarily either urban or rural. Pierre Benabou, Isidora Saavedra de Losada, and Alicia Sánchez live in town, whereas Neli de Salas, Hugo Stringat, and Juan Coisson live in the campo. What it means to be an "outsider" is illustrated by Tullio Gilly's story about a schoolteacher who came to work in San Sebastiano for two or three years and did not like it. "She said that San Sebastiano was the worst place she'd ever been, from all points of view: the degree of friendliness, the stores, the food, everything. But two or three years is too short a time to know if a village is friendly or not." Isidora Saavedra de Losada, a municipal employee in La Paz, feels the same way about the town as the schoolteacher did about San Sebastiano. After four years working in a busy public office where she meets many people, Isidora finds the inhabitants of the town closed and unfriendly. She was born in

Tierra del Fuego, studied at the university in Santa Fe, and received her first appointment in La Paz. She and her husband, who is also from Tierra del Fuego, and their four children live in one of the newer barrios. While they find the youth more open than older people, they feel that both groups are hard to get to know. "Everyone in Tierra del Fuego comes from outside, so they all help each other and are friendly. But La Paz is closed. I have friends here, but that's because I live in a new barrio where life is more open than in the center of the city." The perceived unreceptiveness on the part of the local populace is matched by a strong desire on the part of outsiders to maintain their own perceived distinctness. Outsiders have pushed for what they see as innovation and progress in the community and when their efforts are met with lack of interest, they accuse insiders of being as closed and unreceptive as creoles. Insiders regard outsiders, on the other hand, as well-intentioned but misguided people who lack the knowledge of the area to understand how things work there and what its needs are, and above all as people who have somewhat different values. This is fine with the outsiders: when they measure themselves against creoles or gringo insiders, they see themselves as more progressive than either.

On the Saturday after the auction, Pierre Benabou has to pay a visit to the La Paz museum over on the banks of the river in a small park. As he passes by a butcher's, he chases a stray dog away from the wooden wheelbarrow parked along the curb. The dog already had its paws resting on the sides of the wheelbarrow and its nose under the piece of burlap, nuzzling the side of beef that was on its way to be delivered. At the museum Pierre shares some coffee with the museum workers and explains that he has come for some information on old threshing machines, for a future radio program. He and Alicia Sánchez begin talking animatedly and the subject of the closed nature of San Sebastiano soon enters their conversation. "Did you hear about the show that CANA put on yesterday?" asks Alicia. (CANA is a special school for the mentally and physically handicapped in La Paz.) "One of the children broke her leg when she was tumbling—what a shame—but it's really remarkable what they do with those children." "That's for sure," agrees Pierre, "especially considering how limited the kids are. I understand they've got about thirteen teachers now. It's too bad consanguinity is such a problem here, but you can understand it when you look at the hundreds of Prochets and Baridons there are. The Waldenses are such a closed community, even to people of their own religion from other places. I guess the camps they have where kids from the different Waldensian colonies can mix will help—maybe it will help inbreeding, too."

Out in San Sebastiano, Neli de Salas, at the village school, is among the most outspoken villagers on the subject of the closed nature of the colony. She herself is a gringa and a gallega—of Catholic French and Spanish background—but came to San Sebastiano twenty years ago and still considers herself different from long-term residents. She says that as soon as she arrived in San Sebastiano, she noted a considerable difference between village people (mainly creole) and colony people (mainly gringo and Waldensian). "The people of the colony are self-centered. They have a narrow outlook. They're backward and have no conscience. They lack culture. They're afraid; they're uncomfortable outside their own environment; they're cut off. Why, you know, when they go to the cinema they don't even know where to buy their tickets! Don't misunderstand me, I'm a nationalist—I think there's room for all kinds of people in Argentina. But it was Bunge and Born, those capitalists—imperialists, that's what they were—who started it all in San Sebastiano. The village had a thriving mill and beautiful houses, but when the mill collapsed Bunge and Born went away and then the poverty of the village began."

Gringo insiders' closed, entrenched tendencies carry over into areas like housing. Dora de Micol sketches the history of gringo houses as she remembers it. "When Oscar and I came to San Sebastiano in 1970, the Waldenses were living in very modest houses, almost ranchos. Little by little some people began to fix up their houses, to preserve their ancestral home, qué sé yo? And then everyone had to follow suit. Before this there was no way to tell who had money and who didn't, because they all lived the same! People wanted to hide their wealth, I think so that they wouldn't have to give to the church. That's why it took us so long to get the pastor's house fixed up: they just didn't believe in making houses nice places."

Hurrying to catch up with their neighbors as soon as a new standard in homes was established, the Prochet sisters, Ernestina and Liliana, modernized the kitchen at their family's estancia in San Sebastiano. They put in a stove and refrigerator and laid down linoleum on the floor. By then they were already spending most of their time at their La Paz house, which left their brother Esteban, who was working the farm, pretty much on his own. Esteban prefers to cook the way he always has, over an open fire in the corner of the veranda, and he has little use for a refrigerator. So the new appliances in the kitchen remain unused, protected under a layer of old newspapers, which in the 1970's made the Prochet estancia—albeit unintentionally—one of the few open depositories of forbidden Peronist material.[2]

Pierre Benabou says that the only people who fix up their houses are those who have been to the city or abroad. Pierre is thinking especially of people like Edgar Baridon and his wife María Cesan de Baridon, who have introduced a new outlook to the community. "They traveled a lot in Switzerland and belong to the Hermanos Libres, a group that broke away from the Waldenses. It's the same with María Baridon de Bert, who married a Catholic. They're different from most people because they aren't so conformist."

Like other outsiders, Pierre sees conformism as a negative quality. Gringo insiders do not: they strive for conformity—in what they feel are its good senses—because they see it as an important element that holds the community together. Concealing evidence of one's wealth, for example, or being skeptical about innovations helps keep the community on an even keel. Outsiders with different ideas are seen as a threat to this equilibrium. The threat is probably more imagined than real, however; gringo insiders' values are so dominant in the society that outsiders' criticisms have little effect.

Landowners and Peons

Almost from the founding of the colony, farmers employed peons on their land. Most peons were originally from the La Paz area, but the opportunities for work attracted a large number from Corrientes too. Landowners and peons generally correspond to the two sides of the gringo-creole dichotomy. Occasionally gringos have worked briefly as peons as old-timer Bruno Bouissa did, but they have been the exceptions to the rule and in any case they went on to become landowners. Most landowners in the area are gringos, but there are creole landowners too, some with properties much more extensive than any gringo properties. The mass of creoles, though, are peon laborers, and in fact the words "creole" and "peon" are usually used interchangeably, the ethnic group being equated with the occupation.

If peons and landowners were to pause and consider their history, they would testify to its continuity. In the heyday of agricultural expansion in the nineteenth century, landowners expended little more compassion on their human work force than they did on their animals. The consensus among the old-timers is that peons were ignorant and uncaring. Quite properly therefore they worked at the beck and call of estancieros, of the weather, of international markets; they lived in mud shacks and ate their fatty beef with their work knives; they had a narrow vision of life's possibilities. For the peons working the cattle auction, the situation is scarcely different today. Their status has improved little, they live in similar dwellings, and their work is no more secure, their options no less limited. They could argue that their situation has in fact deteriorated, since agriculture has been in decline for decades. Less land is being worked, which means fewer jobs, higher prices, and a reduction in the social services on which the poor depend. Perón's pro-labor policy promoted benefits such as pensions and family subsidies, even a union, but as one villager comments, "When a poor person lives and works on the land of a patron, what can he expect?"[3]

What *can* a twentieth-century peon expect, someone like Pío Sánchez, a retired San Sebastiano peon of sixty-five years? He has recently lost his sight owing to cataracts, a problem that could have been avoided with a simple operation had he had the money or had there been adequate public health care. He now spends most of his time leaning on his stick as he sits in one of the several straight-backed chairs in the family's "sitting" rancho, the hut that serves as the main living area. The rancho is about fifty square feet, but its smallness gives him a sense of security. He usually sits in the doorway so he can talk to his wife while she cooks or washes clothes under the lean-to in front of the rancho. She is almost always there except when she goes across the yard to the clay oven. He remembers how she looks, plump and always with a colorful kerchief around her head, and her red smiling face. Himself a slight man in a battered hat, he too retains a smiling countenance, though his eyes now water constantly. Pío feels his way around with one hand on his stick and the other extended as he shuffles hesitantly in his canvas shoes. To get from the sitting rancho to the sleeping rancho, he must maneuver around support poles for the thatched covering of the outdoor cooking and eating area; tin cans for fetching water for drinking and washing dishes and clothes; scraps left over from the dog's meals; the cookfire; chickens—a mélange of items that appear to be piles of rubble and suggest his poverty. His loss of sight was gradual, but he is still unfamiliar with total blindness and lacks the confidence to venture to the far corners of the yard to the storage rancho, henhouse, hog wallow, and outhouse. Pío Sánchez has had the outlines of his world drawn even narrower than other peons.

Then there is Miguel Moreno, still working as a peon at age sixty, but looking forward to his retirement and his pension. He has been living in San Sebastiano for a year and a half on a piece of land he rents from the Cerutti family. He has been busy rebuilding the property's two ranchos. When Miguel first arrived, these buildings were only a shadow of what ranchos become when fleshed out with the motley assortment of materials that are used for roof and walls. The departing tenant had disassembled the ranchos, taking all these movable items away with him on his horse—scraps of tin, pieces of cardboard, used grain sacks. Miguel for his part had brought with him all the movable items from his former house. The rancho offers little enough protection, but at least it is more comfortable than the living quarters Miguel typically encounters when he works away from home, at a cattle auction for example or on an estancia. "I like the Santa Aurelia—it's the best estancia around for comforts— because there's a shed for us to sleep in and there's electricity. Too many times, though, I get jobs on estancias where the owner just tells us to sleep outside on our saddles. And the meals aren't good anywhere anymore, not even at Santa Aurelia. They used to give us meat, but now they give us whatever they have lying around. Of course we used to have to go to work at one or two in the morning, but things have gotten better because there are social laws that prohibit this and have improved conditions."

On the opposite side of the village lives Gabriel González, a peon and young father of five, the husband of Teresa. Gabriel does not work far from home, but because his hours are long and the roads are bad, he can only be with his family on Saturday afternoons and Sundays. The González family's entire life is of necessity centered on work: on hoping that Gabriel's employer will continue to like him and keep him on, and on hoping that their twelve-year-old son will be able to get work when he finishes primary school this year, maybe even gain enough weight to get a job clearing land. Teresa's main concern, however, is the problem of caring for five young children when she is equipped with few resources and only a rudimentary knowledge of health and hygiene. Accordingly she spends much of her time at the 9 de Julio Hospital. When the Posadas River flooded, she and her children crossed it barefoot; it was early winter, and the wind and water were cold. Not surprisingly, three days later she was emerging from the La Paz bus (the *colectivo*), all five children in tow. The two youngest had bronchitis, a chronic problem, but nonetheless were dressed in light clothing and were shoeless. Poverty forces her to feed her family first, before clothing them, but on 450,000 pesos ($150) a month it is difficult to do either.

One can hardly imagine a life more precarious and wretched. Probably the deepest expression of sympathy one will hear from landowners is, "gente pobre" (poor people). More often one hears excuses like the following for the peon's situation: "Estancieros don't give peons good places to sleep and good food anymore because of the Perón era when peons would go work for someone, stay with him a while, then leave him and denounce him to the police. Maybe they were paid—qué sé yo?—or maybe they did it out of spite when they got fired."⁴ The middle and upper class are not too curious about peons' circumstances or motives. Analysis goes no deeper than tautologies like, "Peons have little education because they don't go to school." A peon must deal discreetly with his superiors, but his own life is dehumanizingly public. All his basic functions are open to view: his outhouse with its torn rag for a door flapping in the breeze; his rubbish heap poked over by his hog; his fights with his wife and their lovemaking; his meals that are cooked and eaten outdoors to escape the dampness of the rancho—all-too-obvious testaments to his poverty.

Twelve-year-old Jaime Santos's description of his father, "He's a peon, that's all," is as complete a statement of his socioeconomic status as the boy could make. It sums up his father's past, present, and future, and most likely his own too. The most secure position Jaime can hope for is that of permanent worker on an estancia, with a close relationship with his employer like the patron-client relationship formed over two generations between Domenico Antonini and one of his peon families. The family has been with the Antoninis for twenty-two years. Juan, the father, lives near Domenico with his wife and three children, two of whom are his wife's by another man. Domenico's parents are the *padrinos* (godparents) of Juan's own child. Domenico pays Juan the going rate, 20,000 pesos ($6) a day (the price of only four liters of milk in 1981) or about 450,000 pesos ($150) a month. He provides a meal of one and a half pounds of beef per worker at noon, prepared by his wife Lucia or a peon. A regular cook is hired during the busy sheep-shearing period when there are more peon laborers to feed. The cost of the food is deducted from the peons' wages. The pay rate is supposedly based on an eight-hour day, but peons work as many hours as the work demands, often ten or eleven. They have Saturday afternoons and Sundays off. Apologetically, Elsa de Prochet, Domenico's mother-in-law, says that this is not a great salary—and Elsa knows this well, since her own father worked as a peon—but she adds that with the family subsidy and a good patron who sells meat to them cheaply or maybe gives it to them occasionally, a peon family can get by and even, as Domenico's longest employee did, buy a major item like a truck. Juan bought Domenico's old red truck and is now a common sight driving around La Paz on Saturday afternoons with his wife and children crowded together in the cab. Juan probably bought the truck on "credit"; that is, he will work off the cost. Domenico probably could not have sold the truck for cash anyway.

Permanent positions with families like the Antoninis are a rarity, though, and it is more likely that Jaime can expect several years, perhaps even a lifetime, of temporary work or odd jobs (*changas*), working cattle auctions, for example, or driving animals to their monthly tick baths. Between March and May he might pick cotton; in October or November, shear sheep; in winter, clear the land of montes. His monthly wage will be between 300,000 and 450,000 pesos ($100–$150) a month depending on the number of days he works. Jaime might well ask why he should bother to work at all with inflation and wages the way they are.

Like most peons, Jaime will most likely live in a rancho his entire life. There are 145 ranchos in San Sebastiano housing 698 people, compared with 101 *casas*, or simply "houses," the dwellings of the middle and upper classes, housing 483 people.[5] Jaime's rancho will most likely be a shack with outer walls of mud and straw and wooden slats, inner walls smoothed out with more mud. The roof will probably be of straw and the floor of earth. He might very well own the rancho himself, or he might occupy it gratis as part of a work arrangement with his patron. If Jaime has the resources, he might talk of adding "comforts"—an outhouse, for example, since it is unlikely his rancho will have one. Forty-one of San Sebastiano's 145 rancho households do not; instead people use commonly designated spots behind clumps of trees or out of sight in gullies. He might be able to get his rancho connected to the public water supply (only 69 ranchos have their own water supply, either inside or outside the house) or he might move nearer to a public well. He will most likely resign himself, though, to doing without bathing or cooking facilities and electricity. He will continue to bathe with water out of a tin, go to bed when it is dark, and cook his stew—his *guiso* of meat, pasta, onions, and fat, or his *locro*, a more expensive dish made with corn—over an outdoor wood fire and bake his bread in an earth oven in the yard.

Jaime might create another room in his rancho to give an elderly person or an older child some privacy, as Miguel Moreno did for his eldest son. He might eventually even have to build another rancho if his family totally outgrows the first one. Ranchos usually have two rooms and house an average of five people; however, many ranchos house families with ten or more children. When most of Pío Sánchez's fifteen children lived at home, their one sleeping rancho with its two rooms and three beds was very crowded, though three beds can hold a number of people sleeping crossways. Miguel's two ranchos have since been sectioned off to make several rooms for his wife and himself and the five children who still live with them. One is a square rancho of three tiny sleeping rooms with makeshift walls of crates and pieces of material. The other is oblong and contains two rooms: a smaller bedroom in the back partitioned off with a curtain, and a larger front room. The latter contains the all-important radio and is the eating room and sitting room for the entire family, as well as a bedroom and workroom for Miguel's twenty-two-year-old son.

Every so often Jaime, like other rancho dwellers, will have to reinforce the walls of his rancho with more cardboard, grain sacks, or mud, or will improve the straw roof by covering it over with a sheet of tin. He might add an awning to the front of the rancho to protect his family from rain while they cook and eat. Little by little he will decorate the inside, with a picture from a discarded calendar or a matchbook cover or a special tin can. The Sánchez family's house contains postcards from the children who have moved away, two attractive empty wine bottles, a radio, and a clock. Jaime may put up some boards to hold his dishes. The Sánchez family store their cups, plates, and utensils on narrow wooden slats that are unevenly nailed together with broader boards in all four corners of the sitting rancho, conforming to the uneven configuration of the walls.

Probably neither Jaime nor his patron will choose to acknowledge or even notice the particular living conditions of the campo that they share. As a member of the middle or upper class, a patron has a larger house, built of sturdier materials and with more conveniences. Even middle- and upper-class residences often lack indoor toilets (about half of them in fact), but nearly all of them have at least an outhouse, whereas almost a third of the ranchos lack even that. Middle- and upper-class residences are also more likely to have bathing facilities (about half of them), whereas ranchos are not; they are more likely to have drinking water (more than half of them, compared with almost none of the ranchos); and they almost invariably have a kitchen, since there is more room to spare. Interior decorations in all houses in San Sebastiano are likely to be minimal and of somewhat the same type and quality. It is clear that in spite of a great socioeconomic distance between patron and peon, middle- and upper-class housing shares some of the disadvantages of the most destitute type of lower-class housing.

Unlike his patron, Jaime will spend most of his time in subsistence projects: looking for work, growing a little food, waiting in line at the public hospital to see a doctor. He will have few dependable resources to fall back on if he cannot find work or grow enough food. Free milk is distributed for infants and young children through the hospital, but if it runs out, his children may have to go hungry. It is possible that he may not receive a pension—if he becomes ill or handicapped and cannot work, or if he does only odd jobs (or his wife only domestic work). If he has no children who can help him financially, he will be eligible for either a provincial or a national subsidy, but it will be difficult to get. Since 1979, only five or six La Paz residents have received a national subsidy. It is distributed through the Bank of Entre Ríos, and pays a substantial $125 a month. He will stand a better chance of getting a provincial subsidy, distributed by the Department of Social Services and the La Paz police department, but it pays only $13 a month. A peon's pension, on the other hand, is 70 to 82 percent of his average earnings in his last five years of employment, but increased according to the rate of inflation.

Getting a pension will be no easy matter either, but Jaime hopes that he will join the majority of peons in becoming eligible for one when he retires. The lawyers Toni Howard and Rodolfo Guzmán handled eighty-two pension cases in 1980. The process is supposed to take three months from the initial application, but it is more likely to take a year or two. In May of 1981, Toni and Rodolfo still had two cases pending from May 1978. It is not simply a matter of the peon's filing the correct papers, but of confronting a wholly foreign attitude toward the land. Many people in large cities, especially Buenos Aires, trade in land as if it were shares of stock—never seeing it or working it, only holding it for a time and then selling it. Before peons can receive their pension, they must have all the owners of the land where they have worked complete certain papers. This is not a problem in the many cases where land has stayed in the same family and the owners live on the land. But in other cases the peon has to hire a lawyer to trace ownership, locate lost records, and cajole owners who, when they are finally found, are sometimes too preoccupied with their own affairs to fill out forms so that a peon they do not know or care about, on land they have forgotten they ever owned, can receive a pension. Such bureaucratic snags occur at all levels of society, but are particularly frustrating for the lower classes because they have no alternatives, and sinister because they involve the urgent matter of daily living.

Remarks by some of the old-timers, as well as the younger landowners—"They never worked," "They were naive"—recall the long servile history of peons. They are the descendants of gauchos like the central figure of the nineteenth-century poem *El Gaucho Martín Fierro*: nomadic herders, prairie men who gradually became the farmhands of the immigrants, pitied for their poverty but still admired for their horsemanship and the spontaneous repartees they sing around the campfire. Even today, social and work situations have a degrading aspect for the peon, prompting porteños to comment that "Entre Ríos is backward: peons still tip their hats to landowners." But Entre Ríos holds no monopoly on prejudice toward peons and creoles.[6]

Catholics and Non-Catholics

A person's religion, like his gringo or creole background, or his landowner or peon status, adds further roughness to the social texture. Religion, however, is less divisive than other differences. For one thing, "gringo" and "creole" do not correspond to "Catholic" and "non-Catholic," since many gringos are Catholic and some creoles have been converting to Protestant and other sects. Similarly, landowner and peon status do not automatically say anything about a person's religion. Creoles do not connect their differences with gringos to any particular religion. Characteristics they are unsympathetic toward—hard work, progress, exploitation—they do not identify with Protestantism but with gringos. Nor do gringos draw any broad inferences from a person's religion, although they do sometimes refer to creole superstition.

There are other reasons why religion does not generally present problems to the inhabitants of San Sebastiano and La Paz. Officially, Argentina is a Catholic country: over 90 percent of the population is Catholic; the president must be a member of the Catholic church; and the clergy have a role in all major government functions. More important, society is imbued with Catholic culture and values. Package-laden commuters on crowded buses struggle to free a hand to make the sign of the cross as they go hurtling by a church; Mass begins and ends the day for many people; school textbooks are packed with Catholic dogma. Catholicism so pervades society and culture that it is accepted and taken for granted as being everyone's culture, regardless of his religion.

The Waldensian church is the only one in San Sebastiano and La Paz large enough and organized enough to challenge the Catholic church, and even forces it to be something of a missionary church in its own domain. The national Waldensian church is closely linked to the Waldensian organization in Italy and is aligned with other Evangelical churches in Argentina. A Waldensian splinter group called the Hermanos Libres (Free Brothers) appeared in San Sebastiano and La Paz some time ago. Oscar Micol, the Waldensian pastor, considers the Hermanos' estrangement from the main group a reflection of their more spiritual and less materialistic values, which he himself sympathizes with. Some people, like Pierre Benabou, see the Hermanos as more open than the Waldenses. "Their children go away to school and they drink wine and dance, although they say it's better to avoid the dancing. They attach less importance to religion than the Waldenses do—they don't confess to anyone and they don't try to convert people. The Waldenses have laymen going around door to door, just as the Mormons do, only not so aggressively." The parish priest in La Paz uses the rupture as an indication of the problems of Protestant organization. "The problem with

Protestants is that they have no head. If the congregation don't like their pastor, they send him packing or form a new sect! In the Catholic church the pope is the head who unites the church, and the priest answers to his bishop and not to his parishioners, though he must treat them well, of course. I think this hierarchical system has many advantages over the Protestant church." Another factor operating against Waldensian unity is that Waldenses from other colonies consider themselves (and are perceived as) different from the local Waldensian group by virtue of their status as outsiders.

Besides the Catholics and the Waldenses, many smaller sects are active in San Sebastiano and La Paz—notably the Pentecostals, the Jehovah's Witnesses, and the Mormons. In one of the two new barrios of La Paz, four different sects compete for members in a population of only 150. Each has its own meeting place and its own leader within the barrio. The variety of religions in La Paz is not atypical of Entre Ríos as a whole, which also includes a sizable portion of Argentina's Jewish population, and helps reduce the possibility of religion operating as a divisive force.[7]

Sitting on a bench any day in the Plaza de Mayo, La Paz's main and only square, a passerby can observe the community's religious leaders going about their business. Father Franco Cagliero leaves the Church of Our Lady of La Paz on the north side of the square and, beckoned by the police chief, hurries over to find out what his function will be at the May 25 festivities commemorating the 1810 revolution. From Pilar Street comes Pastor Oscar Micol, heading toward Umberto Eckstein's house on Tandil. Umberto will give the sermon on Sunday, and Oscar is delivering some materials to him. On the south side of the square, the Mormon team of young men are pedaling by on their way to the campo, their high rubber boots giving away their destination. The priest and the pastor, from their separate places on the square, watch them go by, speculating as always about their business in La Paz. "People call them 'los rubios que más caminan' (the blond guys who are always on the move), quoting an ad for Jockey Club cigarettes," says Oscar, "because they're always trying to convert people. Sometimes they call them 'los huevos que van de a dos' (the eggs who go in pairs), because they always go around in twos with their hair slicked down like a couple of eggs." He chuckles that "huevos" is also slang for testicles. "They ask so many questions, a lot of people think they're connected with the CIA. You can see how they'd be useful to them, because they can get into people's homes easily and ask all kinds of things about their families and life here. They've even been asking how many police and military personnel La Paz has, as if anyone would know. It seems to me they must be connected with the Right because the Argentine government tolerates them." Franco has heard the same suspicions expressed about the Mormons. "I don't think they've been too successful converting people, but they write lots of letters with lots of information. Qué sé yo?—I only say what I hear." Throughout the day, Pentecostal, Baptist, Congregationalist, Jehovah's Witnesses, and Seventh Day Adventist leaders go by, but none of them elicits as much speculation as the Mormons, and none, including the Mormons, is as visible as the more major Catholic and Waldensian groups.

Even though the Catholic church outnumbers all other sects and denominations combined, it exists in a highly diversified environment and must compete with a variety of minority groups that are all the more zealous just because they are minorities. At the leadership level, Catholics and Waldenses see themselves in conflict and each church has its particular sphere of influence in the department of La Paz. Waldensian strength resides mainly in San Sebastiano, though the La Paz church is important. It is Oscar's base, and many people from San Sebastiano attend the services there. There are also Waldenses in many other colonies. They hold services in members' homes, as the San Sebastiano Waldenses have done for several years since their church was closed down for repairs. Oscar travels to other colonies to perform services about once a month. Catholics are dominant everywhere except San Sebastiano. Franco's parish includes the entire northern section of the department and contains three churches in the campo and six in La Paz plus the cathedral. He serves the rest of the population through the schools. Members are seldom drawn into church conflicts, perhaps because they leave debate to their representatives, the priest and the pastor. Franco and Oscar are public figures, almost a complement to political leaders, vying for constituents, competing to perform charitable acts, and taking stands on major social issues.

Like Franco, Oscar feels life is incomplete without an earthly adversary—something more substantive, less amorphous than "sin." But Oscar finds that a joust with the Catholic church is sometimes difficult because Franco will not acknowledge that a tournament is being held. Instead he alternately ignores Oscar's protests or claims him as a friend, depending on his purposes. Oscar's attempts to do battle are made even harder because the Catholic church, being the official church, is protected by the state. Moreover, after the coup in 1976, and to a lesser extent before the coup, some non-Catholic groups were under suspicion by the military government. Although the Waldenses' activities were within legal boundaries, their antimilitary sentiment and social involvement drew attention to them. Oscar's correspondence was opened, church activities were carefully watched, and openly carrying Waldensian materials was dangerous.[8] While refraining from direct attacks on non-Catholic groups, the government viewed them with suspicion because they opposed the military, aided refugees and the persecuted, and worked for human rights. In 1976 and 1977 the government banned the Jehovah's Witnesses among others. Waldenses in La Paz were outraged at the persecution of the Jehovah's Witnesses. In 1978 all religious groups except Catholics were required to register with the Ministry of Foreign Affairs. Any sect could be banned if it was considered a threat to public order, national security, or morality. Any time Oscar wanted to hold a special function, he had to get permission from the local police. The 1970's also saw a denial of many fundamental rights to Jews.[9]

As for Oscar, his awareness that he was under suspicion did not discourage his tilts with the Catholic church. He was critical of the church's support of the military government. In much of Latin America important Leftist segments of the Catholic church represented a challenge to the government, but in Argentina church and state for the most part worked together. A small group of progressive priests were unable to change this relationship. In 1981, under the military government, Oscar described the church as a handmaiden to the military, turning its back on allegations of human rights violations and more actively promoting the interests and role of the church.[10]

"The relationship between church and state is a symbiotic one," Oscar affirmed. "Appeals to people through their religion have often served governments well and in turn have strengthened the religion. The military emphasize that belief in God, through the Catholic church, helps fight Leftists—that leading a Christian life, possible only through Catholicism, will bring the nation through the crisis—so the church supports them."

Franco protested his connection with the military. "I'm completely independent of the military hierarchy. Before the May 25 ceremonies I had hot chocolate with the military because they invited me and I wanted to go; I wasn't required to go. There were going to be about twenty officials there, and I wanted to attend because it was a good chance to meet them and get to know them better—just as public officials, right? We have our problems here, but the United States, especially Carter, shouldn't have discriminated against Argentina over the human rights issue. Why did he bother with Argentina and not say anything about Cuba, Honduras, El Salvador?" Since he left office, President Carter has of course been credited with having saved numerous lives of political prisoners in Argentina by supporting human rights campaigns. "It's much better now that Reagan is president. The United States under Carter didn't understand our problem—that we were in a war and had to defend ourselves against the guerrillas. They didn't realize that communism and Marxism were not the traditional governing principles of Argentina. Lamentably there were possibly abuses, but the Leftists had to be killed. Argentina is now trying to reach an equilibrium."

Oscar did not accept Franco's denial that he was dependent on the military. The law forbade the church to enter directly into public education (though textbooks in particular had long reflected Catholic dogma), but the restrictions seemed to be slackening under the military as the church became bolder in its more protected position.[11] One of Oscar's principal complaints concerned Franco's use of the schools to hear students' confessions during Holy Week. Oscar labeled it an "illegal invasion," and maintained that it changed and corrupted the role of the schools and gave the Catholic church an unfair advantage. Franco was careful to explain that he heard confessions and performed baptisms and marriages at the forty schools in the area only on Sundays. "On a typical Sunday I drive thirty miles into the campo to some school, hear one and a half hours of confessions, say Mass, baptize some babies, maybe perform a marriage. Usually someone in town invites me to dinner, so I return to La Paz, and then in the afternoon I drive thirty miles in another direction in the campo and do the same thing. On an average Sunday I hear four and a half hours of confessions! Can you imagine—four and a half hours!" Oscar was angered that the director of the San Sebastiano school would not make it available for cultural uses, and made protests to the departmental director of education, threatening to denounce the school (and Franco) to the provincial government. But even he did not expect a response.

Oscar and Franco see themselves as in constant competition with each other, watching each other's moves, jockeying for a more secure position in the area. There is plenty of need for charity work in San Sebastiano and La Paz, and it has become an important arena for the testing of their strength. For many years Waldenses have contributed money to an orphanage, an old age home, and a hospital in Uruguay, and along with the Methodists, Lutherans, and Reformed Church, they periodically send truckloads of used agricultural tools and clothing to the Toba Indians in the Chaco.

Closer to home, they collect clothes and sell them at nominal cost in San Sebastiano and in Barrio La Costa, and help support the hospital in San Sebastiano. Waldensian women in San Sebastiano and La Paz give sewing lessons to poor creoles and have organized an after-school clinic to help Barrio La Costa children in La Paz with their homework. Every year the church holds an asado out in the fields at a member's estancia and someone donates a truck and driver to gather the poor children from the surrounding area and bring them to the picnic. Oscar says that the Catholic church has suddenly started making inroads in this system of charity, which the Waldenses initiated, in order to attract new members. Franco boasts of collecting and distributing food and clothing gratis—unlike the Waldenses, who sell it, he says. "Generally speaking, we don't do much charity work in the campo—it's too hard to organize—but we're active in San Sebastiano." He seems intent on taking on the Waldenses in their own territory and in an area of charity work where they have dominated.

Franco and Oscar differ substantially on most current issues. Oscar takes the Waldensian position on birth control and abortion, for example. Waldenses accept birth control, and though they oppose abortion, they believe it should be a matter for individual conscience rather than legislated by the state. Franco takes a hard-line Catholic position. As he tacks up more posters against abortion around the parish, he asks, "Why did Carter give Argentina such a hard time about its human rights record, I'd like to know! Why didn't he object when Italy legalized abortion—that's killing, too!" As respected and educated members of the community, Oscar and Franco are often consulted on current issues, especially by the radio station.

Oscar and Franco also differ about the origin of certain problems in San Sebastiano. Franco, a gringo like Oscar, says the problems have arisen because poor creoles predominate in a village that occupies a small area; most other villages, he says, are more spread out and have more of a mix of gringos and creoles. He intimates that the proximity of the inhabitants probably contributes to drinking and sexual promiscuity; he cites drinking, along with pregnancies followed by abortions, as two of the village's main problems. Oscar, on the other hand, feels strongly that the gringos' attitudes have played a major role in the impoverishment and corruption of the creoles, and he works toward trying to change those attitudes.

Contributing to his differences of opinion with Franco, Oscar maintains, are the policies of the new pope, John Paul II. "Pope John XXIII ran an open church—open toward Protestantism—but now things have changed. For example, it used to be that when a Protestant died and his surviving relatives were Catholic, both churches would cooperate in the burial service. But the Catholic church refuses to do this any longer. The church is harder now; it pushes more. It's going in for more pageantry, too, centered on the cult of the Virgin Mary. Cagliero delegates someone in each block to be keeper of a statue of the Virgin. This person is supposed to cart it over to one of his neighbors' houses, then come fetch it after a couple days and take it on to a new house. The people pray to it— maybe it's supposed to protect their house, qué sé yo? I think it's very much tied up with fertility. Maybe Cagliero is promoting María because he doesn't have a María in his own home! That man—he thinks he runs the town, that he's the only one who lives here. He plays his María record over the loudspeaker at the church on Saturday and Sunday nights. You can hear it at our service on Sunday nights, it's so loud. Cagliero says he's my friend, but it's not true—he won't even talk to me." [12]

Oscar and Franco take their battles very seriously and personally. Their congregations take them less personally. Yet even though individuals do not feel embattled about their Waldensian or Catholic affiliations, some traditional distinctions are generally maintained; for example, there are few marriages between the groups, and gringo and creole stereotypes may at times be reinforced with religious overtones by each group. Normally, however, it is the gringo and creole stereotypes that are much more significant in the divisions within the community.

Country and Town People

It is rare for an adult in San Sebastiano to idealize life in La Paz, but teenagers, like twelve-year-old Xavier Orlando, commonly do so. Xavier is a student at the village school, still carrying around the chunkiness of a child whose height has not caught up with his weight. He was born and raised in San Sebastiano, in a rancho about three blocks from the school. He lives with his parents and three of his siblings. School is over for the day—classes for the fourth- through seventh-graders are in the morning—and Xavier now sprawls on his stomach on the grass in front of his house, watching the chickens and eating an orange. A fence surrounds the neat yard of citrus trees and flowers, and a nondescript dog lolls on his side asleep in the early afternoon heat. Xavier does not dislike the campo by any means, unlike a schoolmate of his who thinks that life in San Sebastiano is too restricted, but he does envy his contemporaries in La Paz for certain things. He likes to visit La Paz to see the new building that is eight stories tall, and one of his dreams is to live someday high above the ground. He will graduate in a year and would like to be one of the children who go on to study in La Paz—he wants to learn Latin—but most likely he will remain in San Sebastiano and work.

Xavier has heard youths who live in La Paz, both temporarily and permanently, complain about the limited diversions in town. As they say, "If you've been around La Paz once, you've seen it all." But Xavier would nevertheless like a chance to sample La Paz's pinball parlor, coffee houses, and occasional dances and festivals.

Xavier is also acquainted with the discomfort his retired father feels when he must go to town to see about his pension. In Toni Howard's law office, Xavier's father joins the other campo people who have flattened themselves against the walls of the waiting room, too uncomfortable to sit in the chairs. They try to fade into the background, but it is impossible for them to wear their campo culture unobtrusively—above all, their lack of experience and vulnerability, but also their wide thick leather belts, canvas shoes and sockless feet, flat hat, baggy trousers, and neck scarves. The wait stretches on and one of them goes into the secretaries' office to inquire hesitantly if the lawyer will be much longer. Back at home, Xavier's father must sometimes report that his trip and his wait were wasted because the lawyer was called out unexpectedly and he could stay no longer. Xavier's positive feelings about La Paz have not yet been changed by his father's experiences. Xavier also knows that many people in the village, like his neighbor, Iolanda de Gilly, do not go to La Paz more than three or four times a year. They say they go in only when they have to, as when Señora Gilly went to help her daughter after she had given birth. But Xavier is not particularly influenced by such opinions either.

It is just Xavier's vision of La Paz, shared by many San Sebastiano youths, that worries Father Cagliero. In Franco's view La Paz is morally inferior to the campo and has a corrupting influence on people from the countryside. "The best people come from the campo," he maintains. "They keep their traditions. Ah, but when they come to town! It's a shame how often I see an innocent campo girl who has moved to La Paz to do domestic work get in trouble because she is ignorant of city ways and vulnerable. She is susceptible to many influences here. Lamentably, in some of these cases the girl is abused by her employer or his sons." Waldenses in San Sebastiano used to make these same charges against La Paz, and only in the late 1960's did they begin to send their children to high school there.

The corollary of the "pure" campo is the backward and unrefined countryside. The superiority over campo people that townspeople occasionally express is usually oriented along class lines rather than place of residence or origin, since many middle- and upper-class townspeople also have ties to the campo. Sometimes, however, an observation unrelated to social class emerges. Elsa de Prochet, for example, uttered a stereotypic remark about campo people even though she is herself partly a campo person and the remark she made was directed at someone—her son-in-law Domenico—who is her social superior and a relative she likes. "You know what my son-in-law said when he heard Michela crying when she was first born and he didn't know if she was a girl or a boy? He said, 'It must be an old gaucho!' Isn't that an awful thing to say! He's a campesino—qué sé yo?—he's not very refined. It's an ugly saying because 'gaucho' is sometimes used to mean a vagabond." Elsa chuckles, embarrassed at having expressed such a strong opinion. She doesn't like being around people who are too refined, but some of the campesinos' habits bother her.

It is rare, however, for a campesino to be looked down upon

purely for being a campesino, and distinction between town and country in any case pales when people of the area look to the "outside" world. More important distinctions are ethnic, socioeconomic, and religious ones, and even these have little effect on the essential homogeneity of the society.

Public Honor and Social Place

In spite of the real and potential divisive points in the texture of society, San Sebastiano, and to a certain extent La Paz, has a certain homogeneity. Part of the origin of this homogeneity is a shared sense of public honor and social place.[13] Such concerns are common in other societies too, but people in San Sebastiano and La Paz are remarkable not only for the extent to which they respect and adhere to a code but also for the manner in which they have apparently moulded that code from contrasting visions of honor and place. A story recounted by the old-timer Carlos Baridon-Charbonier suggests how the two main codes met head-on in the early colony. Carlos tells of a creole who wanted to be able to offer his friend a drink at a bar but did not have the cash and gave the gringo barkeeper a piece of his land instead. According to the creole's beliefs, he achieved honor by showing generosity to his friend; to have been unable to pay and thus unable to offer his friend a drink, or to have allowed his friend to pay, would have diminished his status in his own eyes and in the eyes of fellow creoles. Besides, one less piece of land did not matter to him. The gringo barkeeper, on the other hand, achieved honor and social place among his gringo friends through his business sense and cunning.[14] It is an interesting labor to find where, if at all, the two codes have come together since the early colony to form a common one for San Sebastiano, regardless of a person's creole or gringo background. One finds, I believe, some accommodation by both groups.

Accommodation has resulted in a hierarchical concept of honor: the type of behavior considered honorable changes with social level but gives each person an accepted position and value in society. A peon's honor is not the same as an estanciero's, a gringo's not the same as a creole's; but all have the possibility of honor and reward. Among the middle and upper class, and thus mainly gringos, the ideal of honor became a necessary component of, and has sometimes supplanted, the ideal of cleverness and acumen in business concerns. A person deemed too cunning will not be accepted. Success is worth nothing—indeed, is not really success—if it is not achieved by honorable means. "In business," says the lawyer Rodolfo Guzmán, "success means having a little more work than someone else. A person's prestige depends on how he makes his money. A lawyer who is wealthier than all his competitors won't have prestige if he makes his money in dishonorable ways." Even in their play, people must be honorable. "In spite of the economy," says Rodolfo, "a lot of people gamble. They play dice and cards and stake their cars, trucks, houses, and businesses. When they lose, though, they don't fight or take revenge. They consider it a matter of honor, if they bet their car and lose it, to hand it over calmly. Otherwise, they'd lose their reputation."

Gringos have also moved toward a creole-style generosity over the years, which, as we have seen, can exist alongside a parsimonious life-style. Taking care of one's fellow man constitutes another dimension of honor. The *padrino* system (or godparenthood) and *compadrazgo* (or coparenthood) are both important in San Sebastiano and La Paz. Both are more common among Catholics, but they exist among Waldenses as well. Elsa de Prochet, for example, has two godchildren, and Aldo has one. Waldenses tend to ask their relatives to be godparents; Catholics also ask their friends. The poorer tend to ask the wealthier because, especially in the campo, when people cannot afford to keep a child they often ask the child's godparents to take him. Children are admonished to pray for the benediction of their padrino each morning, and whenever they meet him they are to ask his blessing: "Dios lo haga bueno, mijo" (God be with you, my son). Voluntary, informal "adoption" of children and adults in need occurs often and is not necessarily associated with ritual kinship. Rather, it is a spontaneous response to someone's immediate need to be taken in and cared for—if, for instance, he has just lost a parent or a spouse—and is distinct from the more calculated behavior of early colonists. An arrangement of this sort can last a few years, as with a teenage girl the Micols "adopted" until Oscar was transferred to another town, or it can last a lifetime, as with a forty-year-old man the Gillys took in and cared for until he died recently.[15]

Honor in business and generosity and spontaneity in personal relationships have become new priorities for gringos, priorities that have joined or replaced the original ones of the early colony and are important factors in the modification of San Sebastiano's original hard-driving immigrant society.

Everyone is expected to be concerned about his honor and place in the community, regardless of his status. It is easy to regard the existence of peons, the lower-class mass of manual laborers, as just another of Latin America's failures. Yet while their lives may seem too precarious for them to be concerned with honor and place, people like Teresa de González, Pío Sánchez, and Miguel Moreno project another image. They live their lives with assurance that these lives have the potential to be as stable, meaningful, and imbued with honor as others' lives. There is often as much honor (as well as permanency and affection) in their little-understood common-law (*unido de hecho*) unions—the most prevalent type of union among the lower classes, chosen usually for financial reasons—as there is in formal marriages.[16] They have tasks, jobs, friends, daily routines; plans, aspirations, and regrets. It is true that society has done little for them, but they themselves have done what they can to enrich their lives and to earn honor and place. Even without government support, without adequate infrastructure and comforts, they feel that this ideal of public honor and a place within the community offers something valuable in itself.

For Teresa de González, there are several ways to attain honor and place. She is proud of her family: she has five reasonably healthy children and a husband who provides for them and lives with her. Her husband has permanent work, though he can only be home on the weekends; moreover, he is so much liked by his patron that he receives his meals free. Teresa has never been outside the San Sebastiano–La Paz area—she is only twenty-seven—but she is certain that San Sebastiano offers much that other villages do not. The village has sixteen public wells, one of them near her rancho; San Sebastiano has a bus service to La Paz, where there is a public hospital; and within the village she has found a reliable midwife. The village is friendly and she has people to visit with at the well, the post office, and the church. Teresa is trying to improve her sewing skills and provide better for her family by taking lessons at Iolanda de Gilly's house. Iolanda has a sewing machine and gives free lessons to the women and girls of the village. Her husband Tullio fixed up a room for her in his family's old house and she holds the lessons there. She mainly teaches the women how to alter used clothing, given to them by a church or perhaps by the employer of a relative who has done domestic work in the city. On Tuesdays Teresa usually goes to the Gillys'. Sometimes she sees Tullio there working on his car or puttering in the yard. On the way home she goes by the police station. Invariably, officer García is out front, and he really seems to enjoy talking with her. She is pleased that these important people take her seriously. Teresa measures her place in society and her satisfaction with it in the terms of a particular segment of her class.

Miguel Moreno is different. What brings honor to Miguel is the fact that he has been able to succeed without compromising his independence, even within a highly stratified class system. Moreover, he has had to learn it all himself. As he says, "The world was my school." It shows in his gaucho bearing. Miguel swings his horse into the yard, within a hairbreadth of the children playing in the mud with a kitten; he dismounts and throws his blankets and saddle onto a fence—in much the same way as his ancestors before him, and this gives him satisfaction. He belongs to the society of roughly-hewn campo men—self-educated and taking orders from no one—he is his own man. "I've been up at the Santa Aurelia cutting trees. I do these odd jobs when they come along, but I'm really mainly a tourist now," he laughs. "I'm not rich but I've never had any trouble—I've never been in jail. I began working when I was eight or nine. No one ever thought about school when I was growing up. We lived way out in the campo. The world was my school. I know how to sign my name, that's all."

The emasculating features of patron-peon society offend him. For example, he shuns the practices of addressing one's superiors as "don" or "doña," doffing one's hat to them, and parroting "Sí, señor" when in their company. But he is not a social reformer or a revolutionary. The situation bothers him to the same degree that conditions in automobile factories concern many urban workers: it is irritating but not cause for rebellion. Within the strictures of his society, he is pleased with the way he has lived his life: he has bowed to no man and has never been in trouble; he is self-reliant; he is soon to retire and be eligible for a pension; and he likes his work and life in the campo. He is also proud of his family—twelve children in all. He still has three children and two grandchildren living at home. His other children are dispersed as far away as Santa Fe and Buenos Aires, but they come back to visit him. He is proud of his son, self-educated too, who is already an enterprising man in his early twenties: only a year ago he began doing leather work with a minimum of tools, and just recently bought an old Singer sewing machine in response to increased demand. Leather belts, whips, horse hobbles, and other equipment he has made cover the wall behind his workbench. But Miguel is proud of all his children. Like him, they had to make their way without the aid of a formal education.

Children are also a source of pride to Pío Sánchez. "We had fifteen," he says. "They live all over now but they write and come back to visit us. One works in a factory in Santa Fe and one does domestic work in Buenos Aires. I also have three in La Paz—one works with motors, one works in the hotel by the plaza, and one works in the prefect's office. We still have three at home, but only the sixteen-year-old girl is ours. The other two are relatives' children who live with us while they are going to school in the village."

Pío finds community life as well as family life supportive. He is pleased to be accepted in the social hierarchy of the village, even though he is near the bottom of it and had no hand in creating it. He feels that he has cooperated with the system and been able to use it to achieve a position for himself. He is what is known as a "good" peon, a mixture of creole and gringo values that, according to gringos, occurs only occasionally. Since the early days of the colony, Waldenses have always welcomed opportunities to get together and exchange information—often, in the early colony, at church functions and services, perhaps fitting business matters around the "hallelujahs" of hymns and sermons—and such exchanges have allowed them, among other things, to guarantee a pool of proven workers by an informal screening out of the "bad" peons from the good.

The creation of a good peon, however, is far from being a celestial miracle. Pío, for example, made accommodations to please his patrons—he learned to work in a different manner and appreciate different qualities in the land and aim for different goals. And so he became numbered among the proven workers. He cultivated ways of behaving that won him approval and brought him close to his employers' ideal. He was a good worker. "I did all kinds of rural work in my time and worked for lots of different people, good people like Piero Prochet and Renato Baridon. I cut down trees and sold the

wood; I transported people and crops; I built and repaired fences—
I guess I did just about everything. And I liked all of it because I
liked to work." Every so often one of Pío's former employers has a
reason to visit him and this pleases him. Before he lost his sight he got
about more and visited with the Baridons, the Gillys, or the Prochets if he saw them abroad in the village. He completely accepts his
role in this stratified society and unlike Miguel he willingly doffs his
hat to his superiors, but he does not lose self-respect on that account, or the respect of the village. Rather, this is how he achieves
respect. He has had his work, he has his family, and he has his customs: all of them contribute to establishing his social place in the
community.

Peons must have a developed sense of social place, because patron
and peon live side by side in San Sebastiano, they have similar life-
styles, and the immediate demands of the environment and of farming tend to blur class distinctions. They share certain similarities
in their housing that belie their socioeconomic differences. Their
clothing differs more in state of repair than in style or fabric. Patron
and peon both drink maté and eat fatty, salty beef and rice or
pasta—though patrons prepare these foods in a greater variety of
ways—and when they are in the fields together, they eat the same
food. They often work side by side, defying a storm to get the harvest in or straining to extricate a cow from the mud, and they share
a pride in being campo men. In large cities, a worker is unac-
quainted with the daily life of his employer, and his employer with
his. Worker and employer may also have different work environ-
ments. Moreover, distinctions between them as socioeconomic
classes are more obvious because middle- and upper-class residential areas are separate from each other and from the shanty barrios
(the *villas miserias*) ringing large cities.

The proximity and similarities of patron and peon life in San
Sebastiano call for a great deal of discretion on the part of the peon,
along with tact and strategic inattentiveness to the living situations
of the middle and upper classes. Pío has been especially adept at not
presuming too much familiarity, sensing the delicate balance between the classes. There is a tacit agreement that to question this
balance is dishonorable and threatens everyone's place, though
within these bounds people like Pío and Miguel can have varying
degrees of satisfaction with the social system. San Sebastiano is not

the place where challenges are going to be made to society or where social inequities are going to be settled. In different ways, Teresa, Miguel, and Pío have adjusted to a gringo code of honor and place; gringos, too, have adjusted their behavior of the early days. While it would perhaps be difficult to claim that gringos have met creoles half way, it can be said that each group has made accommodations that reach deep into the values of the other.

FOUR

A Personalized World

THE MORNING BUS to downtown Buenos Aires was perilously crowded as usual. No one noticed that four-year-old Fabio Bounous's leg had become trapped behind a woman's plastic bag of produce so that the great bunches of greens sticking out of the top brushed against his face and blocked his view. It had been a confusing morning. In the store the clerk had spoken angrily to his mother. And he didn't understand why they'd had to stand in the long line at the Ministry of Economy. That morning something else had happened, something that had become a part of daily life. The police had stopped the number 87 bus and hurried the passengers outside—all except two men in the back, whom they shot.

Fabio's world in 1981 had become rigid, closed, and impersonal. Across the nation, the military government meant death squads, unexplained imprisonments, mass arrests of cordoned-off pedestrians, and constant checking of documents. Argentina has a national registration system that begins at birth when a child is registered in his parents' *libreta de familia,* a pocket-size record book. Control begins in the parents' selection of a name for their child; the Civil Registry Office, the Registro Civil, has an approved list and does not accept foreign or nonsensical names that might be an embarrassment to the child. Fabio already has his own identity document, which he will begin carrying himself when he is about twelve. When he is eighteen, he will have his fingerprints taken and will be issued an adult libreta with a new photograph. During his lifetime, all changes of civil status, military status, and residence, as well as an indication that he has voted in each election (since voting is mandatory), must be recorded here by the Civil Registry Office. "The police are always checking our libretas," says Eside de Bounous. "Once Adolfo got caught. It was during Onganía's time, when there were all the strikes in 1969 and there was a police crackdown.[1] They were stopping everyone in the streets and checking their libretas, and Adolfo didn't have his. I had to go down to the police station with it to get him out! Now we know we always have to carry our libretas with us."

To combat the negative image that such treatment engendered, the military government tried various means to instill in the public a trust and confidence in the police. A poster campaign in the early 1980's pictured policemen helping fire victims and lost children. The caption under the poster read, "Autoridad y algo más (Authority and something more), Policía Federal Argentina."[2] Many civilians had also become defensive about Argentina's reputation, even when they acknowledged the atrocities of terrorism. In referring to the worst periods of terrorism of the mid- to late 1970's, they protested that, "Argentines aren't really like this—this wasn't the true Argentina." A campaign was begun in the later 1970's to boost morale in the face of accusations of human rights violations. It featured stickers (in blue and white like the flag) declaring that "Los Argentinos—somos derechos y humanos" (The Argentines—we are right and we are human).

In spite of the propaganda efforts, Argentina continued to be perceived at home and abroad as an impersonal military state—and indeed, at many levels it was. In Paraná, the military state meant fourteen-year-old boys—with boys' inexperience but with orders to kill like men—posted in front of public buildings or on second-floor patios, dangerously over-alert with their fingers playing on the triggers of machine guns. Even in small-town La Paz the military government meant a garrisoned town and surveillance of groups like the Waldenses and radio requests for denunciations of one's neighbors. At the police barricades at the entrance to La Paz, the soldiers usually waved through trusted locals but stopped all unknowns, all trucks, and all cars with out-of-town license plates. In the fall of 1976 security had been even tighter because rumor had it that the deposed Isabel Perón was being held under arrest at the nearby military base. Yet at the same time the local soldiers' pride in the base's officer housing was such that guards allowed townspeople to drive around the base and show off the beautiful homes to their out-of-town visitors.[3]

People commented on the military only in private. A villager's friendly wave to the soldiers at the entrance to town might later be offset by a caustic remark about their waste of time. Another villager might grumble that it was his hard-earned money that paid for the military officers' elegant homes. Generally, though, people were afraid and respectful of the military. During one of the frequent floods old-timer Carlos Baridon-Charbonier looked out his window and saw the corpse of his neighbor's dog floating by. Later he saw the military arrive and try to help the people living down the road from him whose furniture was floating out to the Paraná. The rains were early this year. "It'll probably break up as soon as it hits the river, but what do I know? Might go on down to Paraná. End up in my cousin's house." He chuckled, but not without sympathy. Oscar Micol had been helping the flood victims and was up at Carlos's house complaining that townspeople were already on the scene helping but then the military arrived and no one dared continue rescuing the household goods floating away in the swift current for fear of being shot for stealing. Not only that, but the soldiers were totally ineffective encumbered with their machine guns.

People who tended not to stray far from their houses or go to public buildings and events might never actually have seen the military. But they would have known about them from radio requests to denounce anyone acting suspiciously. Only one resident of La Paz was imprisoned at length—and it did not occur in La Paz. Annina Pascal, a young woman studying at the university in Córdoba, became a victim of the last period of Peronism in the early 1970's. Unsuspectingly applying at the police station for a certificate of good conduct—a *Papel de Buena Conducta*, which she needed to get a job—she was arrested and sent to prison, where she remained for the next three years. Her former boyfriend belonged to a reputed terrorist group in Buenos Aires, and it was thus considered prudent to imprison her. Her relatives in Córdoba were notified and told to bring her clothes and food. She was one of the more fortunate victims of the Dirty War in that her arrest had been formally recorded, which meant that she had a much greater chance of eventual release instead of disappearance. After her release she returned to La Paz and became one of Toni Howard's secretaries, but she talked about wanting to return to Córdoba.

Government

While it is true that San Sebastiano belonged to the same military state that produced Annina Pascal's imprisonment—that its administration functioned under a provincial government ultimately responsible to the national one—it also managed to transcend that state. In part, this is because of San Sebastiano's position on the periphery. It has relative autonomy because of neglect and disorganization at the national level and lack of infrastructure at the local one. In a country where there is a wide gulf between city and countryside, rural society necessarily becomes less tied to national society and the central government. San Sebastiano also transcends the national state because of the personalized nature of village life. Government in San Sebastiano means government by people who see themselves as public men serving the interests of their community as a whole. At the same time that Argentina was a military state, then, it was also something more, and it is this that one must remember when one considers the people who had no choice but to watch uneasily and keep on living.

People in public positions in San Sebastiano are community members and are connected to their clients through family and friends. They respond to their fellow villagers as relatives or neighbors, rather than as impersonal employees. Thus just when it looks as if nothing could possibly work in San Sebastiano—with flooded roads and downed electric lines, and with the upper levels of government in such chaos that even if they could reach out to the periphery they would be ineffective—someone like Hernán García or Tullio Gilly appears.

Hernán García is a policeman in San Sebastiano, a public official and thus a figure whose place of work becomes a gathering point in the village—even when it is in the middle of a river, as happened during one of Hernán's errands of mercy. Undaunted by the washed-out road, he had driven his 1960 Pontiac into the swollen Posadas River where it flooded the asphalt entrance to the village. Having watched a pickup truck make the crossing earlier, he had been confident that his car would make it too, now that the river had crested. The car sailed out into the deepest water, only to stall and die. It was quickly surrounded by Teresa de González and her five children, who were crossing the river on foot. For the past few days they had been carrying their shoes more than wearing them because of the heavy rains. The water and wind were cold, but Teresa and the children were eager to stop and talk with Hernán García while he worked on his car and dried various engine parts under the raised hood. The peons José and Julio, who were riding by on horseback, also stopped to pass the time of day with Hernán. The group of nine and the Pontiac were still blocking the road when Renato Baridon drove up to the water's edge in his pickup and prepared to cross. Hernán rallied everyone behind the car, exhorting them to push hard, and even against the strong headwind they got the car moving and up on dry land. The old woman Raquel de Luna had sat patiently in the car the whole while. Hernán was driving her to the hospital outside La Paz for some tests; she could not take the bus because she was too arthritic. This was the third time in one week that Hernán had driven someone to the hospital.

It is easy to tell that Hernán prefers the service part of his job to the law enforcement part. "Not a lot happens here," he explains, "and that's why I like San Sebastiano. The three of us, the senior man, a guard, and myself, can handle everything. We don't get a lot of business—people come here to get a driver's license or permission to sell something. The government doesn't care if a farmer sells a cow to his relatives or his peons, but he can't sell it at an auction without coming here first to pay the tax. As for crime, people are too poor right now to drink much, so there aren't too many fights. It's not like it was two years ago when farmers here hired a lot of workers from outside the colony to clear the land of montes. Boy, were we busy then! Eight people died in the fights. There wasn't anything like that last year, but we did have some deaths from car accidents and there were a couple suicides—there always are. It's a wonder we don't have more deaths, with the fights that occur at soccer games and horse races. You wouldn't believe how excited the spectators get! Of course, we've always got one or two animal thieves we're trying to track down—young boys, you know, who have stolen some sheep or some horses."

Hernán likes conversation and is so far removed from central authority that he seems to escape the tight lid of security that is usually placed on police business. The official statistics for 1980 are even prominently displayed on a large piece of cardboard mounted on the otherwise bare wall of his office. He takes the crime report down from the wall and goes over the cases, hoarded memories from the past. Fifty-four people were arrested and jailed, most of them men between the ages of fifteen and twenty-five. Forty-three were arrested for disorderly conduct and/or molestation, and all but seven were also charged with being under the influence of alcohol. There were seven cases of illegal carrying of arms and one of armed aggression. Finally, there were three thefts, two of them of livestock.[4]

With the exception of one theft, all the crimes occurred in February and March, the months when many people from outside the area are recruited to work in the fields. Disorders often seem to accompany two events: the arrival of people from outside the village, and payday splurges at the local bars. The rest of the time peer group pressure makes the village more or less self-disciplining, which suits Hernán very nicely. He is more concerned with enjoying the natural tranquility of San Sebastiano than with either demonstrating or increasing his power. "The bigger the town, the more problems I'd have. Besides, I like it here—I get to do a bit of everything." He especially enjoys the public aspect of his job. He likes standing out front of the police station under the Argentine flag, now balancing himself against the wall with his foot, now strolling up and down the short stretch of sidewalk that begins at one end of the building and stops at the other, chatting with the sentry, with passing villagers, or with the woman who prepares and delivers the prisoners' meals. And when one of the cells has an occupant, it is hard to conceive of Hernán declining to share some rounds of maté with him.

Around the corner from the police station in the same field as the school is San Sebastiano's new town hall—its first town hall, in fact, since village government used to be housed in the home of one of the officials. The building, completed about five years ago, is no more imposing than any other in San Sebastiano. It has just three rooms, opening onto a common veranda, and is small and low, an unpretentious oblong of concrete maintaining its space as best it can in the midst of the prairie vastness of brush and trees. To the side and in back are some cinder blocks that mark the first stages of what may finally be San Sebastiano's first realized village square. Tullio Gilly, the secretary of the village junta, goes to this building each day, even though he hasn't known for the better part of a year whether San Sebastiano's *junta de gobierno* is still recognized by the provincial government. He keeps on working because, as he puts it, "the people in San Sebastiano are good people," and "a place is what you make it."

Like Hernán García, Tullio has very few traditional bureaucratic duties. Rather, his duties range from road maintenance to meter reading, from accounting to general repairs, from care of the cemetery to legal advice. Though the government now has a permanent office, Tullio is more likely to be found trooping through the village helping people. His work is as personal as his private life, and the line between the two is not easy to draw.

One day after a storm the early morning found Tullio briskly sloshing his way through the mud. He had just gone to check for messages at the junta office. As he headed home across the field a barefoot child ran up to him and greeted him with a breathless, "Adiós, señor." The boy swelled with importance, ready to deliver his message. "What's that, mijo?" exclaimed Tullio. "The storm knocked down the line again? Well, come on, I'll get the car and have a look."

The junta represents the utility companies in San Sebastiano; hence Tullio's concern over some downed lines. The first lines appeared in the early 1970's, and by the early 1980's seventy-eight buildings had electricity. Rural electricity is all local. The village of San Sebastiano has one transformer, and Tullio reads the electric meters each month and repairs the lines. The colony farms have their own transformers, and the La Paz cooperative for electricity reads the meters every two months.

As the boy and Tullio were about to get into the car, Tullio remembered that he didn't have all his equipment. He called to his wife Iolanda, who was in the doorway of the house waiting to see them off. "Mamita, bring me the screwdriver. I'm going over to the far side of the hospital to fix some wires. Why don't you get me a plastic bag, too, while you're in the kitchen. I'll be going by the butcher's and might as well stop. Maybe the truck will have come this morning."

Once they were under way, the boy took the opportunity to question Tullio about one of the week's big events, officer García's unsuccessful fording of the flooded river. Driving out to the downed line in Tullio's familiar '67 Ford Fairlane was an additional reward for the small messenger. Accompanying the señor adds to the boy's feeling of importance and increases his stature among his peers. It is a mutual feeling, however, because for all his fussing Tullio immensely enjoys the role the villagers have assigned him as "padre de la villa" (father of the village). "Someone has to do it—isn't that so?—and I enjoy it. I'm retired from the store now—worked there for thirty-two years. My brother Italo handles it now. Sure I help out when he has to take Inés to the clinic—they're afraid she has cancer—but my time's usually my own. Actually I'm busier now than when I worked at the store.

"I like the job I do now. I came in when the new junta was formed in 1976. Before the military takeover we had a *junta política* chosen by representatives of the people. The new one was formed by the military with the help of Dr. Saavedra, who was a former military man himself and could act as an intermediary. He's got an office in La Paz, but he holds a clinic at the San Sebastiano hospital twice a week, so he knows both the military and the people here. When the military asked him who would be good people to appoint to a junta, he suggested Hernández, Baridon, the Sabelli brothers, and me. Hernández didn't stay long; he resigned after a couple years when he found he couldn't profit from his position. Orlando became the new treasurer. The Sabelli brothers are no longer members either; they both work in Italo's store. We don't know what's happening just now. When Viola's government came in recently, we renounced our commission to the provincial government in Paraná like we're supposed to, but so far they haven't asked us to resign. Qué sé yo?"[5]

Tullio's commitment is not to a superimposed government structure but to the villagers, and he feels that his job is to keep life moving in San Sebastiano. In fact, his feelings are well-founded since the junta performs nearly all the functions of municipal, provincial, and national government itself and thus touches on all aspects of villagers' lives. In the area of health care, for example, the junta pays a dentist—in this case Dr. Saavedra, the military man—a monthly stipend to run a clinic at the hospital on Wednesdays and to take care of the children at the San Sebastiano school. Most of the hospital's clinic patients are poor. Thanks to the junta's subsidy, dental care is virtually free. The junta also takes care of village maintenance—cleaning cemeteries, digging trenches, laying drainage pipes. Tullio is just as likely to perform these tasks himself as to hire peons to perform them; it depends on the junta's finances and the size of the job. The government runs on a shoestring budget, so that even the simplest projects take a long time. For example, San Sebastiano has no road machinery and no access to any, so all repair and construction work is done by hand with a couple of shovels. The few kilometers of asphalt desperately need repair. The low section over the Posadas allows seasonal flooding of the entrance into

San Sebastiano. What would be a minor repair job in another context can create havoc in San Sebastiano: while the stream is rising, children cannot get to school in La Paz, and mail and delivery trucks cannot get through to the village post office and stores.

The junta has recently completed an important village improvement project. It has built several three-sided concrete shelters, and when buses are able to enter San Sebastiano they pick up and discharge their passengers there. Moreover, plans are under way for an enclosed bus station to be built opposite the town hall. The materials and labor will cost $3,000, a large amount for a village government, but the junta has been accumulating the materials for several years, through purchases when the cash is available and through donations from residents who dismantle buildings on their property. Bricks, lumber, and sheets of galvanized tin are piled in various storage spots around the village. The junta's priorities may seem strange at first. Surely road repair should come before bus shelters if the bus shelters are to be completely useful. But perhaps, in the logic of San Sebastiano, a new addition to beautify the village does seem more of an improvement than the repair of an old, already-built road. The asphalt was once an innovation, but now it cannot compete with the novelty of bus shelters. More important, repairing the road over the Posadas would cost a great deal, and even rounding up road machinery would be difficult.

Tullio pulled up in front of the butcher's and allowed the car's engine to stall out next to Lucio Orlando's cart. "Why don't you run ahead and tell the Bareas I'll be there to inspect the lines shortly," Tullio suggested, and the boy was off in a dash. It was evident that the meat truck had finally arrived because Lucio was hefting a side of beef for his family into his cart. His horse ignored the interruption and continued to graze in the grass in front of the store. The butcher has no phone, so he never knows when deliveries will be delayed. Lucio and his other customers had been coming to the store daily to see if his stock had arrived, and had been going away empty-handed. They are used to these uncertainties, however, and they are adaptable. Tullio was nevertheless relieved to take away with him the pieces of beef the butcher put in his plastic bag. The odor of raw meat quickly filled the car as Tullio accelerated in the direction of the Bareas'.

Parking the car in front of Miriam de Barea's property, he found Miriam hanging wet laundry on the fence. She insisted that they talk a while, in her son's house because her rancho was still damp from the rain; the two houses were only a few yards apart. "How's your family, señora?" inquired Tullio. "My son's with a road crew up toward Feliciano this week and my daughter-in-law's feeling much better," said Miriam. "Haven't these storms been bad though! We were watching the floods in Santa Fe last night on the TV. The helicopters were trying to rescue the people and they were running away because they were afraid of them! Can you imagine! What people!" she laughed. She assured Tullio that *she* would not be so backward. Tullio was not eager to dally, partly because of the work he had to do on the lines and partly because of Miriam's demeanor. Although she spoke with him as though they were social equals— she avoided addressing him as "Don Tullio," for example—she also made a point of drawing attention to the differences between them. "Oh, no, here she goes about the economy," cringed Tullio. Miriam ran through a list of complaints—about her small pension, the well-being of the landowners in the colony, and the plight of the peons. Tullio replied with a slightly defensive recitation of his own expenses with his livestock and mentioned *his* small pension and the economic crisis. "Well, anyway, Martínez de Hoz has money," Miriam laughed. Everyone disliked the former Minister of Economy, and Miriam's comment cleared the air. Tullio soon excused himself to go fix the lines.

The repair took longer than Tullio expected, and he was in a rush when he drove up to the gate in front of his house. Iolanda was in the front yard weeding the flower garden. "Here, mamita, take the meat. I'm late to read the meters. I'll be back about twelve-thirty for dinner."

It was still brisk late in the morning when Tullio began tromping through mud and fields prying open the meter boxes with his iron pipe and using a magnifying glass to read the numbers, chatting along the way. Occasionally villagers commandeer him to carry messages or the postmistress gets him to deliver an urgent-looking letter or telegram. Tullio recorded the meter readings in his pocket notebook. After the noon meal he finished reading the meters and checked in at Juan López's house. Juan is paid by the junta to add chemicals periodically to San Sebastiano's water supply. The position of water sanitation inspector used to be held by a provincial employee until the province recently declined to continue the service. Juan got the job primarily because he lives next door to the village's water tank, an old converted grain silo, rather than because of any special training, but the arrangement seems to be working quite well.

At home that night—ironically, by the light of a kerosene lamp because the lines were down again—Tullio transferred the meter readings into the weathered official record book. The next day, if the river was down enough, he would drive into La Paz and deliver the book to the company office. Some weeks later, when the company finished printing the bills, Tullio took care of delivering them. "The largest bill for April was Santucho's, for 600,000 pesos ($200). I'm worried. I don't know how they're going to pay this bill when they haven't been able to pay last month's yet. The junta's responsible for the entire village, so if someone can't pay we have to make it up out of our own pockets until they can pay us back. Most people pay, though, and a more usual bill is about 45,000 pesos ($15)—and sixteen people just pay the minimum of 7,500 pesos ($2.50). Sometimes they come to the office, and sometimes they catch me when I'm out around the village or in front of the house working on my car."

Villages like San Sebastiano may seem to be ill-served by the tenuous links that connect the countryside and metropolises like Buenos Aires. But they keep going, not by virtue of their resources or an independent bureaucracy, but by reason of the good will of their people and the direct, immediate assistance a Tullio Gilly can offer. Performing all the functions of a patriarchal centralized government, Tullio does not perceive any drawbacks in the limited size and potential of San Sebastiano. He does his job "because the people here are good people and helping them promotes harmony in the village."

In 1981, people in San Sebastiano had faith in their local government and were tolerant of inconveniences. People in towns and cities had a very different attitude toward their leaders, and jokes about government incompetence were common. "In the last Argentine election," went one joke, "*many* years ago, of course, a very stupid man was elected vice-governor of the province. When they went to interview his mother, she said that she was very proud of him and if only she'd known he was going to become so famous, she would have sent him to school!"

Health

It was still dark when Filipa de Malvasio went to the shed where they kept the chickens and goat. The day before she had gathered the thickest parsley stalks she could find. Squatting on the dirt floor, she inserted the stalks into her vagina, hoping that either the thrust itself or the substance secreted by the white inner part of the stem would induce an abortion. Parsley had worked before. It was a good time to do it because Pedro was away picking cotton and the children were not up yet. About noon her efforts were successful, but she began to bleed heavily. Her daughter ran to fetch officer García to drive her to the 9 de Julio Hospital. Filipa hoped she would have a doctor who would not be suspicious and report her. In any case, the other women said it was hard to prove anything with locally-induced abortions. The pain seemed greater than last time—couldn't Señor García drive any faster? At last the blackness came, and she woke to find Laura De Pereda at her bedside. Ah, Dr. De Pereda—she's good—she doesn't believe in abortion but she would never tell on her.

The government, buttressed by the Catholic church and nuns on hospital staffs, tries to get doctors to be vigilant about ascertaining if an abortion has occurred and to report it. Laura, although she herself does not perform abortions, does not believe in reporting her patients to the police. "Lots of women come to the hospital hemorrhaging," she says, "and claim they've fallen or something and lost their baby. It's my legal obligation to denounce them to the police if I think they've intentionally aborted, but who's to say really? I'm certainly not going to report any of my patients; they'd stop coming to the hospital and would die. I'd like to be able to give my patients contraceptives, but I can't—for one thing, we've got four nuns here at the hospital. Back in the early 1970's a hospital in Paraná gave out contraceptives to its patients, but it stopped after a couple of years—I don't know why. It seems unfair. I'd say 70 percent of the middle and upper classes use contraceptives, but most poor families don't have that option and have five or ten children. People have to resort to abortion. There's a high percentage here, but I couldn't say what it is. It would be very hard to know. Many doctors perform abortions, but they would never tell because they'd be subject to prosecution. The government is cracking down."

Even though the government has become more vigilant about abortion since the military junta took over, women in the countryside continue to use a variety of herbs and other agents to bring on uterine contractions to induce abortions. Filipa's choice, the parsley plant, is a popular one because parsley is believed to have a double effect. Women hope that either the mechanical action of insertion or the chemical action from the apiole secreted by the stem will produce an abortion. Apiole by itself, which is sold in pharmacies without a prescription, is often taken orally to cause toxic abortion. It is dangerous because it can cause serious damage to the liver and the kidneys, which is almost always fatal. Filipa could also have chosen other plants like nutmeg, rosemary, and the male rue, or coniferous plants like the thuja, also used to burn off warts, and the savin. Some of these plants are used both orally and locally. Occasionally a concoction of mashed insects is ingested, but insects are far less frequently used than plants and other substances. The introduction of irritants into the vagina with a syringe is another popular method of abortion, since most of them are commonly available, like quinine, disinfectants, boiling water, and alcohol, and they can be difficult for doctors to detect.[6]

Once Filipa found herself in Dr. De Pereda's care, she did not need to fear exposure. But she had taken care this time to hide what she was doing from her daughter. Ever since the girl next door started going to high school in La Paz, she had filled Filipa's daughter with ideas that angered Filipa. Her daughter accused her of having no maternal feelings and even hinted that she thought her a murderer. She showed her a passage in her friend's textbook that pronounced abortion and contraception to be selfish, unnatural, and criminal.[7]

Within six months of her abortion, Filipa found that she was pregnant again. She tried the parsley, but it cheated her—it did not work. A week later she tried lysol and boiling water and waited. Her pregnancy must have been further along than she thought. At any rate, Pedro would be happy with another baby. He had been disappointed at her losing the last two. One day toward the end of her pregnancy she walked over to see if Juana Inés Vilas would help her when the time came. Juana Inés's grandmother had practiced midwifery and had taught Juana Inés the profession. Midwifery is technically illegal, but non-professionals still deliver many babies. In the department of La Paz in 1979—the most recent year for which statistics are available—1,441 out of 1,870 total births were attended by a doctor, 377 by a midwife, and 35 were unassisted (in 17 cases the circumstances were unknown).[8]

Many women put a great deal of trust in midwives like Juana Inés. She boasts that she has delivered more than fifty babies and all were born alive. Local women also go to a midwife rather than the hospital for the sake of convenience. Cost is not really a factor since the hospital outside La Paz is public. "With the mud and bad weather," says Juana Inés, "it's no wonder women have their babies at home sometimes. I always deliver my babies as a favor to people—I can't let them suffer—but sometimes they give me a bag of maté leaves or a few centavos."

In Filipa's view, doctors and hospital personnel never have the time to spend with their patients. As she approached Juana Inés's rancho, she clapped her hands to warn Juana Inés that she had a visitor. She walked through the line of chickens that followed Juana Inés from the lean-to kitchen up the step into the bedroom-sittingroom of the house. The chickens found little to interest them on the brick floor but stayed nevertheless, seeming not to tire of checking out chair legs and rug tassels. Had they been allowed to move up a level, the possibilities would have been increased a hundredfold—all manner of objects fill Juana Inés's room. She has had a wider experience than most women in San Sebastiano; her father was widowed early on and she spent much of her youth as a servant for a family in Paraná.

"Don't worry, Filipa, I'll be here when your time comes. I hardly ever go out now. I never visit my neighbors, but sometimes they come here. I only go to weddings and to the lawyer's office. Look here." Juana Inés gets her purse, which she treats as a kind of safe-deposit box to store her valuables in, and pulls out a piece of paper. "This is my property title. See, here's my name. I've been trying to get this house transferred to my name alone ever since my husband died. It's been two years now that the lawyer's been working on it and nothing's happened. I go see him every couple months, but otherwise I'm here working in my garden. On May 25, because it's a holiday, my son-in-law is coming by with his patron's plow to plow my garden. I never go to the store, you know, I grow my own vegetables. I like planting vegetables—I guess I'm half gringa! We have a pig again, and I had sixty-odd chickens, at least till a while ago.

With all this rain we've been having, we've eaten a few. Anyway, you just get your daughter to come for me when the time comes."

Juana Inés went to Filipa in late May and delivered a boy. Four days later, just to be sure he was all right, Filipa took him to the 9 de Julio Hospital to be checked by a doctor. Dr. Marina Merati de Howard was on duty. "How was the umbilical cord cut, Señora? With scissors?! Were they sterilized? Over the cookfire?! Well, let's see how he's doing," Marina sighed.

It was early June and the winter rains had begun. The streets were flooded and roofs were leaking. The blue neon sign from the Hotel Mesopotamia across the street from the Howards' house flashed a bleary message on the pavement. Marina decided to wait until the rain let up a bit before she tried to go to her car. She planned her trip to the hospital carefully to avoid roads with low spots that would be under water. It seemed impossible that she would have clients today. But as she entered the administrative wing of the hospital, Zurita López handed her a clipboard with a long list of people who were waiting to see her. Marina groaned—it was already late.

There were fourteen doctors on the staff, but the busiest were the pediatricians. About three-fourths of the 120 daily patients come to see Marina and the two other pediatricians. The hospital functions more as a clinic for the poor than as an in-patient facility—in 1980, only 46 percent of its 95-bed capacity was occupied. It admitted 2,120 persons that year, and 80 of them died there; most of its long-term patients are elderly people who have nowhere else to go.[9] The hospital in San Sebastiano has similar functions, and part of its title is Home for the Elderly. There is no comparison, though, between the San Sebastiano Hospital and the larger 9 de Julio Hospital. The latter is new, better equipped, and well staffed by La Paz physicians who divide their time between the hospital and their private practices. Still, it is a public hospital and has its limitations. One of its main problems is a shortage of medicine, since it has to rely on what the provincial public health office sends. When the hospital's supply of a particular medicine is exhausted, the patient it is prescribed for is sent to Señora Galdós's house in La Paz; she heads a women's charity organization that will buy the medicine with its own funds from a local pharmacy. The hospital's supply of powdered milk often runs short, too. Every child under two years of age is entitled to two and a half pounds a month, but when the hospital runs out, people must buy it at the store or feed their children something else. The middle and upper classes typically do not use the La Paz hospital and go instead to specialized clinics elsewhere, particularly for the more serious illnesses.

The wait at the 9 de Julio is sometimes long. When Marina went through the consultation room set aside for her and opened the front door, she saw about thirty people, mainly women, waiting in the corridor, their bare feet muddy from their walk. Among them was Filipa with her new baby. He had diarrhea. "Señora, we will have to keep your son here and feed him liquids through his veins or else he will die. He's so dehydrated already." Filipa was frightened of the needles, though, and moved toward the door, thanking Dr. Merati but taking the baby with her. Hoisting the screaming child into the sack tied around her neck, she started off across the field to the house of the *curandera,* the woman in the village who knows about healing.

The next day the baby was worse. Pedro stayed home from the fields even though it would anger his patron. He had to get food for his son. He rode his horse first to Vicente Salas at the San Sebastiano Hospital and Home for the Elderly, but received an officious reply that the hospital was out of milk. He had more success at the 9 de Julio and rode home with the milk. The following day Pedro went to work—he'd done what he could. That night the baby died. After Pedro returned from work the next day, he and Filipa buried the baby in the campo. There was no record of the child's ever having entered or left the world.

It is understandable why many births and deaths of babies and young children are not registered in rural areas. Registration means a costly and time-consuming trip to La Paz and the payment of a fee. If Pedro and Filipa had registered the birth of their son, for example, it would have cost them about $1.80; for $1.80 they could have bought more than a liter of milk.

The evening after their baby died, Pedro bought some rum and he and Filipa and their neighbors gathered to drink and play the guitar in a sad tribute to the sacrifice they had made to God.[10]

The rate of infant mortality has decreased markedly in San Sebastiano and La Paz since 1970, a reflection of better health care and services, especially for residents of La Paz, but parents like Pedro and Filipa remain inured to the death of infants all the same. Diarrhea, the cause of their son's death, is the most common illness in children of the area and the leading cause of infant mortality—in 1980 the doctors at the 9 de Julio Hospital saw 1,045 cases of it, many of them complicated by malnutrition—and grippe and respiratory diseases are a distant second and third.[11]

Diarrhea is most virulent during summer (hence its common name, *diarrea estival*), but it is a year-round problem. Most of its victims survive if they are hospitalized, but many parents react like Filipa to the thought of hospitalization and their children often die. The infection results from contaminated water and food. The National Institute of Agricultural Technology advises people to boil their water and milk, to boil the nipples of baby bottles, to remove human excrement, to keep flies away, to wash their hands after using the toilet, and to practice general hygiene, but such instructions presume a life-style impossible for rancho residents. It is enough of a problem to haul drinking water from the public water supply; river or rain water is usually used for washing dishes, food, and hands. Marina believes there must be a problem with La Paz's public water supply as well, since she sees many cases of diarrhea among the middle-class townspeople who come to her office. "For my hospital patients, though, it's a matter of training. They come to see me and then don't follow my directions. Lots of times they just turn around and go to a curandera." Until the early 1970's the family record book, the libreta de familia, still carried a statement advising mothers against consulting curanderas and *parteras*, or midwives, warning that they often mistook diarrhea for indigestion and treated many of their patients incorrectly. And at least as recently as 1977 the libreta's section on the care of newborns advised women to breastfeed if possible to avoid contagion, to wash their hands when handling milk and baby bottles, and to control flies. Diarrhea can be over quickly, and sometimes disastrously, but it does not become a life-long problem as does another common disease in the San Sebastiano–La Paz area.

Later in the year Filipa's two-year-old son—actually her daughter's illegitimate child, whom Filipa and Pedro have adopted—awoke one morning with an insect bite near his eye. It was the bite of a bedbug, a *vinchuca*. Filipa hoped it was not infected with Chagas-Mazza disease, but a few weeks later the symptoms began to appear: fever, chills, headache, sore muscles, and loss of appetite. She knew the disease would become latent after the first month and most likely would remain so for the rest of the boy's life. It would weaken him, but perhaps not enough to make him unable to do heavy campo work. Filipa hoped the disease would not become a chronic condition in his later years, as it does in about 15 percent of all cases, producing palpitations, pain in the liver, and heart lesions.[12]

Lower-class rancho housing is particularly hospitable to bedbugs. Since about 60 percent of San Sebastiano's population lives in ranchos and about 20 percent of the La Paz population, the disease is endemic to the area. The bedbug lives in the mud and straw building materials of ranchos. It emerges at night to infect the sleeping inhabitants by sucking their blood, and people use mosquito netting or keep a light on at night if they can. Generally, there are no sanitation facilities for ranchos, and human waste infected with the bacteria of Chagas-Mazza empties into the ground water flowing into rivers—water that is then used for cooking and washing. Insects in subtropical regions like the northeast are almost all infected and have been transported all over Argentina, with the result that 10 percent of the nation's population now carries the disease.

The Social Services Office in La Paz and the fumigation team of the National Chagas-Mazza Service, which work together, recommend that the best way to prevent the disease is to eliminate the bedbug's place of refuge—by plastering and whitewashing walls and roofs, by periodically cleaning and ventilating all buildings, and by using insecticides. Even in ranchos, a good application of mud for the plastering, followed by a whitewash of the same material and one or two coats of lime, is said to be enough to keep out the vinchuca. But it is difficult to seal all cracks, to ventilate a building that has at most only one tiny window and a door, and to keep clean a house that has a dirt floor and is crowded with people and animals. The fumigation team tries to break the cycle of infection by advising the use of these methods, but its most effective tactic seems to be the burning of heavily-infected ranchos.

During a nine-month fumigation campaign in 1980, Rosa Lorenzo, the head of the Social Services Office, was in charge of identifying infected houses and relocating people whose homes had been burned. "Now that we're in the second stage of the campaign," she reported, "we're finding that 90 percent of the bedbugs are infected.

In May it seemed it was only 50 percent. That means the fumigation team is probably going to have to burn down a lot more ranchos. The people bring us the bugs here in the office. They're very good about this because they really want to know. And then if the bugs are infected, we prepare the people for fumigation and relocation if necessary. The town gives them some land and some materials for a new rancho, but it can't give much because the materials are too expensive. A rancho with about 200 square feet costs 1,950,000 pesos ($650). This seems high but that's because the materials are good: cement, asbestos, brick. Now, a person could build a rancho this size for 975,000 pesos ($325) if he used cheaper materials like cardboard, sacks, and straw, but it wouldn't last. It's hard to build a rancho for 975,000 pesos today, though, because the town doesn't allow people to cut straw on the islands any more; the straw just adds to the bedbug problem. For the same reason the town won't distribute any more straw either."

In September, Filipa's mother, who lives on the other side of the village, became ill and asked the old man next door to go to the Social Services Office in La Paz to get the ambulance. The old man shuffled into the office. He seemed intensely worried but was unwilling to interrupt what was clearly only a casual conversation between Rosa and her co-worker. Neither paid any attention to him for several minutes. Eventually he coughed, they noticed him, and he requested an ambulance for his neighbor. A good deal of time had already elapsed since the man had left home, and now Rosa told him that his neighbor's doctor must make out a request form for him to take to the hospital. Then the hospital would send the ambulance. This was the only way a poor woman like Filipa's mother could hope to get an ambulance. Luckily, he knew who her doctor was and went straight to his private office since his clinic hours at the 9 de Julio Hospital were over for the day. Finding the doctor's office would not be open for another hour, the neighbor waited outside the door, where other people soon joined him in a line against the wall. The doctor was reluctant, since he did not know the nature of Filipa's mother's illness, but gave the man a note, which he took to the hospital. The ambulance was out on a call, but Filipa's mother would be next on the list. By then it was early evening and the old man returned to the bus stop to wait for the San Sebastiano bus. His experience with the bureaucratic entanglements that arise when two different agencies must cooperate (in this case the Social Services Office and the hospital) had not been good.

While Filipa was away visiting her sick mother a few days later, Pedro, who had no work for the day, forced himself on their thirteen-year-old daughter again. He had last done this when Filipa was pregnant. Their daughter had been a student then, and there was a scandal when word got around the school. Pedro denied the charge, got drunk, and started a brawl at the Cerutti's bar.

The social worker Rosa is daily involved with problems like these. Rosa, like many gringos, regards common-law marriages as little more than concubinage and views this living arrangement as a major factor in family problems. "Living conditions foster promiscuity," she says. "It's easy for fathers to take advantage of their daughters or their neighbor's daughters in a dark rancho. They do it when their wives are sick or pregnant or maybe with another man. It's an awful problem. It gets around the school, the police confront the father, he denies it, and that's the end of it. What are you going to do! These people have their own culture—they're marginal people, so theirs is a marginal culture. It's their custom not to marry—concubinage is the rule." Rosa understands, however, that there are advantages to a common-law union. "It's not just for the advantage of men; the women want it, too. They don't want to be tied to a man who turns out to be worthless and a drunk, for example.

"Alcoholism is a real problem here—they drink wine usually, but rum too if it's cheaper. Drunkenness is especially common at the end of the week or, for that matter, any time anyone gets paid. At La Paz's School for the Handicapped alcoholism is one of the most important factors in the children's mental disabilities. So are malnutrition—maté cocido is often a child's entire breakfast and supper—and lack of pre-natal care. La Paz has the highest rate of alcoholism in the province. Malnutrition and alcohol are a bad combination: one glass of wine for a malnourished person and he's drunk. We don't have many statistics, but I know that between September 1977 and September 1978, for example, the La Paz police made 241 arrests for drunkenness in town and 1,138 in the campo. We have an Alcoholics Anonymous chapter here now; the town provides a meeting place for them but no money, so I don't know how effective they are. There's no drug problem here, though; people are too poor. A man is doing well if he gets to work fifteen days a month—he'll earn about 150,000 pesos ($50) and if a woman has regular domestic work she can earn 240,000 pesos ($80) a month. That's not much money to go around when a family has seven or eight kids. And some families have a lot more, like one I visit that has seventeen. The kids don't even know each other's real names, they just use nicknames.

"Some people try to better themselves even in these conditions. In fact almost all rancho families send their children to school through the third grade. Then they drop out to work, though, and eventually they forget how to read and write. The children are also too malnourished to learn. We don't have any statistics, but the signs are there—bloated stomachs and thin fingers, arms, and legs. Except for sending their kids to school, most people don't try to better themselves. It's true that there isn't much work and the pay is bad, but I still see ads for people to look after a small farm sometimes, for example. It's just that our clients don't take advantage of the opportunity. Frankly, they don't have to work because our office provides everything. We give them land and building materials, medicine, caskets, shoes and notebooks for the kids, bus tickets to Paraná if they have to go there for medical reasons or for legal reasons—because there's no Juvenile Court in La Paz—or so a child can participate in a school sporting event. We distribute milk through the hospital and provide the meals at the schools. So why should they work?"

The social welfare system is designed to provide a better life for the poor of the San Sebastiano–La Paz area, and to teach them to pursue the admittedly limited opportunities open to them. In many areas of social welfare, however, they are still left to their own devices. Even in health care, some things have changed little since the days when Eduardo Howard's father used to take time out from herding cattle to pull teeth on his ranch in San Sebastiano. He had had some training, but it was experience on the job that made him, in a sense, one of the colony's first curanderos. This personal aspect of health care still carried out by local healers and midwives is at least as important to the people as any agency that works in La Paz. Villagers have a narrowed frame of experience, but they know how to take care of themselves in their society.

In November, Filipa and Pedro and the children watched the flames spread over their rancho. Some of their neighbors were with them; their own homes were on fire too. The fires were brief, since there was little to burn. The fumigation team had come early in the month and given them a week to remove their belongings. Filipa and Pedro had moved in with her mother. It would be the same old story: the province would promise them materials for a new rancho, they would return several times to the Social Services Office to ask when the materials would arrive, but in the end they would have to scrounge for wood and straw and cardboard if they hoped to have a house in the near future. Then in a few years it would be the same fiery spectacle all over again: the fumigators would come, find the insects, and torch the ranchos.

Education

Education provides an example of the personalized village's bureaucratic side. In government, policeman and junta official do their jobs unaided but also unhampered by externally-imposed structure. In the area of health too, personalization predominates, this time along with some hierarchical structure to facilitate matters. But in education, external influences ranging from the departmental to the national level have been allowed and even encouraged to dominate.

One Thursday morning Neli Rivera de Salas, the director of the San Sebastiano school, panicked and rang up Pablo Rodriguez of the Education Office for the department of La Paz. He was just walking into his office, nodding perfunctorily in the direction of his employees' "Good morning, chief," when he heard the phone. The Education Office is on the second floor of the La Paz school, and Pablo was already in a bad mood because he had been held up by the crush of youngsters in the school yard. Why hadn't they rung the last bell yet? Now the bustle of the clerks in the room to his right and the noisy chatter of the women about an upcoming meeting distracted him. And here was Neli de Salas blabbering about some problem. His anger was mounting rapidly as he continued meditating on a problem of his own: "Why can't these book vendors ever learn. I can't give them permission to sell books here—they have to go to Paraná. They always want me to make just one little exception. How am I to know if something's just been put on the proscribed list? It's better just to say no." Suddenly he found himself listening more closely to Neli, his anger now fueled by paranoid suspicions. Finally he responded: "Someone, a foreigner yet, wants to ask some questions and see our records? Well, everything under my command is top secret and no one talks. I won't budge an inch until I get direct, written orders addressed to me personally.

And even then, what if he got permission and wrote something bad about my schools? Would I ever be in trouble! I don't like to bother the police, but I'd better be safe. They're always telling us to report anything suspicious anyhow."

Pablo lost no time in bringing the foreigner's presence to the attention of Luis Morales of the Prefect's Office in La Paz, an office much more concerned with national security than Hernán García's office in San Sebastiano. Luis quickly received confirmation about the foreigner from the public telephone employee in San Sebastiano—a reliable source, his wife. The foreigner had been asking questions and taking pictures. Now Luis's task was to find out everything he could. How, he wondered, could this have happened while he was in charge? Things had been going so well, too. Why hadn't the foreigner reported to the La Paz police immediately upon arriving in town? Then he, Morales, could have been monitoring his activities all along. His task was also to convince the foreigner that the police regretted the bother they were causing and to make sure the foreigner would not say anything about La Paz or Argentina that would damage his country's reputation. He rehearsed a carefully phrased repertory of excuses for the actions of an underdeveloped country living under a military government. "Many countries are more developed and Argentina is poor by comparison, but one must take this into consideration. Besides, all countries have their rich and poor classes." Many times he repeated that the military government was necessary to maintain order and explained that every country has its good and bad points. He emphasized the need for a balanced view. "There are two groups of Argentines worried about human rights: those who want to publicize the issue and those who feel it has been exaggerated." Luis, as a representative of the military and like many others protective of Argentina's reputation, would like to see the human rights issue forgotten. First, it is an embarrassment, and second, it means constant surveillance of people like this foreigner to make sure nothing negative about Argentina is leaked to the outside world.

In the end, Luis points out, he is only doing his job—and jobs are hard to come by. He and his wife are both fortunate to have work, even though it means they cannot live together and really have no home of their own. Because of the bus schedule, his wife, who works in San Sebastiano, and his daughter both live in the colony during the week with his wife's parents, visiting Luis in his rooms in

La Paz on Saturday afternoon and Sunday. They have never lived together during their five years of marriage.

People's explanations of the commotion about the foreigner—the kind of episode that is repeated daily all over Argentina—range from "It reflects a general fear" to "Schools feel a great responsibility for their students" to "Something funny may be going on," perhaps a reference to Neli's husband's illegal but as yet unacknowledged expropriation of village building materials in San Sebastiano. Toni Howard's view was that, "The police are more scared of the foreigner than he is of them, you can believe me. You can imagine they don't want an international incident in La Paz—an ambassador's car coming up from Buenos Aires, a big black limousine driving through the middle of La Paz with some foreign flag waving, especially to have it out with the La Paz police! How embarrassing it would be!"

The people may be unconcerned and Toni may chuckle, but Neli and Pablo and Luis are worried and not at all amused. They seem to stand apart from the personalization of rural life. It is an interesting juxtaposition to see officer García in San Sebastiano carrying out his duties like an amiable shopkeeper tending his store, coaxing cooperation from his clients, tolerant of their idiosyncracies and peccadillos, while the educator Neli de Salas fulfills her commission like an imperious general. Now that the foreigner threatens her domain, Neli responds with what might appear unwarranted zeal for her situation. She is at the bottom of the hierarchy and director of a peripheral school, yet she acts as if her mission is much more important and far-reaching. Admittedly she must be careful because the government insists that education be treated as a matter of top national security necessitating strict adherence to rules at all levels, but Neli seems to believe that the task of preserving the country's reputation rests solely on her shoulders.

Early in Argentina's history, education came to be considered an important component of a civilized nation. Indeed, the Argentine government first emphasized education for the same reason it promoted European immigration: it was a tool to free Argentina from its "barbaric" past and place it within the "civilized" world of Western Europe and North America. Today, with Argentines chafing under the negative judgment of much of the world because of the nation's economic and political crises and its human rights record, the government continues to promote education in order to justify its claims to be part of the civilized, progressive West.

In the past, government efforts have been largely successful, and Argentina is known as one of the most literate of the Latin American nations. Something that threatens to tarnish that reputation, however, is the extraordinarily high drop-out rate in primary schools— and this is undoubtedly another reason for educators' attitudes in La Paz and San Sebastiano. In the early 1980's the drop-out rate in the province of Santa Fe was 45 percent; in 1977 in Entre Ríos, 72 percent.[13] The single most important cause of the high drop-out rate was the economy. Not for several decades had the need for extra income earned by children and the expenses of even "free" education been so great. The military government took note of the situation, made all the more apparent by improved reporting of school attendance, and in the spring of 1980 the National Office of Education launched a campaign against desertion from the schools. In part, the campaign may have been encouraged to increase the military's control over the populace, or to divert attention from economic problems or the human rights issue toward an issue on which people could rally in support of the government, as they did over the Malvinas issue. But though these motives may have contributed to the original decision to launch a campaign, the fact remains that school desertion was and is a real issue, and that its causes were primarily economic.

Educators are also affected by state censorship. The ideas that students—and the populace in general—are exposed to are strictly controlled. Neli keeps her copy of a two-page list of proscribed books handy in the top drawer of her desk; the first entries are the works of Paolo Freire, the leftist Brazilian sociologist whose methods of teaching reading and writing to peasants using class struggle analysis are well-known and controversial. The books approved for Argentine students are quite different; they are designed to instill respect for the ordering and disciplining institutions of society— the family, the church, and the state—through the medium of the military. The textbook used for third-year secondary school students in civics classes, for example, is based on a government interpretation of Catholic dogma and of political history. It singles out the Christian family as the basic unit of society, and discourages individualism. It rejects anything that threatens Christian morality and the family, such as pornography, divorce, adultery, abortion, and contraception. It portrays the military government as sharing and promoting the Christian values of the populace, and good Christians as upholders of the State.[14]

The textbook exhorts students to oppose materialism, subversion, individualism, and totalitarianism, and to shun any subversive act or idea, whether in the form of disrespect, disobedience, or illegal action, that is designed to overturn established authority and values.[15] The stated reason for these instructions is that subversive acts are always followed by anarchism, as happened at the end of the nineteenth century and the beginning of the twentieth. Contemporary European terrorism is also cited as a consequence.[16] The book describes these terrorists as leftists, international Marxists, who are trying to undermine non-Marxist countries. Marx is analyzed as a kind of Antichrist who denies God and whose ideas are contradictory and impractical. The text points out that in communist countries the means of production are not in the hands of the workers but in the hands of the state; that workers are constantly improving their situation in capitalist countries; and that Marx ignored the middle class, which is now growing even in communist countries. The text continues in this heavy-handed and dogmatic vein. This is the type of education the young teachers of San Sebastiano have themselves experienced, and it is what they must teach their students. Questions, discussions, and differing views must be delicately handled, and thus it is no surprise that educators feel tense and vulnerable when confronted by someone who seems to threaten the established order.

Neli de Salas' paranoia is perhaps understandable because the government holds her responsible for the propagation of orthodox thinking in her teachers and pupils. Children are hardly encouraged to be inquiring free spirits, and neither are teachers. Neli's pronouncements are a good example of the misinformation that is passed on under the isolation and indoctrination of censorship. She declares authoritatively that people in the United States must be very poor indeed since they can afford only one meal a day (here she has misinterpreted the North American custom of eating the main meal in the evening instead of at noon as Argentines do); that children there have to eat out of tin boxes (that is, lunch boxes) sitting at their desks; and that fathers sometimes do not see their children for days at a time because they get home late at night. In her desire to gain respect for her country, Neli says she hopes that people in foreign countries will not see pictures of Argentine village bars, the *pulperías*, lest they take her countrymen for drunkards. The extent of her preoccupation with such issues in the midst of the "disappearance" and torture of thousands of Argentine citizens is frighteningly close to that of the military. Authoritarian interference is nevertheless only one side of education in San Sebastiano and La Paz.

Like the areas of government and health, education also has a more constructive, personalized aspect. Argentines are deeply committed to education, even beyond their ability to pay for it. In March 1982 the Minister of Education issued the schools a list of instructions designed to limit the demands on a family's income and make it easier to comply with the law requiring school attendance until age fourteen. "Free" education had become a luxury for many Argentines, even for some members of the middle class. The Education Office calculated that even if a family could cut down on the purchase of special clothing or items for extracurricular school activities, the initial outlay for sending one child to a free state school would come to about $160. To put this figure in context, a worker in a textile factory at the time earned about $250 a month, a peon perhaps $150 a month.

For many poor families "free" primary education is still unaffordable because of the cost of school supplies and clothing and because it entails the loss of a potential wage earner. In rural areas especially, school attendance has always been erratic and has typically ended altogether at the third grade. The effect of the high drop-out rate is devastating. In San Sebastiano in 1980, 54 percent of the population aged fourteen and older had not finished primary school. By the time they are forty, many drop-outs have become illiterate adults; the illiteracy rate in San Sebastiano in 1980 for the population aged fourteen and older was officially 20 percent.[17]

Every morning except Sunday, Neli sets off through the grass of her yard early. This particular morning the road was muddy; it would dry out a little before she had to return to prepare the midday meal at twelve-thirty, but her shoes would be wet and muddy all morning. She squished by the pasture that lies between her house and the school, picking her way carefully around the puddles. One of her students rode by, seated behind her father on his horse. "Say good morning to the señora," he prompted his daughter.

At the school the nine teachers were helping the three cooks make maté cocido in a large black iron pot over the wood fire in the shelter behind the school. The maté was for the children; the teachers were drinking coffee, a privilege of their superior position. It was a cold early winter morning; there was no heat and the doors were all open to let in fresh air. It was break time between classes, and the white-smocked children were playing in the school yard. The din of their voices was ear-splitting as it echoed off the walls, but no one seemed to notice. The teachers, all young women, were trying to warm themselves around the fire, huddling in layers of sweaters beneath their smocks. They wore blue and white ribbons in honor of a national holiday. A group of boys ran off in the direction of the outhouse, stopping to explore the interesting debris hidden in the long grass of the school yard: cow skulls, broken tools, someone's bike. The children tried to gain some extra playtime by ignoring the custodian's bell, but were eventually herded back into the five classrooms.

By noon the cooks had finished preparing the meal for about 120 children, students of both the morning and the afternoon classes. The children were served a stew (a guiso), bread and crackers, and water. Their families were too poor to feed them at home. Neli knew which children were entitled to the meal and sent any intruders packing.

From Neli's viewpoint, class attendance at the village school is high. "Ninety percent of the children attend regularly. The biggest problem is that they don't have help at home, so they don't study." Actually, attendance varies a great deal, according to the weather and to the demands of farm work. In addition, some of the morning students routinely arrive late to school because of farm chores such as milking the cows. The school's statistics for the past ten years quickly reveal the problem of desertion. One example is the drop-out rate for the 1981 seventh-grade class. In 1975, 46 students entered the first grade; in subsequent years their number declined to 38, 35, 33, 33, 23, and finally, in the spring of 1981, to 16 students, a drop-out rate of 65 percent. The drop-out rate between first grade and completion of the seventh grade ranged from 50 to 70 percent in the 1970's: 60 percent of the students who began first grade in

1971 failed to complete primary school (33 out of 55 students); 50 percent of those who began in 1972 (21 out of 42); and 71 and 61 percent of those who began in 1973 and 1974 (14 out of 49 and 19 out of 49). All the indications are that the trend continues. In the spring of 1981 there were 52 students in the first grade; 42 in the second; 26 in the third; 37 in the fourth; 27 in the fifth; 19 in the sixth; and 16 in the seventh. Most drop-outs go to work picking cotton or doing domestic work to help their families. About 70 percent of the village school's students are from lower-class families. Only 25 percent are from middle-class families, and 5 percent from the upper class.

There is evidence of attrition in the colony school too, though to a lesser degree. The situation there is somewhat different, however, because most of the colony population is upper class and is also Waldensian. What appears to be attrition is usually a matter of students transferring to a school in La Paz. For example, the Ecksteins' three granddaughters live with them during the week in La Paz and attend primary school there. Their parents found this preferable to driving the dirt roads each day to the colony school. There is a great difference between the village and colony schools, reflecting the different populations of each. The village school, the Luis de Góngora, has a morning session of about 100 children, grades four through seven. Grades one through three, with 120 children, meet in the afternoon. The colony school is across the Posadas River opposite the Waldensian church. It has only 16 students in grades one through three and 19 in grades four through seven, and all classes are held in the afternoon. The school has two teachers. Classes are larger in the colony school, but the student population is much more socioeconomically homogeneous, and scholastically at a higher level.

Of the people censused in 1980 in San Sebastiano, only 76 had ever enrolled in any kind of high school—usually one of the public schools in La Paz—and 29 of them had not graduated. Twenty-five of them were still in school, and they made up just 18 percent of a censused population of 139 people aged fourteen to nineteen. San Sebastiano teachers maintain, though, that most students who remain in primary school through seventh grade do go on to secondary school in La Paz.

The first real separating out of students occurs in the third grade; the next at the end of the seventh grade. Xavier Orlando, a twelve-year-old student at the village school and the son of a peon, made it past third grade but will probably not be so fortunate when he is ready to go to secondary school. Secondary education is really a luxury, and usually only the middle and upper classes can afford it. Since rural areas tend not to have secondary schools, a secondary education often means living away from home. It became common for middle-class San Sebastiano residents to send their children to secondary school only in the 1960's; initially they had been reluctant to do so because of their distrust of the town and because of the expense. Now that more people are familiar with the town, or at least have overcome their reservations about it because they realize the value of a secondary education, they are more willing to send their children there. In addition, a whole structure has developed to assist campo children attending school in La Paz. Elsa de Prochet, for example, "pastures children" from San Sebastiano, that is, she provides room and board to them.

People are much more concerned now about getting as much education as possible in order to get a better job. Night school is a popular way for adults to continue their schooling. Many teenagers also prefer night classes, so that they can work during the day. Juana, the Howards' sixteen-year-old live-in babysitter, decided to resume her primary education in night school. She had attended two years of classes in the campo before dropping out. Now, between 5:00 and 8:00 p.m., when classes begin, she proudly practices forming her letters at the Howards' kitchen table.

There are several elements in society that operate at a personal, individual level to increase children's chances of succeeding in school and completing their primary education. Schoolteachers, although they are subject to the same censorship as school administrators, nevertheless seem not to let it get in the way of their concern for their students and their teaching. Teachers are among the most professionally committed and enthusiastic workers in Argentina, and this can be a boon to children. Because Argentina has few universities, secondary school teachers have the status a university professor would elsewhere. Most secondary school teachers are *docentes* (meaning simply "teachers"), and a few have the still more respected rank of *profesores* (signifying that they have a university education). La Paz has seven profesores, compared with twenty medical doctors and twenty-four lawyers. The figure reflects a limit imposed by the Education Office, as well as profesores' preference for positions in larger towns. Primary school teachers are also respected as professionals.

Respect is one of the few benefits of a career in teaching. The training is long. To become a primary school teacher, a *maestro*, takes two years in a teacher training school; to become a secondary school teacher takes four years. At the university level, it takes four years to become a *profesor superior* (who holds the equivalent of a U.S. bachelor's degree); two more years to earn a *licencia universitaria* (a master's degree); and two more years to earn a *doctorado* (a doctorate).

Few people from La Paz have attended a university. It is not easy to obtain a higher education in Argentina. There are few schools to choose from, and they are located in major cities where the cost of living is high. Universities used to be tuition-free, but in the early 1980's a law was passed obligating students to pay a small monthly fee toward the cost of the instructors' salaries.[18] Moreover, books are expensive, library collections meager and disorganized, and support facilities for study lacking.

A teacher can expect a low salary, and most teachers' incomes are second incomes. Paychecks can be late, often by months; in 1976 in particular, paychecks stopped at about the time of the coup in March and still had not been issued in October. Albertina Bounous teaches high school in Paraná. She is the head of her family—she has three children of her own and two "adopted" children—and her teaching salary is a second income; her main income comes from another government position. She has been hired to teach a total of twelve hours a week at two different schools in the campo, and her workday is very long. She stops in at Mass at 6:15 a.m. because by 6:30 she is supposed to be at work at the office. The day begins slowly, and she and her colleagues spend a peaceful half hour drinking maté with something from the breadshop, but by 7:30 or 8:00 it is in full swing. At 1:00 Albertina goes to eat with her mother, whose house is nearer than Albertina's to her office. She must eat quickly because her afternoon class in the countryside begins at 2:30. She does not have a car, so she must take a bus. She will not return home until 7:00.

Albertina does not teach every day; on her free afternoons she prepares for her classes. This is not easy, because she has few books of her own and the libraries in Paraná are inadequate; she wants to teach her students something about the ancient world, for example, and for some time she has been looking for a book on Egypt—not one particular book, not the best book, just a book. At other times she prepares her lesson plans, which go to the departmental Education Office for approval; she attends meetings; she helps take the census; and on national holidays she marches with her students in parades. Intellectual growth requires motivation and persistence since information circulates with difficulty. Albertina is finding it difficult to plan a workshop on new teaching methods, but feels there must be alternatives to the *enciclopedismo* methods (rote-learning of facts dictated by the teacher) that are still used in secondary schools.

School teachers in La Paz work after hours to improve the rancho barrio children's chances of success by helping them with their homework. It is here, in poor barrios, that the sacrifice to obtain an education is greatest. Dora de Micol, one of the volunteer teachers, who are mainly Waldenses, often deals with less-motivated children at her job during the day. She blames her regular students' apathy on their parents' lack of interest in their education and on the influence of television. "The children in my classes aren't interested in anything that goes on in school anymore," says Dora. "They only want me to tell them stories or sing songs. And most mothers work now and don't care about their children's education either; they just let them watch TV. Television has two problems: it's passive and it's violent. I'm so glad we don't have a TV. My children read instead, even the three-year-old." In poorer barrios like Barrio La Costa, however, education is still valued, and Dora encounters a very different situation when she does her volunteer work there.

María Carmen García lives with her parents and five siblings in a one-room rancho next door to the one-room renovated building where the teachers help the rancho children every afternoon after school. Proud of having completed primary school, María Carmen now watches over her sisters' and brothers' education. Since she graduated four years ago she has been doing domestic work, as her mother does. Her father gets jobs through the agricultural cooperative of La Paz, that is, when there are jobs to be had in the campo. At the moment he is picking cotton; he leaves at 7:00 a.m. one day and sometimes does not return until 3:00 a.m. the next. María Carmen is the surrogate parent and seems to accept the responsibility willingly.

María Carmen spots the teacher coming along the path about

5 : 30 p.m. The word passes that she has arrived and will unlock the door of the school. Several of the children already cluster in front of the wood building, still dressed in their regulation white smocks, swinging their plastic briefcases while they wait. Others have stacked their things against a tree and are playing. María Carmen disappears into the darkness of her family's rancho and reappears with her younger sister, pushing her out the door toward the schoolhouse. The school, even this one set among ranchos, far surpasses in elegance any other building in the neighborhood with its metal door, glass windows, brick floor and walls, electricity, and eight rows of wooden desks. It sits on the upper edge of the highest shelf of the barrio, overlooking the ranchos which spill down the steep ravines toward the river.

Bedlam soon reigns in the school, as each of the twenty to thirty children vies for the attention of the teacher and a friend who helps her. The women move between the desks as quickly as possible, trying to ascertain what each child is working on in school and where he needs help. Younger children, wanting to be part of the grown-up world of school, wander in and out of the school, shoeless, noses running, with bits of half-eaten food in hand. Sitting on the doorstep, they amuse themselves by making designs in the dirt with their food, chewing on scissors, or poking sticks in their ears.

The children's families have forfeited potential workers and spent money for smocks, shoes, books, and supplies to send them to school. Most likely they have several children in primary school at the same time, all unproductive members of the family. Smocks are obligatory, but it is evident that the family's resources often run out at this point, because under the smocks the children's clothes are barely held together with ties and pins and on their feet they wear an assortment of tennis shoes in different colors and in a variety of sizes unrelated to the actual size of their feet.

The light is fading and it is getting difficult for the children to see by the one weak lightbulb hanging from the ceiling. The day is ending for these scholars. It is also ending for seven-year-old José, returning home along the path by María Carmen's rancho with his basket empty. He spends his day selling *churros* (balls of fried dough rolled in powdered sugar). His is a different world from that of his playmates. While they are at school, he joins the group of young children who work the streets of La Paz. They go from door to door selling churros and other pastries made by their mothers and sisters. Small boys barely taller than their three-tier tiffin carriers deliver hot meals to the elderly or to sick people, meals that again are made at home by the women or sometimes by restaurants. José dumps his basket alongside his friends' plastic briefcases, back under the tree, and begins to play. Even after a day of walking the pavement barefoot, the churros vendor has energy to spare for play. He and his friends engage in the usual friendly banter with the darkest-skinned child in the group: "Hey, morocho" (a common nickname for a dark-skinned person), "you can't play soccer—you're too dark!" Tomorrow perhaps, one of these children will have to quit the school, but possibly, just possibly, the churros vendor will have a chance to attend school himself.

Information Systems

Almost all information systems are personalized in San Sebastiano, whether they originate within the village or outside it. Even some of the "modern" tools of communication become personalized in the hands of the villagers. Like junta secretary Tullio Gilly, postmistress Teresa Angelini reports to the town hall each day. She has reigned over the San Sebastiano post office for seventeen years now, and no one need worry that an impersonal postal service will misplace an important letter. On the contrary, Teresa efficiently files away in her head all the details of the written communications of her village. She says that she has had opportunities to leave San Sebastiano but that she never will. "I was born here, my mother is still living here, and most of my family is here. My husband grew up in a big city, but he likes it here too. It's tranquil. Life has always been nice here, even when there was no electricity or asphalt road. We were with our parents so nothing else mattered.

"The post office moved into the junta building three or four years ago. Before that I'd had it in my house. The railroad brought the mail in then, and I built up my muscles carrying the mail sacks back and forth to the station. It was thirty blocks from my house. They took out the railroad in the 1960's. Now the mail comes in by truck, twice a week, on Wednesdays and Fridays. Beginning next month, mail is supposed to be delivered on Mondays too."

The one-room post office is a popular place on delivery days. A man comes by in his pickup truck and calls in through the open doorway asking if he has any mail. A woman checks in as she passes by on her way to the public well. A child who has been sent for the mail hangs around for the better part of an hour, uncomfortably shifting from foot to foot but too curious to leave. Like most shops and offices, the post office has a set of standbys throughout the day, though the composition of the group is likely to change hourly. One of its members, a deaf mute, remains longer than the others; he is an established member of the village. He migrates between the half-dozen public places in San Sebastiano, conversing with the people there in a mixture of gestures and gutturals. He and Teresa communicate quite successfully as they discuss the delay of the mail truck caused by the flooded stream.

Between conversations Teresa attentively registers incoming mail, and hands it over to its owner with a grand gesture, delivering her pronouncements on any letter that strikes her as out of the ordinary and often announcing in a booming voice its provenance as well as her analysis of its contents. Since most mail is certified and she must record names and addresses for it, Teresa necessarily comes to know something of her clients' lives—where relatives live, how often they write, whether an estranged spouse is keeping in touch. She often holds the missing piece to a local puzzle. By putting together the Santuchos' correspondence with various bits of gossip about their lawyer in La Paz, for example, she has a pretty good idea of their current financial crisis.

Actually, the national postal system is often bypassed and written messages are delivered by hand. Many people lack confidence in the mail, and they also like to avoid paying the postage, so they often wait to send a message until someone they know is making a trip. They work out elaborate plans to take advantage of anyone traveling anywhere, and people with cars and trucks find themselves very much sought after. The law team of Howard and Guzmán are known to make weekly trips to Paraná for their practice, and it is a rare Friday when they do not carry with them other passengers, packages, written letters, verbal messages for family and friends, and even birthday cakes. People rely upon them for this service. For their part, carrying news increases their knowledge of the town, as well as their importance to the community, and in addition builds good public relations, all of which benefits their law practice.

Even the road on which Toni and Rodolfo travel each week is part of the personalized world. Man tried ten years ago to tame the dirt road that lies underneath by covering it with macadam, but the original form keeps asserting itself. As they drove back from Paraná near the beginning of winter, Toni and Rodolfo found the road more uneven than usual, expanding and contracting with the wet and the cold. Toni's Dodge compact hesitated at the top of each ridge, at one point threatening to drift across the road into the path of an on-coming truck, until it pitched instead into the gaping trough on its own side of the road. The original dirt road refused to succumb to the impersonality of asphalt. Its roughness penetrated to every spring in the car as it jounced the passengers along the corrugated surface. Toni entertained his passengers with jokes, juggling a maté gourd and a thermos while he steered. Once, he opened the car door to throw out a used gourdful of maté leaves. Midway through the trip, he pulled into a gas station with a bar—the only commercial establishment on their route—and treated Rodolfo and their passenger, a friend's daughter who needed a ride home to La Paz, to a Coke. A group of people from the nearby campo sat at the tables watching the new color television set at the end of the room. Color transmission began in 1980, so it was still a novelty.

As they resumed their drive, Toni used the rough road as an occasion to poke fun at the government. "Did you hear the one about the bus driver who was elected governor of the province? One day he told his chauffeur to take the day off, that he was going to drive the car himself. But he couldn't get the car started, so the chauffeur advised him, 'Turn the key, teeth up.' The governor, thinking his chauffeur meant the teeth in his mouth, threw his head back!" Toni doubled over the wheel in laughter and just managed to wrestle the car back from its ricochet across the road. National Route 126 is the main artery between Corrientes to the north of La Paz and Paraná to the south, yet it is still virgin territory to road repair crews. After years of inattention, the road more closely resembles its former grooved track than current paving technology.

The telephone, like the road, has been made to accommodate to the state of technology, limited resources, and the personal nature of the town and village. La Paz has two phone companies, neither of them national. Entre Ríos, along with the provinces of Salta and Tucuman, has a private company, the Entrerriano Telephone Company, owned by a Swede. La Paz also has the Provincial Telephone Company, which serves the rural zones. Calling out from the province or receiving calls can frequently be difficult because there must be a balance between the number of incoming and outgoing calls over a given period. With a complicated system that pastor Oscar Micol likens to a child's game, the Entre Ríos company keeps track of calls and refuses to complete a communication if the tally is out of balance. Even if a caller is fortunate enough to encounter a balanced period, the chances of his actually being able to talk to someone in La Paz are still slim because some of the lines are likely to be down. It is not unusual for the lines between Paraná and La Paz to be down at least part of every day, and sometimes an entire week goes by when calls cannot get through to Corrientes.

The demand for residential telephones is not great—only about a third of La Paz households have one, and most people would prefer to do their business or socializing in person or send a message with someone—but businesses do need phones. It can take two to three years to get one, however—so infrequently does the phone commission from Paraná visit La Paz to take applications—and directories are almost always out-of-date. Toni and Rodolfo depend on the telephone, but theirs is not a typical system. They have had their second-floor law office for several years, but they are still waiting for an official phone. Meanwhile, they have installed a system of phones and buzzers and connected it to the phone of the Coca-Cola distributor on the first floor. When a call comes in for the lawyers, the Coke distributor buzzes their office upstairs. After completing a call, the lawyers buzz their secretaries, who buzz the Coke distributor to let him know to replace the receiver. The system works, but it scarcely guarantees lawyer-client confidentiality.

In the colony of San Sebastiano, phones are homemade internal ones—installed by farmers to link up neighboring farms and not hooked up to the official system. The village has six phones, but five belong to government offices and businesses: the police, the hospital, the Gillys' store, the Ceruttis' store, and Filipe Santucho's auto body shop. The other is the public phone, in the village's public telephone office. Calls are made from a lightweight plywood booth that offers little privacy, especially when a caller must shout to be heard over the static on the line. The office employee (whose husband happens to be Luis Morales of the Prefect's Office in La Paz), as well as anyone else standing at the counter passing the time of day with her, does not have to strain to hear the conversations. The public telephone thus contributes to the stockpiling of village gossip.

Probably the best example of the personalization of a formal means of communication is the radio. It too is a good source of gossip. In communities like San Sebastiano, which are ineffectively served by roads, telephone, and mail, the radio is the main way of "communicating with the tribe," as Toni puts it. Radio station La Paz is one of the largest employers in the area. Seventeen people keep the station broadcasting daily from early morning to late evening. It reaches listeners within a radius of forty miles, announcing births, deaths, and times of funerals, warning them when they can expect to become mired in mud in the campo, informing them when they must move their cars for the streetcleaner in town, and entertaining them with music, farm programs, and campo lore. But it is not only a medium for information and diversion; it also serves as a kind of messenger service. Argentines rely to a great extent on telegrams, and in rural areas like San Sebastiano and La Paz they prefer to send them by radio. They pay for the telegrams at the post office as usual but then take them to the local radio station to have them read over the air. Radio La Paz carries on a brisk daily correspondence between listeners in a program called "Rural Post Office," which in 1980 broadcast 9,000 telegrams. Listeners in San Sebastiano in particular, with its infrequent postal service, may thus receive messages days earlier than if they were delivered by mail.

In a small rural community, major life events, such as births, marriages, and deaths, are to a great extent public knowledge already, but the "Rural Post Office" service provides additional information exchanges like the following:[19]

> La Paz to San Sebastiano:
> Ramón—Come at 4:00. I'll have
> the cattle together.   Ernesto

> San Sebastiano to La Paz:
> Ernesto—Can't. Too much mud.
> Tomorrow at 1:00.   Ramón

> Negro—Come home. Mother needs you.
> Juan

> Jorge—Present yourself at the lawyer's
> office for your trial.

The brevity of telegram messages does not at all reflect their complexity and depth of meaning or their interest to listeners other than the recipient. A simple message from Juan to Lahitte that "the truck goes today" informs the knowing listener of a whole string of facts.

Today, Juan and Lahitte will be passing through La Paz and will of course stop by Juan's brother's house. This tells one of the listeners that she can take the sweater she has knitted for her granddaughter over to Juan's brother's house, where Juan will pick it up, delivering it to his neighbor, the listener's son, on the return trip. Or there is the message to Hipólito, in Tacuara Yacar, from Faustino: "Impossible to travel Saturday 30th. Will travel Saturday 6th." It alerts another listener, not the one the message was intended for, that Faustino's mother must be feeling worse. Again, a message to the friends of Alberto and Elvira, that their wedding reception will be at Elvira's house instead of in the campo, advises listeners that the rains have made the road in the northwest section of the colony impassable.

Three times daily the theme music from *Star Wars* announces the feeding of such personal messages into the community, replenishing the stock of information available. Thus the radio is part of the most effective system of communication in La Paz and San Sebastiano— the personal one.

Gossip, the classic example of communication on a personal level, is not just a way for housewives to pass time; it is even part of the business world. "Gossip is not idle," Toni Howard explains. "Society demands that people gossip in order to keep informed. People know each other through gossip—and because they know each other, they pay attention to gossip. The more information a person gathers, the more important he becomes. In a small community, you can learn a lot about people just by keeping your eyes and ears open. Details are hard to miss. From the day a newcomer first sets foot in town, for example, he is scrutinized and catalogued. His appearance sets the system in motion; by nightfall everyone who cares to will know who he is—his family background and his purpose and how he fits into the community of La Paz and San Sebastiano. Not every outsider is interesting to all people, unless it's a woman who's pregnant or a man who's driving an unusual car— they're interesting to everyone."

Since Toni has access to a great deal of information about fellow townspeople and outsiders, a chance meeting with him on the street can be very profitable. The casual greeting he is met with, "Qué tal? Cómo estás?" is not a call for the perfunctory reply that "How are you? How's it going?" might elicit elsewhere, nor is it just an overture to a longer conversation. Rather it is an invitation to provide a substantive account of his activities. "With a lot of delicacy a person can be evasive if he doesn't want to talk," says Toni, "but usually he can't get away with this."

Little escapes the notice of townspeople, nor should it, since it is a duty to be informed. Only rarely does a person say that he does not want to become involved or to know something. One day Rodolfo Guzmán's wife noted that someone with a car called for her neighbor, who has no car, and dropped him off again later. In the evening another neighbor, who had noted the same thing, came by to see if Señora Guzmán knew what was going on, and offered her own version of events. She said she had heard from the pharmacist that one of the man's relatives was ill and that was why he had been seen leaving his house uncharacteristically in a car. Anything out of the ordinary is cause for comment and analysis. La Paz extends only twenty blocks by twenty, and news travels fast even though many townspeople seldom go outside their three- or four-block living radius.

The spread of gossip is fostered not only by the smallness of the town but by a particular architectural feature of Latin-style houses, the courtyard. Whereas houses in San Sebastiano are detached, in La Paz they have common walls. Rooms usually run along three sides of a house and open onto a central courtyard, separated on the fourth side from the neighbors' courtyard by a wall. Though the wall is seven to eight feet high, it does not block out the passage of sound between two houses. Across the common wall from Elsa de Prochet's house in La Paz, Elsa's neighbors happen to be her son-in-law's grandparents. Elsa does not enjoy visiting neighbors and rarely leaves the house, so weeks may pass without her seeing her neighbors; when she does see them, it is at a family gathering at her son-in-law's estancia, half an hour away. But she often hears them—surreptitiously, because it would be improper to acknowledge that their conversation was being overheard or to speak to them over the wall. Neither Elsa nor her daughter Lucia out on the estancia has a phone, but although they cannot communicate directly, Elsa can pick up bits of news about her daughter by listening in on her neighbors' conversations. One day she learns they have been out to Domenico and Lucia's place over the weekend and hears them discussing their news in the courtyard—Michela's new tooth, Lucia's search for a good maid, and so on. Elsa also learns that Domenico is coming into town on the following Wednesday, and knows that Lucia will try to come with him to spend some time with her mother.

Toni and Elsa are opposite ends of the spectrum in this system of information gathering. Toni is party to most of the main sources of information in La Paz and San Sebastiano—as a lawyer, the legal counsel for a local bank, the husband of a physician, and a personal messenger—and he necessarily creates some gossip himself. Elsa, on the other hand, avoids attracting attention to herself. She keeps to her house and gets her information from within her four walls— from the radio telegrams, from her courtyard, and from occasional visitors. Though her means are more limited and her field of vision more confined, she is usually as full of news and information as Toni is and feels as much a part of a community as Toni does. In San Sebastiano and La Paz, gossip, which to an outsider might seem annoying, even harmful, and a reflection of rural isolation, actually creates a rich environment where each person contributes to the processing and distributing of information throughout the community.

News from the outside world also becomes personalized in San Sebastiano and La Paz, defining the community's relationship with the larger world. Television illustrates well this particular relationship. The television came to the area in the early 1970's, and Ernestina Prochet was one of the first to own one. The TV set arrived as a status symbol, rather than a consumer item, and as such was placed under a piece of plastic in the seldom-used living room, much as Ernestina's brother's modernized kitchen lies buried under a layer of newspapers. At this stage the TV played no part in Ernestina's life: there was little to watch, and it had no bearing on her ideas or knowledge. Later, television became more relevant as it became more popular, and Ernestina rescued her set from its protection of plastic and began to watch it. Recently, it has become part of the important world of gossip. The TV now resides in the busy kitchen, and the four Prochets, together with a neighbor and the Prochets' tenant, regularly gather to watch the eight o'clock evening news. Ernestina was once a knowledgeable village informant in San Sebastiano, and in La Paz she has adapted her news-gathering skills to her enlarged world.

For most of Ernestina's life, the borders of her world were the borders of San Sebastiano; then they expanded to La Paz; now they extend far beyond. Once a major source of information in San Sebastiano, she found the challenge of La Paz difficult at first. Its larger population meant more information to learn and keep track of, and its more varied news sources presented new forms of competition. She had to know what to pursue and what to ignore; otherwise she could waste time carefully gathering a piece of information or reconstructing a story, only to have it become totally worthless as it was suddenly broadcast to all via the radio. She adjusted, though, and now she watches the TV news as avidly as she gathered gossip in the campo. Her former training has served her well, and TV has merely expanded her area of operation. The possibility of being in touch with the outside world on such an immediate and understandable level amazes Ernestina and the rest of the household. They are as zealous about filing away tidbits on world figures as on their neighbors next door. In 1981 the Prochet household watched a news broadcast that showed the shooting of President Reagan. "What a terrible thing!" said Ernestina. "This would never have happened here!" Then Reagan was shown entering the hospital and making a joke to reporters about his wound. After the news the Prochets moved their chairs outdoors to the street, as they were accustomed to doing on a nice evening. Interrupting their conversation with an occasional "Adiós" to people who drove or walked by—and carefully recording their movements—they discussed the behavior of the U.S. president much as they discussed that of their neighbors. They decided that Reagan should not have joked at such a critical time; it indicated that he was distracted and not being serious about the business at hand. If Reagan had been running for public office in Argentina at the time, they maintained, his inappropriate behavior would have cost him some votes. Whether as a TV audience or as curbside spectators, people like Ernestina are active participants in their world. They receive, develop, and pass on both local gossip and world news. Instead of replacing old patterns of information gathering, television has enabled such people to be in touch with the world on their own level. They zealously arrange the news of an outside world, encountered through TV and other media, but in the process reorder it so that instead of challenging the order of their world it becomes in many ways just another part of it. In the end Reagan's quip is evaluated from Ernestina's curbside perspective on the correct behavior for a person in a position of responsibility in rural Argentina and found sadly wanting, much to her satisfaction. Ernestina is not threatened by Reagan and the outside world. Why should she be? She is after all the judge of it, not its victim, from her perspective at least.

Government employees, local healers, schoolteachers, radio listeners and television viewers, and gossips all participate in making a personalized world in La Paz and San Sebastiano. Officer García is not a vigilant upholder of military rule aggressively ferreting out the state's enemies. Junta member Tullio Gilly acts not as a distant functionary of a government imposed from above, but as an individual interested in making San Sebastiano a good place to live. Another bureaucrat might well stand aloof from Tullio's unconventional activities—tramping about the village, dropping into ditches, and climbing onto rooftops—as unbefitting to a government official. But these are the things in the village that need doing. Even Filipa de Malvasio in San Sebastiano, and the lower-class school children in La Paz find some satisfaction of their needs in this personalized society. Communication methods, too, are personalized. Telephones, the mail, and the radio have as much of a personal and public aspect as an impersonal and private one. We can point to Toni Howard's makeshift phone in La Paz, to letters that are hand-carried rather than sent through the mail, and to telegrams that are read over the air for all to benefit from rather than delivered privately.

Personalization may sometimes break down and cause pain or discomfort: San Sebastiano may never get its access road repaired; more infants may die because a curandera has failed to diagnose diarrhea; a local bookseller may run into the Education Office's paranoia; gossip may be used to harm someone. For the most part, however, personalization is a positive feature of this society and is as effective as more formal systems. Most important, it is a part of the essential character of San Sebastiano and La Paz society and is one of the principal agents in keeping life going when the nation as a whole is floundering in a sea of political and economic crises.

FIVE

Family and Community

THE WEDDING of Alberto Gilly and Elvira Musset in 1981 marked the formation of a typical family household unit in San Sebastiano. An immoderate amount of rain had left the dirt road to the Musset farm a sea of mud, but there was no question that Alberto and Elvira's wedding would take place. At 7 : 00 p.m., an hour and a half before it was to begin, the Waldensian pastor and his family were already piling into their Citroën to get to the farm before the road became heavily rutted and impassable.

As the car turned off the pavement and sank into the dirt road's muddy recesses, Oscar stepped sharply on the gas. The car skated from side to side, throwing its passengers against the doors, triggering the windshield wipers and loosening the window latches. Oscar joked that one of the tests for a prospective pastor in the Argentine campo is mud driving. "The best machine in the mud is a horse, but after that comes a Citroën; it won't tip over." The car continued on laboriously, with wipers running, windows flapping, and the Micols laughing somewhat nervously. The going was slow, Oscar gripping the wheel tightly the whole while, weaving back and forth through the ruts. His assertion about Citroëns was in danger of being proved wrong.

Halfway to the house, the Micols met an obstacle that threatened to stall their progress altogether: a pickup truck was parked across the road. But Oscar rose to the occasion. It was his kind of challenge—a tough play for victory over the adversity of nature, where nothing else counted except getting through. He enjoys being as hard as his environment. "We can't stop or we'll be stuck," Oscar yelled over his shoulder as he swung the car into a skid around the truck, steering out into the sodden fields. Beginning to sink dangerously, the car gave a lurch and the wheels tipped back up onto the road again as Oscar applied the gas. Dora and the girls waved hello to the people in the truck. With a final acceleration, Oscar brought the car hurtling into the farmyard, where he jerked it to a stop. Other early arrivals who had braved the same road stood in the entrance to a large hangar-like shed, crowding the edge of the concrete floor, cheering as they directed Oscar to a place to park. He drove once around the yard sizing up the different approaches to the shed and managed to drop his passengers off within leaping distance of a board that had been laid across the mud at the open end of the galpón, where the wedding was to take place.

Dora de Micol talked with the other women for a while and then moved off toward the card table in the corner, where the wedding gifts were displayed. Some blue china plates and some drinking glasses were wrapped in plastic; they were the kind found in most middle-class homes, and were probably bought at the stationery store in La Paz. There were also a couple of serving dishes and some silverware. The men meanwhile remained at the entrance to the galpón, still cheering the new arrivals, each of whom had had a more difficult time than the last getting through the deepening ruts. The shed became crowded and the women were having a hard time squeezing between the rows of tables and chairs to greet one another. Somehow the children still managed to race through the aisles, only occasionally ducking under the tables when the aisles became too clogged with adults. The Musset family's collie surveyed the whole scene from a safe spot near the wall. All of Alberto and Elvira's aunts, uncles, and unmarried cousins had been invited, as well as all the children in the Waldensian church, because a wedding is also a party and children are always invited to parties. If it had not been for the weather, some four hundred people might have come. In a closely related society, family events are community events.

Talk of the mud threatened to overshadow the wedding, but Oscar's activity let no one forget the purpose of the evening. He was busy setting up the portable organ, rolling out a red strip of carpet, and adjusting the wiring for the loudspeaker. The speaker took several attempts to be coaxed into working, and from time to time during the process the electric bulbs hanging from the ceiling went out, causing the children to squeal with excitement. The main table had been placed at the closed end of the shed, set off from the guests' tables by a backdrop of blue cloth hung on the wall with red and white carnations pinned to it. Pine branches and oranges stuck with toothpicks decorated the guests' tables, though the toothpicks also had a practical use.

About 8:30, Oscar's voice boomed out asking everyone to sit down. After a loud scraping of chairs on concrete, everyone turned toward Oscar and the table of honor, and he signaled the organist to begin the wedding march. Alberto, thirty-four years old, and Elvira, twenty-seven, entered from the yard and began the march together up the carpeted aisle. In between hymns, prayers, and a special performance by a three-person choir, Oscar delivered a full sermon on the importance and meaning of establishing a family. The couple stood patiently during the sermon, and by the end of the service they were soaked with perspiration, Alberto in his suit and Elvira in her handmade white gown. They parted immediately and began to greet their guests.

Oscar had been quite caught up in the service and seemed impervious to the odor of the asado. But his audience had not missed the smell of the beef being grilled over a wood fire outside the window. As Alberto's and Elvira's brothers began bringing in the bottles of white wine and the mixers—soda water and sweetened grapefruit juice—the guests scouted around trying to find the eating utensils they had brought with them from home.

For the first course the hosts had chosen the traditional "mayonnaise"—chopped carrots, peas, and chicken mixed with mayonnaise on a bed of lettuce—rather than the alternative empanadas. Not until the second course did Oscar slip into a chair across from Dora; their children were eating with some friends at another table. After a few bites of salad Oscar was off again. "It's not in his character to sit down and eat calmly, that man," declared Dora. "He keeps going on nervous energy—goodness knows it's not from the food he eats." By the time the large pans of grilled chorizo sausages and pieces of beef came around for the second time, Oscar was back at the table, but he gave them no more attention than before. This was more than Oscar's normal preoccupation, however, because tonight he was the master of ceremonies, and the master of ceremonies is sometimes even more the host than the bride and groom's parents are. This was a meeting of friends at a festive religious rite marking an important beginning in society, and Oscar had made it his show.

There was much activity besides Oscar's popping up and down:

servers rushing in and out of the galpón; children chasing one another; the dog hunting for scraps; and frequent scrapings of chairs as guests rose to shout their toasts to the wedding couple. After the asado had been handed around for the last time, the hosts brought in Sneider beer for the interlude before the cutting of the wedding cake. Pastries and other sweets were put out with the beer. The wedding cake cannot be cut until after midnight, and it was only eleven. In the meantime people circulated and talked to friends and drank beer. Finally midnight arrives. Teenage girls have been grouped around the main table for the past half hour holding onto the ends of ribbons baked into the cake. At midnight they can at last try their luck at extracting a prize; the one who gets the ring will be the next to marry, or if she is already married she will never be without a husband. This can also be a risky business, since whoever pulls out the nail will supposedly never marry. It has been a night full of risk and ritual, first the trip to the farm and then the marriage itself. With the cutting of the cake, Elvira performs her final duty as a bride. Slicing off pieces of cake decoration, she distributes them to her special friends around the room via envoys who announce, "Sent by the bride." Now Alberto and Elvira can at last see the night's end approaching.

The Family Household

The personalization of the village reflects the special relationship between family and community. The true center of community life in San Sebastiano and La Paz is the community of people living under the same roof—the family household.[1] The communal aspect of Alberto and Elvira's first night together as husband and wife did not significantly diminish with the departure of their guests from the wedding party. To begin with, the rest of their wedding night would be spent in the bosom of the family, at Elvira's parents' house. Originally, they were to have gone away, but their car broke down earlier in the day and the mud probably would have prevented their leaving in any case. They were not concerned, however, about this end to the evening. After all, they intended to live with Elvira's family for the first year or two, and perhaps they would have their first child there.

Theirs will be a traditional rural life much like Domenico and Lucia Antonini's. Alberto will work the land which he holds in common with two of his uncles, his mother, and his four brothers. Together they own 2,750 acres: 2,000 in San Sebastiano and 750 in a colony recently established on land that was once owned by a large estanciero before it was purchased by the government and subdivided. Alberto and Elvira will eventually move into a house on the smaller property, but at present there is someone else living there. An interim arrangement with the bride's or the groom's parents is a common beginning for newlyweds—indeed, a marriage means the physical expansion of an already-existing household group as often as it does the creation of a separate one.

The new Gilly/Musset family will most likely retain its communal character through much of Alberto and Elvira's life together. According to San Sebastiano's 1980 census about half the households in the colony were communal households, containing, among others, extended family networks. The other half were contracted, or nuclear, households.[2] The composition of households changes frequently of course, but the 1980 figures reveal some interesting patterns. About two-thirds of the communal households belonged to the census category of multi-generational households—like the new Gilly/Musset household where Elvira and Alberto will live together with Elvira's parents and her two brothers. In a year or two Elvira's aging grandmother may well move into the household too, and if Alberto and Elvira have had a child in the meantime, the household will contain four direct generations. The "multi-generational" category also includes families that contain a single generation plus additional family members, like that of the Mussets' neighbor Aldo Prochet. Aldo is married, but his wife lives in La Paz and he lives with his brother and sister on their ranch in San Sebastiano.

Fully one-third of communal households (and about a sixth of all households) included non-family members, a striking feature of the household's role as a center of community life in San Sebastiano. Non-family members are not limited to one particular age group, but they are usually male and tend to be of three main types: workers, who are paid members of the household; boarders, who are paying members; and informally "adopted" children and adults. Workers, typically peon and domestic laborers, are the simplest category. Peons usually live in their own ranchos on estancias (the Antoninis have five such peon families), but occasionally they live with their patron and his family. Tullio and Iolanda Gilly had a peon who lived for many years in a rancho so close to their own house that he became part of the family and ate with them. Maids, however, almost always live directly with their employer's family. They are fairly easily affordable because wages for domestic help are low. Some maids become a part of the family more than others. Lucia de Antonini's chica, for example, found little favor with the family, and was not expected to stay with them long. Her room was on the other side of the courtyard from them and was definitely inferior to theirs. Toni and Marina Howard's live-in maid Juana, on the other hand, sleeps in the Howard children's bedroom a short two steps across the hall from the Howards' own room. This arrangement stems partly from the smaller size of the Howards' house; it is a small house in town, not an estancia in San Sebastiano. But Juana is also more a part of the family. They have encouraged her efforts to complete primary school by way of night classes and have even given her time off from work to study.

The role of boarders in family households, to an even greater extent than that of workers, has as much a communal as a financial aspect. Most boarders are students who live with relatives and friends to be near a school. Thus someone like Elsa Martínez de Prochet in La Paz, who is technically a landlady, is also a surrogate parent for her boarders. Indeed, someone from outside the community would often find it difficult to distinguish between family and boarder in her household. Emilia, Elsa's boarder, has returned from school for her noon meal only minutes after her schoolmate and fellow boarder Claudia. Emilia is related to the Prochets; Claudia is not. "Wonderful, potato pie." Claudia smiles approvingly at the casserole of mashed potatoes with tomato and beef sauce. There is a great flurry as Elsa, Emilia, and Claudia ferry food up the two steps from the kitchen to the table. Embarrassed by the girls, Antonio, Elsa's son, tries to slip into his chair unnoticed. Emilia carries in a small plate of chopped lettuce and an apple compote, and Elsa brings in the bread and water and grapefruit juice. Elsa closes the curtain that hides the kitchen, asks Claudia to say grace, and then begins to question Emilia about Alberto and Elvira's wedding. "What was her dress like? I heard she made it all herself. How many cows did they roast? Only one? Well, I suppose lots of people couldn't get there because of the mud." Antonio eats quickly, occasionally exchanging conspiratorial giggles with Claudia, and then dashes off to his classes. He goes to the same school as the girls, the Colegio Nacional, which in the afternoon becomes the Colegio Comercial. When Emilia and Claudia finish eating, they hurry to do their chores so as to get to gym class by 2:00. "Is there anything else, señora?" the girls ask, before they change into their sweatsuits and run out the door.

Emilia and Claudia are both campo girls. Their parents pay Elsa for their room and board, often paying in kind or performing some service or other. But the girls also make a point of helping around the house generally, not as part of their payment but as an act of politeness that befits their special status as more than boarders.

The place of informally adopted children and adults in family households is more difficult to ascertain than that of workers or boarders. These people, more often children than adults, have been invited to live with another family, usually because their own family has broken up, perhaps following the death of one of the parents, or has experienced some financial setback. Non-family children are frequently called "chicos" (kids) to distinguish them from family "hijos" (sons and daughters), but "chicos" is also commonly used of family children. The official term for informally adopted children is "hijos de crianza," children one "brings up" but has not given birth to. At any rate, the different designations do not appear to reflect differences in the way the children are treated.

The inclusion of non-family in a household was characteristic of creole families when the immigrants first came to San Sebastiano and La Paz. Many creole households were made up almost entirely of unrelated persons. Usually these were single people, often males, who lived together and perhaps did similar work. Occasionally such a household contained one or two women who cooked, cleaned, and washed for the men and perhaps for other households as well. Non-family members were generally unrelated, although sometimes they had children if they were widowed or separated and sometimes they were siblings.[3] This household type is still common among creoles in San Sebastiano, but today it is also found among gringos, along with the more frequent contracted and extended families containing non-family members. It is possible that the amoebic characteristics of contemporary gringo families are related in some way to the gringos' contact with the creole population.

The inclusion of non-family within a family household may well be interpreted as an adaptation of a creole ritual kinship system or of creole generosity. It may be a response to the isolated environment. Or it may be a response to the perceived necessity of placing everyone in a family household, as a method of social discipline perhaps, to ensure the harmony and homogeneity of the village. "Adoption" may have any or all of these aspects, but its practice in contemporary San Sebastiano and La Paz appears to be largely an uncalculated, spontaneous response to someone's immediate need, and not, as is often reported for other societies, a practice designed to exploit young children. One sign of the built-in egalitarianism of San Sebastiano and La Paz society is that a household's inclusion of non-family seems to ignore socioeconomic differences and gringo-creole divisions. Often a middle- or upper-class gringo family will adopt someone from the lower-class creole population.

Five-year-old Nicolás waited, scared and cold and naked, wondering if he could trust this woman. She had said it wouldn't hurt. He was alert to every sensation. The metal walls, the wooden slats on the floor, and the dampness were ominous. She turned a switch. He screamed as the force of the water hit him, and tried to squirm out of her arms. It was his first shower, and the woman was his new mother, Rosa Collet de Baridon. Rosa and Marco Baridon already had four children of their own, all girls, when they decided to take in Nicolás, whose father was widowed. Nicolás came from a peon household and was only familiar with rancho life. He had never seen a shower, and had to get used to other things as well, like wearing shoes, when he moved in with the Baridons.

But Nicolás was a young child, and he probably had an easier adjustment period than the man Tullio and Iolanda Gilly took into their home in his adult years. The Gillys had three children of their own when they invited the man's son to live with them. "The boy's mother had left his father and gone off with another man," says Iolanda, "so we took the boy in. He was one and a half then. My sister-in-law took in another of the man's children. But their father didn't do very well by himself, so later on we asked him to come live with us too. The boy and his father lived in the room in back of our kitchen for years. The boy had to go off to do his military service in Tierra del Fuego, but his father stayed on with us till he died last year. My husband Tullio is now helping our chico build a house. He dismantled one of the bedrooms in his family's old house and saved the material from it—the zinc for the roof, the bricks, and the wood—for the boy. Our chico has had a girlfriend for two years but he says he won't marry her until the house is ready."

In trying to account for the inclusion of non-relatives and additional generations of relatives, it is tempting to attach too much importance to the exigencies of rural life, especially when one notes too the high birth rate in San Sebastiano (28.0 per thousand in 1980) and the large number of children couples often have (the average number of children in nuclear households in 1980 was 5.7).[4] Certainly additional children and live-in peons do help meet the needs of farming families, but non-farming families are similarly expanded. In Paraná, Albertina Bounous, long separated from her husband, had three children of her own and needed two jobs to support them when she decided to take in twelve-year-old Angelina, an orphan with muscular dystrophy, and Benita, a fifteen-year-old domestic worker whose parents had barred her from their house when she became pregnant. Albertina explains that since her own children were growing older and going out more, she missed having children around the house. In Buenos Aires, where living patterns are different, Albertina's porteño brother and sister-in-law think that she is foolish to live in crowded conditions trying to stretch her income among six people.

The formation of family households seems to be determined not so much by agricultural life as by the family's function as a non-private group and its place as the most important institution in society. This means that households tend to be large and integrated with non-family for three reasons. First, the family does not necessarily break up as part of the rites of passage—that is, when a youth reaches a certain age or when he marries. The custom of living at home or with a relative until one marries persists in the current generation. Young people usually continue living at home until at least age twenty-five and may never move away if they have to care for their parents. Even marriage does not necessarily mean a break from the family, since many couples begin conjugal life within the household of the husband's or the wife's parents. In fact until about age forty, a fairly sizable portion of single people and married couples live at home with their parents or parents-in-law.[5] Economics undoubtedly plays a role, but more important is the fact that youths say they are happiest when they are with their families. Some chafe under certain restrictions, such as being forbidden access to the pinball parlor, cafes, or public dances, but generally they maintain traditional patterns even while participating in activities unheard of when their parents were their age. To the youth of San Sebastiano and La Paz, a society in which young adults live independently of the family or challenge its code of rules, or where the family plays a reduced role and is not a center of one's community—a society such as they might see in a Doris Day movie or in a television series like "Three's Company"—seems strange and unacceptable.[6]

The second factor contributing to large households is that the concept of a relative, whether by blood or by marriage, can be very far-reaching, drawing even distant relatives into the family, or it can be ignored altogether, permitting the inclusion of non-relatives. The third factor is that because most of life is lived within the family rather than other institutions, most people expect and desire membership in a family. Family households, in turn, welcome additional members because they reinforce the feeling of community that is held to be desirable in a family.[7]

Frequent changes in household composition are a normal part of life. The changes are prompted partly by a desire to place people in households and to complete "part-households," that is, households in which a parent or spouse is missing. Family composition also changes because of the necessity of living close to a workplace, a school, or a health facility. Even with improved roads, access to cars and buses, and the short distance between San Sebastiano and La Paz, transportation remains a problem and affects people's perception of space and distance. As a result, people move regularly between various family situations during the week to reflect their work locations and other needs.

These frequent changes help make the society one large group, and they help explain the apparent contradiction between the society's fluidity and variety on the one hand and its stasis and homogeneity on the other. In changing households, people experience different living situations and create movement in the society, giving it fluidity and variety. But although they change households, they are in reality just moving within "family," both in the sense of a blood or marriage group, since much of the population is related, and in the sense of a community, which contributes to stasis and homogeneity.

The ease with which households form and re-form, and their strong communal aspect, are partly explained by people's feelings about living space and privacy as well. The dimensions of houses do not necessarily limit the size of households. The average number of persons per household in San Sebastiano in 1980 was a modest 4.8, but the number of rooms per dwelling ranged from 3.5 (casas) to as little as 1.6 (ranchos)—thus a range of 1.4 to 3.1 persons per room.[8] Houses seem especially crowded considering the great expanses of land surrounding San Sebastiano and La Paz. The size of homes is affected both by the cost of materials and by attitudes toward space. Rosa and Marco Baridon, for example, live with four girls and Nicolás in a two-bedroom house in La Paz. The house has only a few feet of frontage and sits almost on the curb, squeezed in between two neighboring houses. The front door leads directly into a sitting room that contains an upright piano, a desk, three shelves of books, and two red plastic living-room chairs—furnishings that reflect the Baridons' middle-class status. Marco has an engineering degree and works for the electric company, and Rosa is a teacher and school administrator. The two bedrooms in their house are small and windowless; the adults' bedroom connects to the sitting room, the children's to the kitchen. The bathroom is in between the two bedrooms and it adjoins the kitchen. The four girls have bunk beds and store their clothes and shoes underneath. Until recently Nicolás shared the girls' room, but now that he is eleven he has moved into what used to be a workroom, outside the house proper, that is reached via a small section of covered patio in back of the house. Opposite Nicolás's room on the patio is an old wringer washer and a tub. Clotheslines criss-cross the small backyard made up of dirt, some grass, building debris, old flower pots, and remains of the Pekinese's dinner. For the past six years the family has been building a home in the next block, in the shadow of the watertower of La Paz. The work goes slowly because Marco is doing much of the construction himself and because he has to save up some extra money to buy materials a little at a time. The house is of major proportions for La Paz: two stories with four bedrooms. Since the children will most likely remain at home until they are in their mid-twenties (their eldest daughter, who is studying music therapy in Buenos Aires, is already making plans to return to La Paz to work at the school for the handicapped when she finishes her studies), the new home should have many years of use even if Marco does not complete it soon. Rosa comments that although it seems a great sacrifice to be involved in building a house so long, in fact the family is not living for the day when the house will be finished but treats it more as an interesting project that occupies spare time. Small though it is, the Baridons' present home is adequate and they are happy there.

Albertina Bounous decided to expand her family despite the lack of room. She has a condominium in the Barrio Nuevo Rocamora in Paraná, a complex of ninety-two one-story units, many housing five and six persons. Albertina's houses five or six, depending on whether her son Manuel sleeps there or at his grandmother's house, which is on the bus line to the base where he does his military service. Albertina's eighteen-year-old daughter and twenty-year-old son share one of the tiny bedrooms in the condominium; Albertina, Angelina, and Benita share the other. The rooms are only large enough for two twin beds. Albertina sleeps with Angelina in one, in part to help her through the hard transition from the orphanage. Perhaps Benita will have married her boyfriend and moved away by the time Angelina outgrows this arrangement, though she may not outgrow it. Albertina's thirty-year-old sister and her mother continue to sleep together because of Señora Bounous's weak heart, and not because of lack of space. Theirs is a large old colonial-style building with big rooms and high ceilings. Albertina's house is quite small by comparison, not much larger than a rancho. It does have the advantage of being new, but it has no heat or hot water. In addition to the two bedrooms, there is a bathroom, a kitchen, and a *comedor*, or dining room, which also serves as living room and as a garage for Albertina's son's motorcycle. What their house lacks in space the Bounous family make up for in their flexibility.

Living arrangements reflect an acceptance of a limited physical space, but they also suggest a different vision of self.[9] Society's ideal is that a person try to accept and adapt to others. In a way there seems to be a desire and an ability to share what might be called one's mental space much as one shares one's physical space—and tight little households especially in a place like San Sebastiano seem to foster and reward just such sharing. The accepted individual act is one that fits with and supports family and community. And most people feel most comfortable when they succeed in merging personal, individualistic motives with public (that is, family- and community-centered) and altruistic ones.

The many people who spend their whole life in San Sebastiano and La Paz remain integrally linked to their parental family. A person's reputation depends to a large extent on that of his family. When people first meet, notes the lawyer Rodolfo Guzmán, they usually begin by establishing each other's genealogy, partly to avoid a faux pas in the subsequent conversation. At Alberto and Elvira's wedding a woman who had been introduced to Toni Howard began their conversation this way: "Oh, you're Toni Howard. Who are your parents? What Howard family is that? Oh, of course, you're related on your mother's side to the Von Bergers. I think I might have met your uncle once. Isn't he the Alfredo who lives on the main road in San Sebastiano?" "People need to know each other's lineage," jokes Rodolfo, "so that they don't go criticizing each other's relatives! A person may not like all his relatives, but he still doesn't want to hear anything bad about them!"

Outside of first meetings, genealogies also crop up in conversations in general and are used as short descriptions of people, much more often in fact than their residence or their profession. With only three main families in San Sebastiano, and a great deal of intermarriage among them and a finite number of first names, the same combinations of first and last names are bound to occur. Usually another last name is tacked on to distinguish between them. This is how Carlos Baridon came to be named Carlos Baridon-Charbonier; Charbonier is his mother's name. Carlos and his wife themselves increased the number of duplications by naming one of their own children Carlos. Less often, profession is used to sort out people with the same name. There are two Marco Baridons in the community: one is Marco Baridon and the other is Marco Baridon the engineer. Other, more fanciful designations describe some special characteristic of a person. Oscar Micol one day referred to a paunchy youngster as "that canvas sky" (cielo raso de lona). This is his "official" nickname, at least to Oscar; others may give him different nicknames. The most important designation, however, is the one that places people in the context of their family—and therefore in the context of the community.

Society never allows a person to forget his lineage or the people he associates with. People call San Sebastiano and La Paz "a big family," and maintain that the intimacy this creates should not be a concern if a person has a clear conscience. A popular saying, "A person who goes about like a duck, walks like a duck, and defecates like a duck, is a duck" (Si anda como pato, camina como pato, caga como pato, es pato), emphasizes the difficulty a person has in distinguishing himself from his family or from the larger village family. The saying also indirectly underlines the necessity of identifying with family and community for moral, physical, and economic support—in fact, for an identity. "Tell me who you go around with and I'll tell you who you are" (Dime con quién andas y te diré quién eres) is another popular saying. It can have either good or bad connotations. By associating with important people, one can be considered important too, as Tullio Gilly's small friend was. This is part of the rationale behind godparenthood and coparenthood. On the other hand, if a person's family or friends have a questionable reputation, he too may be held in disrepute. The same applies to the community as a whole. The social workers at the school for the handicapped were terribly upset when a former native of La Paz criticized his home town in *Gol* magazine: "He said the streets weren't paved here and the sidewalks were always torn up. Well, that's just not entirely true." Family and community define one's existence from birth.

Maté and the Embrace

The communal aspect of society is reflected and reinforced by two very important customs. The first is the "ceremony" of maté, the strong, non-alcoholic tea. Wherever maté is made and drunk, it creates an automatic center of community feeling. Of all the activities that take place in the home and community, drinking maté occupies the most time and is the most communal. It is more than a drink; it is a ritual of sociability that originates in creole and campo culture. But though it has aspects of ritual and ceremony, it is completely classless: lower, middle, and upper classes drink maté, and there are no "priests" who hold its secret. It is drunk throughout Argentina, but it is more in evidence outside the large cities, in places where the pace of life is more relaxed. Reserved neither for adults nor for males, it bridges generations and sexes. It is a social leveler, an expression of community and of the sharing instincts in society. Its communal aspects mean that it is basically not a commercial beverage. It is not served in restaurants, though there are vendors in Buenos Aires who go from office to office selling it. It is drunk in cars and on horseback, in the home, at work, in the park, and at soccer games. It can accompany other activities—working, talking, watching television, listening to the radio, reading—but it is never secondary to them.

One reason it takes precedence is that it is generally shared—it is a communal rather than a private drink, and everyone uses the same gourd and straw. Moreover, it takes two hands to manipulate the gourd and hot water and pass the maté to others. Even if a person is not the maté maker, the ceremony requires that one be more attentive to the person making and passing the maté than to whatever other activity one may be engaged in. The maté maker, too, must be attentive and must perform the ritual with care, and not be diverted by things going on around him. One day Rodolfo Guzmán choked on a mouthful of maté and good-naturedly yelled at Toni Howard, "Hey, Toni, what are you doing? This maté's been burned!" Toni had not noticed that the water he had poured onto the yerba was so hot that it had scorched the maté leaves. As Rodolfo threw the whole gourdful into the wastecan, he laughed and said, "We live in a poor country, but I'm going to throw out this yerba anyway!" When it comes to maté, the highest standards are upheld even during an economic crisis.

It is easy to err in the small but important details of the ritual. The maté maker must pour the water close to the bombilla, or straw. A participant must not absent-mindedly stir the yerba with the straw while sipping the maté. If the same yerba is used for a number of rounds, the straw should be removed at some point, rotated a hundred and eighty degrees, and then returned to the maté. Maté that has been prepared incorrectly is said to be "maté que corre," maté that has a diarrheic effect. The maker of the maté must in addition be aware of how he serves the gourd around a group. Age, sex, guest-status, and social status must all be observed. Among relatives and close friends, it is polite to remember who prefers sweetened maté and thus needs his own gourd, because the sugar is added to the yerba before the water is poured. Because of its social importance, people seldom refuse maté, though it is acceptable for children and teenagers, like Antonio Prochet, to do so. Many people enjoy maté equally in their childhood and adult years. Maté, even if it is unstirred, is thought to have a diarrheic effect, so diarrhea is also an accepted reason for refusal. The common cold and other contagious diseases, however, are not valid reasons to refuse; if offered by outsiders, such excuses are brushed aside.

The other important expression of community is physical demonstrations of closeness, such as hugging and kissing. They occur daily in a variety of ways and are not determined by family membership or gender. Unrelated men, women, boys, and girls kiss each other in greeting; students kiss their teachers; colleagues and fellow employees kiss each other; teenagers kiss their parents' friends. The lawyers Toni Howard and Rodolfo Guzmán might kiss each other in greeting, and so might Elsa de Prochet and her neighbor down the street. A teenage boy meeting his schoolmate on the street might kiss her, with nothing beyond friendship intended. If Albertina Bounous receives a visit at her office from some of her students, whether boys or girls, she holds her face out for a kiss. When Albertina's twenty-year-old daughter comes by to pick her up for lunch, she kisses all the male and female employees in the office. At the Social Services Office in La Paz, Rosa and her male and female colleagues kiss each other in greeting in the morning; they are also apt to kiss each other when they meet by chance in the street. When people are introduced by a third party who is a mutual friend, they kiss, sealing the introduction. Thereafter, they are likely to kiss whenever they meet, even if they meet every day. In addition to kissing, people also express closeness and community by hugging, holding hands, and touching. They share their homes and families with others who have none; they share maté; they share items that in another society might be personal: a washcloth, a glass, a comb, eating utensils.

One might view these physical demonstrations of closeness as a public display of a private emotion, namely affection. But they might better be viewed as an expression of closeness for the sake of community and harmony. Such demonstrations of closeness are understandably seen much less often in the big cities than in the countryside. And when city dwellers do openly kiss or hug or hold hands, these physical acts may not have the special meaning they have in small towns and villages. In a rural society they are spontaneous, not perfunctory, and are perceived as strengthening community feeling.

Women in the Community

Women are integrated into the family household and community in a particular way.[10] The home is important to them, as to other members of the family, as the site of a community rather than as their personal domain. A home is not a woman's showplace; in fact, its personality is one of asexual austerity. It gains character and color, not from its furnishings and decorations, but from its occupants—such as Elsa de Prochet.

The late morning light catches the hints of auburn in Elsa's hair as she sits at the wooden-frame Singer sewing machine. She is surrounded by flies; a large window that opens onto the courtyard gives them easy access to the house. They ride to and fro in the soft breeze on the scratchy orange synthetic-lace curtains behind the Singer. They move on to the faded piece of material that is used to cover the machine, left over from making a dress; on to Elsa's spectacles; on to some mending. They rest a moment on the discolored, peeling, light green plaster walls; on the one long fluorescent bulb in the sloping ceiling; on the brown plastic sofa and chairs. They inspect the checked plastic tablecloth for crumbs, parade onto the piece of heavy cloth that is hung from a metal bar to hide the stove and sink, and chase each other into the kitchen. "Oh, these flies!" Elsa sprays a stream of insecticide at them. It has no lasting effect except to mix its fumes with the lingering odor of moldy dishrag. Quickly the status quo is restored: the flies reassemble and Elsa returns to her work.

Living rooms are usually the only rooms with any decoration. In the Prochets' living room, a dark brown strip of paint has been added around the base of the wall. The humidity has produced unplanned additions of patchy stains on the walls. Elsa has also hung two wooden oblong plaques painted with Alpine winter scenes and two plates depicting the Dutch countryside on the walls. She will most likely never see these scenes for herself, or even in books. They do not exist for her as representations of something real; they represent instead the La Paz stationery store's available stock of items to hang on the wall of a living room. Hilda Costantino de Coisson, whose husband works for the Animal Health Office, has exactly the same items on her wall. Like her neighbors' living rooms, Elsa's contains no excess, almost no knickknacks, mementos, or items with a purely aesthetic appeal. There is a small alarm clock and a ceramic vase on the coffee table. The furniture is made of plastic, which the middle and upper classes favor over wood and leather, materials available in the campo. Instead of colorful and inexpensive rag rugs, Elsa lays old burlap sacks on the floor, at the street and courtyard entrances to the house. It is as though she believes it would be excessive for objects to be both utilitarian and aesthetically pleasing.

Uniform and characterless home furnishings and decorations reflect the society's particular concept of communal life. A house like Elsa's offers no immediate clues to the lives of its inhabitants as individuals. In a way, the search for clues to the household is made easier by an absence of clutter and the predictableness of houses. There are no projects left around in various states of completion, few games and toys, few books (except for schoolbooks), few magazines and newspapers. One usually finds, however, a wooden-frame Singer, a maté gourd and thermos, a radio, and a Waldensian calendar or a Catholic cross. Occasionally the spareness and predictability of a home cause some clue to a person's life to stand out by its incongruity. In the home of Miriam de Barea's daughter-in-law, a person quickly passes over the regulation plastic furniture, the naked lightbulb, the faded pastel walls, a framed ad for a Peugeot car, a picture of some birds with a religious message underneath, and a calendar, to a certificate for typing of which the family is very proud. Usually, however, there is merely a sameness about houses—a sameness of austerity and grimness rather than familiarity. The focus is not on the house as a showcase of goods and interests and not on the individuals who reside in the house, but on the family as a community.

As the family is a communal group, the work of women, which is often done in the home even when it is more than "housework," is more communal than private, both in its goals and in its performance. Work in the home falls into three categories: housework, household work, and family work. Housework covers the essential activities of preparing and cleaning up after meals and washing clothes. There is little other housework because houses contain almost nothing to dust, polish, wax, shine, or straighten up. After dinner and supper each day, Emilia, Elsa de Prochet's boarder, sweeps the floor around the table. The long-handled dustpan kept in the kitchen is already full from a previous sweeping, so she first empties it into a small plastic pail that is kept in the courtyard. During the meal, Elsa has been heating dishwater, and now she pours it into a tin can in the sink—an old dulce de membrillo container, about the size of a large cheese round, such as commonly serves housewives (even those who are less frugal than Elsa) as a dishpan. While Elsa washes, Emilia dries, stacking glasses and tin cups in a drawer beneath the silverware. "It's hard to get them all in there, I know, Emilia," Elsa always apologizes, "but I've just never gotten around to getting anything else to put them in." Elsa cleans up the sink and the stove while Emilia puts the clean plates back under the bread basket and the cloth napkins in a corner cupboard in the storeroom—a room off the kitchen where Elsa keeps potatoes, onions, and fruit and dries orange peels to add to maté. Their housework is finished. Elsa can now begin her household work.

Women's household work is economically important to the family. There are two ways a woman who stays at home can help with the family income. She can be frugal and make her family's clothes and certain foods like butter and chorizo sausages, in a sense making money by saving it. She can also take in boarders, give sewing lessons, make take-out meals for people, or make sweets to sell door-to-door. In such cases she may actually make money or may take agricultural products or services as payment. Elsa de Prochet does both kinds of household work. She is frugal to the extreme, boils the family's own raw milk, makes the butter, and sews clothes for the entire family. She also earns money directly by taking in boarders. Most Tuesdays Elsa makes butter. On Saturdays Aldo brings the milk to her from their ranch in San Sebastiano and she boils it Sunday night. Then she leaves it for a day in the refrigerator so that the cream can rise to the top. "Boiled milk isn't as rich as raw milk, so the butter won't be as good, but it's good all the same and it's cheaper than at the store." She skims off the cream into a large bowl and stirs it until the milk separates out. She pours off the milk and adds water until the remainder of the milk is washed out, stirring constantly. "I have to be sure to get all the water out so the butter won't be acrid," she explains to her son, Antonio, who likes to watch her create butter from milk.

One important type of household work in San Sebastiano and La Paz, sewing, is a solo activity and might be a lonely one if it did not usually accompany a communal activity. After siesta time on Tuesday, Elsa's neighbor comes to pay her a visit. They kiss, and Elsa invites her to sit down and offers her maté. Elsa continues to sew while her neighbor takes her turn with the gourd. "What do you hear of Santucho in San Sebastiano? Not Felipe who owns the body shop, but his cousin, Roberto, who lost his father. What bad luck that family has! The man cared for his father his entire life until he finally died. I heard he was ninety-seven. Then two years later the son is stricken with arterial sclerosis and has been flat on his back with his mouth open for the past four years. The only thing he can do is eat—he can't talk. I heard he's getting worse and has bad bed sores. The doctors can't do a thing for him." Elsa and her neighbor talk on about other people for a half hour or so. By five the stores are open again, and the neighbor kisses Elsa goodbye and leaves to do her errands.

The last type of work women do in the home is family work, work that is not strictly necessary but helps cement the family as a community. Lucia de Antonini's three-layer birthday cake for her daughter, Michela, can be thought of as family work. It was not necessary work; indeed, Lucia's husband's grandmother thought it an extravagance. A very important kind of family work is done by the Prochet sisters as caretakers of their paternal family.

The day of the Gilly/Musset wedding, Italo Prochet had been much worse, and his sisters, Ernestina and Liliana, had been unable to attend. Liliana was not holding up well under the strain. She pushed through the barrier of colored plastic strips hanging from the casement of the patio door. There was something the matter with her nerves—she couldn't move properly and the look in her eyes suggested that she wanted to be somewhere but couldn't find the way. Ernestina was hanging a sheepskin on the line to dry, laughing at the gaudy shade of pink she had dyed it by mistake. Italo had been quiet all morning sitting on the patio, but began his howling speech, the result of a stroke, and had to be taken to the bathroom to see if that was what he wanted.

As the oldest daughter, Ernestina never thought much about marrying. At an early age she became accustomed to taking care of her siblings; then it was her parents; and now it was her siblings again. Liliana had intended to marry, but when her engagement to a San Sebastiano man did not work out she retired back into the family to help Ernestina. After the death of their parents, Ernestina and Liliana were spurred to become the first Prochets to move to La Paz when their brother Italo's health began to deteriorate. They found two houses for sale across the street from each other. Italo moved into one, promptly coating its new appliances and floors with protective newspapers, and Ernestina and Liliana moved into the other. The sisters tended to their brother across the street. In the late 1970's Esteban's ill health forced him to move into La Paz to be close to his sisters, and he died within a few years. Soon after, Italo had a heart attack. No longer able to live alone, he moved in with Ernestina and Liliana. To help take care of him, a third brother, Andrés, moved into the house too. There was always a constant movement of Prochets through Chaco Street, and the house across the road did not stand vacant long. A sister who had had cancer surgery moved into it. Unexpectedly, Liliana herself became one of Ernestina's patients when she suffered a mental breakdown. Ernestina remains healthy and resilient, however, and is still dedicated to caring for her parental family.

These three types of work all have a communal basis. In general, the communal nature of the household and of work in households does not break down when women have a career. Unlike San Sebastiano women, La Paz women have work outside the home. On a walk through town one may encounter women who are traffic police, schoolteachers and administrators, government employees such as social workers and municipal clerks, utility company employees, secretaries, nurses, doctors, and merchants and store clerks. But they do not consider a job satisfying without the communal context that a home provides. They live with parents or other close family or they have families of their own. Many have several children, but because "a life without chicos is inconceivable," they do not find any difficulty combining them with a job. Their task is made easier, however, by the low cost of domestic help, by the limited size of La Paz, and by the presence of other family to help with child care.

Many women have jobs that allow them to remain at home. The pediatrician Marina Merati de Howard keeps office hours in her small house on Bariloche Street. A visitor will usually find the street gate open and the front door ajar. The entranceway is the waiting room for Marina's office. Perfunctory protests can be heard behind the office door from Ernestina's cousin, who has brought her baby in for a checkup. Marina has had to give her small patient an injection because the baby needs it immediately and she cannot find any of the town's nurses at home; she speculates that they are probably all out shopping for supper. Marina does not normally give injections and feels she does not do it well.

From the living quarters beyond come more serious screams. It is nearly 8:00 p.m.; office hours are over and Jaime is impatient to be rid of the babysitter and try his demands on his mother. During the day he and his brother Fernando had put Juana, their live-in babysitter, through her paces, and now they were trying the patience of Rosa, who replaces Juana from 5:00 to 8:00 while she studies for night school. The boys were formally adopted when they were babies and are now five and three years old. Juana is strictly a sitter and earns $80 a month, plus free medical care and room and board. Another woman comes several times a week to clean. The Howards' small house of two bedrooms, a bathroom, and a kitchen would seem larger if Marina's office were located elsewhere, perhaps in one of the clinics, but she prefers to sacrifice the room and work at home. Her days are varied and are organized to accommodate her roles as doctor, mother, and homemaker. She sees patients between 8:00 and 10:00 a.m., does her shift at the 9 de Julio Hospital between 10:30 and 12:30, and returns home for the midday meal and a siesta. Most days her husband Toni is there to join her. Between 5:00 and 8:00 p.m. she again has office hours. In between seeing an average of fifteen patients a day, she can retire to another room to cook or knit, or make a quick trip to the store, or take the children for a turn around the park.

Fita Gilly de Baridon, Tullio's sister, has a similar arrangement in San Sebastiano: she has a job but rarely leaves the house. She manages a small general store, a dispensary, in her home in the village. "Ordinarily I have about thirty customers a day, so I can be cooking dinner in the back when I need to. But at the end of the month I get busier because that's when people get paid. My children help me when they're not in school, and my husband helps out when he's not out picking up the farmers' milk for the dairy cooperative." Women workers, like Marina and Fita, then, are also involved in the communal life of the family.

With certain qualifications, one could say that there is a female counterpart to male machismo in San Sebastiano and La Paz society. There is an emphasis on personal pride and toughness, which develops out of the society's emphasis on community. Work done in the home is not by definition female. Although women are at home more than men and do most of the work in the house, there is nothing inherently feminine about cooking over a fire or making maté. The work done in the house is more communal than female. Moreover, the fixtures and decorations of the house do not represent a feminine touch or a feminine world: the home is the site of gatherings, not a showcase. In the end, women do take responsibility for the home, but in a frugal and ruthlessly pragmatic way that seems almost macho. Their homes are lean and spartan, proudly stripped to the minimum, suggesting the life-style of the gaucho or the campo man. They are content to do without heat; at most they have a space heater, which they use rather like the fireplace to warm their hands over occasionally, meanwhile leaving the door of the house open. They explain that the smoke from fireplaces is unhealthy and that, in any case, heat is unnecessary and using space heaters is expensive. They are content to do without hot water, another convenience they feel is unnecessary and expensive. Though many middle- and upper-class people in La Paz have hot-water showers, they prefer to sponge-bathe in cold water daily, taking a hot shower just once a week. Heat and hot water are luxuries as are appliances like clothes washers. Smaller, less expensive items, however, are also considered extravagant. Elsa de Prochet proudly describes herself as primitive and rustic. "There are people who have saucers for their cups and all, but that seems like too much luxury for me." She apologizes for her "ugly" house, for not having a phone, a television, hot water, and other conveniences, but she prefers her sense of economy and style. The achievement of a woman like Elsa, her "conquest" in a macho sense, is that she gets the most out of the least. She accomplishes this with a verve and vigor that reveals her toughness in the face of rural life, even when her economic status would allow her much more.

Elsa constantly challenges herself in the most basic of her activities. After a long rainy spell, she takes advantage of the sun's warmth to shower and wash her hair. First she bathes in the cold shower—a shower head appended to the bathroom wall with a drain in the floor underneath it. When she finishes she pushes the excess water into the drain with a rubber "broom." The tiles will be wet and slippery for some time, so she leaves the bathroom door open onto the courtyard to dry them out faster. Meanwhile she has been heating some water to wash her hair. She pours it into a small plastic bowl set in a low metal stand, which she places over the open courtyard drain, trying not to breathe the odor of sewage. Her hair will be dry by supper. Elsa apologizes for her house to an outsider because she thinks she should, not because she questions her way of life. Ultimately, the measure of a woman is sterner stuff than a well-decorated and comfortable home—even an outwardly diminutive and traditional woman such as Elsa.

Women also have a public aspect, much as men do in a macho society, and it has its own distinctive character.[11] The public aspect derives, once again, from women's concern with promoting the communal aspects of society. Public life is more difficult for women; they must be more guarded than men because much of the public domain is off-limits to them. Public life in Latin countries is often described as traditionally male-dominated, and to judge from what women like Fita de Baridon say, the description is accurate. "I almost never leave the house. There's lots to do here, qué sé yo? I haven't been to La Paz for, let's see, three months at least. I hate to leave home. Once I had to go to Rosario and once to Buenos Aires to take care of my cousin who was sick. There's so much to do here. I almost never watch TV even, unless it's the news sometimes. I'd rather talk to my brother or my in-laws—I prefer the friendships I have in the family to any other." Men, in contrast, live a good part of their lives in the public domain. Their work takes them out of the home: they are out with other men rounding up cattle, tending stores, defending their clients in court. During the workday they are in numerous public places: in the fields sitting around cookfires, in offices and banks doing business, in stores buying supplies. Much of their leisure time is spent in public: they gather to talk in the stores—in San Sebastiano a store's clients are largely male—and to drink in the pulperías, where women do not go at all. They pass the time leaning against store fronts or standing on street corners or sitting on park benches—none of which is an acceptable pastime for women. Even a more worldly woman than Fita would be uncomfortable going to a cafe or restaurant alone, or sitting in a park by herself without children or a male companion whose presence would justify her being there.

While women have less of a place in the public domain than men, the place they do occupy is a very important one. An important center of community for women outside the home is the church. Lay participation in the Waldensian church is strongly encouraged. Iolanda Avondet de Gilly in San Sebastiano, for example, teaches Sunday School and works at church socials, making pizza and empanadas to sell. She also belongs to the Women's League of the church, one of whose activities is to collect used clothing and sell it at a nominal price or give it away. Iolanda coordinates this activity and keeps people informed about upcoming sales.

Since the roads still ooze mud at every step, Iolanda walks as far as possible on the asphalt though it takes her out of her way. Head bent, arms folded across her stomach, she carefully picks her way in an old pair of loafers. The usual campo cacophony of animal and human sounds fills the village roads. In fact, there is a surprising amount of noise considering the lack of movement. Iolanda's passage is interrupted only by a child and a dog. She spends the rest of the walk trying to remember the child's Christian name. Past the butcher's and one block toward the river brings her to Hilda de Coisson's gate. Two blond-haired boys stop their play by the side of the house and shyly greet her. It is cold, but the side door is open to let in the late-afternoon rays of the sun. Iolanda claps her hands to let Hilda know that she has a visitor. Hilda, a tall blond woman, gets up from her sewing and invites Iolanda inside. "Abuela," she shouts, bringing Iolanda to her grandmother's attention. "You remember Iolanda Avondet, wife of Tullio Gilly, don't you?" She turns to Iolanda and says in her normal voice, "We have my abuelita living with us now." The old woman smiles from deep in her rocker and huddles down further into her blanket, drawing closer to the iron pot of coals on the floor. Her heavy dress, stockings, and scarf cover all of her except for her wrinkled face and her hands. "Abuela has low blood pressure and likes to drink cognac and milk—she's creole." "Really creole," echoes the old woman grinning. "My mother still lives by herself in the campo, you know," says Hilda. "She's more than sixty years old and she goes out in the fields by herself rounding up cattle like a man! If anything should happen to her, there would be no one around, I tell her. And she has no one to keep her company. So finally she's agreed to move to the Orlandos' lot when they leave. She's going to put a prefabricated house on it." Iolanda studies the plans for the house; it will contain four rooms plus a bath and will have about four hundred square feet. This is more room than her mother needs, explains Hilda, but she wants to have room for her grandchildren to visit her. After enlisting Hilda's help for the clothing sale, Iolanda returns home. Iolanda's world may be narrowly circumscribed, but that does not detract from her effectiveness as a member of the San Sebastiano community.

In La Paz too, the church is one of the main centers of community, especially for women. Back in town one evening, Ernestina and Liliana Prochet, a neighbor, and Elsa de Prochet are sitting in Ernestina's car in front of Doña Carolina's house on Pilar Street. They have been patiently waiting for her for several minutes. They echo each other's indecision: "Well, I wonder where Doña Carolina is." "I wonder if she's even home, there's no light on." "I'm sure she knew what time we were going to pick her up." "I wonder if we should knock at the door?" "Ah, here she is." The porch light comes on and Carolina shuts the door behind her. "Sorry, I didn't hear you pull up. I was watching 'Bonanza.'"

Ernestina starts the car and continues on up the dark street to the Waldensian church, where the Women's League is having its Friday-night meeting. She still does not understand the clutch, and no one mistakes the identity of the driver of the green Fiat being coaxed up the street in short bursts and stalling at every intersection. When they finally arrive in front of the building that is both the church and the Micols' house, Ernestina lets her friends off at the door and drives on a few yards to park. As the women move across the court-yard toward the iron gate that leads into the pastor's living quarters, they hear the normal bedlam of the Micol household. The collie Tango is barking, and Dora, the pastor's wife, is engaged in separate arguments with each of her three daughters. She is not a Waldense but participates in most of the church's activities. Her daughters know they will win their arguments because Dora must quit to help set up tables for the meeting. Oscar is away this evening, but in any case this is a women's gathering.

As the courtyard begins to fill with women and girls of all ages, Tango drops his guise as guard dog and retreats to a safe corner. Slowly everyone drifts into the sanctuary. It is a small room, bare except for two plaques, some flowers, a Bible on a stand, and ten rows of wooden benches. The sparse furnishings do little to absorb the noise of the children who fidget impatiently; they envy Claudia and Vera Micol who can be heard playing in the background. As the formal part of the meeting comes to an end with the motto, "Everyone needs someone to love, something to do, and something to hope for," the children make a dash for the door. The League is celebrating its twentieth anniversary, and the children have been looking forward to the cakes and crackers and maté cocido.

Dora and Rosa de Baridon, who teach at the same school and are good friends, sit down together at one of the tables. "Alberto and Elvira's wedding went very well," Dora reports. "Too bad you couldn't have been there. The dress she made was beautiful. Do you know, Vera passed up the wedding in order to stay overnight with a friend of mine—you know, Elvira. Vera worships her. She's a very independent woman and I admire her. She's had some boyfriends, I guess, but she won't have anything to do with any man who doesn't want her son. She has a ten-year-old who's illegitimate, you know.

'If he doesn't want my son, he doesn't want me,' she says. She refused to marry the boy's father because he wanted her to get an abortion. I started right out taking birth control pills, because I wanted to space my children, and never had any trouble with them. I guess Elvira can't take them. You can't either, can you? Now I'm using a cream and I'm having trouble getting it in La Paz. None of the doctors or pharmacists have ever heard of it here!"

The other women have finished talking and are getting ready to leave. Some are already standing around in the courtyard waiting to kiss the pastor's wife goodbye, so Dora excuses herself. By the time she returns, Rosa and fifteen-year-old Mirta have put the tables and chairs away. The noise and confusion of the meeting have subsided, the girls for a moment contentedly playing in their room, Tango asleep again at his post at the gate, waiting for Oscar to come home.

The church's social function is as important as its religious one. In fact, for Dora, who is not a Waldense and does not regularly attend services but does attend activities like the Women's League meetings, the church is primarily a social center. The church is a place for the exchange of information on the running of families and other important issues, a public place of communication and socialization.

For the most part, middle- and upper-class families exhibit few of the characteristics attributed to macho Latin American culture. There is open, genuine affection, little disagreement, a sharing of some tasks, activities enjoyed in common, and joint decision-making.

On Saturday, Elsa de Prochet begins to speculate on when Aldo will arrive in La Paz to spend the weekend with her. She heard on the radio yesterday that he will be coming in to town; she knows he is planning to sell some cattle at next week's auction and has to get the papers. At mid morning Aldo pulls up in front of the house. His son Antonio runs out to meet him and embrace him. When Aldo and Elsa are settled in the living room, Antonio gets out his schoolbooks. He finds studying lonely, and anyway he wants to take advantage of the time his father is there. He is having an exam in geography on Monday and has opened his book to a map of the Americas. It takes Aldo some time to locate Argentina because he does not have a clear idea where to look. Elsa finds it and laughs that there is so much water surrounding them that she doesn't see why they all don't drown.

Before starting dinner, Elsa takes advantage of the dry weather to wash Aldo's laundry of the previous week: a pair of bombachas, a blue and white checked shirt, a pair of undershorts, an undershirt, and a handkerchief. The washtubs are at the back of the courtyard. Elsa has heated some water and scrubs the clothes with a cake of rough soap and a piece of sponge plant extracted from the stalk's inner husk. After she hangs the clothes on the lines in the courtyard, she takes the little teakettle into the kitchen to heat water for maté. While she drinks and talks with Aldo about which cattle they will sell at the auction, she works on some pajamas for her grand-daughters; she is making them from some material she found on sale at the discount store in La Paz.

After his siesta, Aldo suggests taking a ride in the truck. They pile into the cab with the thermos and maté. Elsa has not been out of the house all week except to attend a church function one evening. She has few errands—Antonio takes care of most of them, and Aldo brings most of their food in from the campo. On their turn around town, Aldo takes the usual route—practically the only route, in fact—hitting all the main points of interest: down to the port to see the river; over to the new barrio of houses; then to the other new barrio with the four-story condominium; out the paved road to the army barracks. On the way they see a man in a Superman T-shirt and wave to him; he is Elsa's cousin. When they return home, Antonio gets permission to drive the truck around the block.

Aldo and Elsa have a strong relationship based on mutual respect and shared responsibilities and interests. There are many such relationships in San Sebastiano and La Paz. The role of these men and women in the family and society, and their goals and methods of attaining them often seem unaffected by gender stereotypes. At the same time, however, one finds among some people a particular attitude toward the sexes which tends to reinforce a more macho pattern. Women, for example, are often blamed for men's actions, especially in sexual matters. Father Cagliero blames women for sep-arations and for the infidelity of their husbands. "The family is still strong here, but there are many separations, in all social classes. This is because parents set a bad example themselves by separating. How a woman can live lying to her husband, I don't know. And kids see things on TV and in films that don't reflect their own reality. And another thing: women shouldn't bring chicas into their houses—the woman of the household just doesn't realize the danger she puts her family in by introducing a young country girl into her home." It should be emphasized, of course, that the speaker is the Catholic priest of a small town, but the view that a woman's virtue represents family honor is shared by others as well.[12]

In the provincial capital of Paraná, a thirty-five-year-old government employee had been engaged for nine years to a man who in the end decided not to marry her. Her family forbade her to date another man, insisting that she had had her chance. The woman resents her parents' decree and is hurt by the implied judgment on her morality. Her parents suspect, or worry that others suspect, that she has had sexual relations with her boyfriend or that she has some flaw, again perhaps something that mars her purity, that caused him to refuse to marry her. They blame her completely for the outcome of her engagement.

A different perspective is offered by the obstetrician and gynecologist Laura De Pereda, who notices some changes in sexual mores. She maintains that pre-marital sex is more common than not in San Sebastiano and La Paz. "I've been called in on three pregnancies of high school girls in La Paz. The school makes them drop out while they're pregnant, but they can go back afterward. Generally the girl's parents adopt her baby as their own. Nowadays I don't think parents pressure their children to get married as they used to." Moreover, birth control is common among the middle and upper classes, abortion is discussed openly on the radio, and some women are choosing to raise their children without a husband.[13] Although the presence of a male-dominated society cannot be denied, women's position in this society is more complex than a simple dichotomy might indicate.

In San Sebastiano and La Paz society, the lines between family and community are intentionally blurred and the communal aspects of each are reinforced. This is true of men and women alike. The fact that a large portion of the population is related tends immediately to broaden the concept of family, as does the inclusion of distant relatives and non-family in households. The flexibility and egalitarianism of this society, and a particular attitude toward individual needs, encourage a kind of communal spirit in households.

The communal sense of a "private" home, manifested in both its furnishings and the activities that take place there, is carried over into life outside the home, in drinking maté and demonstrating physical closeness. The portraits presented in this chapter are not meant to suggest that San Sebastiano and La Paz society is agreeable in all ways and acceptable to everyone, or that tensions do not exist. Rather, the purpose has been to identify one of the keys to the functioning of society—the communal bond between family and community—and its effect on personal relationships and private lives.

Conclusion:
And Here the World Ends

IT IS SEVEN o'clock in the evening at the well in San Sebastiano. The sun is going down on Teresa de González as she hurries back to her rancho with water for the evening meal. In the corner of the Gilly yard, it holds Tullio in view as he fixes a pipe. Miguel Moreno stops repairing his fence for a minute to look up at the sun, and knows he has only an hour more to work. Soon the village will be in shadow, lost to the outside world.

One can only conceptualize a world like San Sebastiano as the villagers would. It is a world that is difficult to label as traditional, transitional, or modern; San Sebastiano is all of these at the same time. People are traditional; they believe in custom, in a familiar way of life. Farming may no longer be as profitable as it once was, but is still the preferred way of life. The society is in a sense in transition, but people are not deserting the countryside; on the contrary, they still see themselves and San Sebastiano in their rural context. Rural-to-urban movement has not resulted in the eclipse of San Sebastiano by La Paz, but rather in the overlapping of the two. There are indications of modernization: in communication, with paved roads, buses, radios, and television; in farming, with new machinery, seeds, and fertilizers; in life-style, with electricity, sewing machines, plastic packaging, and synthetics. These are all familiar signs of a modern, industrialized world, but somehow they become less familiar and more complex in San Sebastiano. People integrate them into their world in unfamiliar ways. Ernestina Prochet incorporates the world of television into the world of local gossip; after watching the nightly news on the television she retires outdoors to reestablish her curbside relationship with the community. Her television does not replace her traditional way of relating with her world; instead it brings her in touch with the world on several levels. Cars and horsecarts sharing streets, modern appliances lying protected under a layer of newspapers with ads for Florida's Disney World, rock music blaring out the door behind a man drinking maté, unisex clothes from the used American clothing store being worn by a stereotypical macho campo man—these are daily reminders of the complex relationship between tradition and modernity. This is a culture that accepts innovation, but largely on its own terms.

An observer might take such innovations to mean that the village desires to move toward the world outside its borders. But people in San Sebastiano and La Paz prefer their own world. They point to the paranoia of porteños and the fact that in La Paz, no one is afraid; no one locks his door, because everyone knows everyone else. And they are not at all attracted to a world where there are racial problems and where presidents and popes get shot. These people do not define a "good place to live," then, by the presence of amenities, nearness to a big city with its diverse cultural life, or good job opportunities. A good place to live, to them, is one where people are good and get along with each other.

For all of the limitations put on this world by the perceptions of its own inhabitants and its particular situation on the edge of Western civilization, it is a complex society. Indeed, a society that functions through personalism, good will, and a sharing of individual expertise in different areas is really no less complex than a society that functions primarily through bureaucracies and laws. San Sebastiano and La Paz also have complex modes of dealing with conflict and control. More formal, institutionalized means are apt to be rejected here in favor of a shared respect for public honor and social place. A commitment to harmony—a method of building a livable community rather than a utopia, a mode of operation rather than a moral principle—provides order and symmetry for people's relationships with each other. And while homes, and activities in the home, are pared down to their essentials, the families occupying those homes extend the idea of "family" to encompass even nonfamily. The familial and community closeness that people work to achieve while still maintaining their own individuality is not a simple matter. But most impressive of all is the way San Sebastiano and La Paz have retained their own mechanisms and even developed them amid the intolerance of a harsh environment where life is sometimes not much respected; amid the cruelty of the military regime with its requests for denunciations and its "disappearances"; amid the wasting away of great natural potential through economic crises.

This is the world in the 1980's—in San Sebastiano, in one of the mainstreams of Argentine national life. As the villagers say, here the world ends; but here it also begins.

Notes

Notes

Chapter 1

1. Most of the published information on Waldensian colonies like Colonia San Sebastiano is included in works written by the Waldenses on the general history of their settlement in Latin America. These include Emilio Ganz-Bert and E. Rostan, *Il centenario della colonizzazione valdese nel Río de la Plata* (Torre Pellice, 1959); Ernesto Tron, *Historia de los Valdenses* (Colonia Valdense, Uruguay, 1952); Ernesto Tron and Emilio H. Ganz, *Historia de las colonias valdenses sudamericanas en su primer centenario (1858–1958)* (Colonia Valdense, Uruguay, 1958); and N. Tourn, *I Valdesi in America* (Turin, 1906; published by the Comitato "I Valdesi all'Estero" for the Exposition of Milan of 1906).

There are also some individual studies of Waldensian colonies by Waldenses, such as Elio Maggi-Pasquet, "La colonia San Gustavo," *Boletín de la Sociedad Sudamericana de Historia Valdense* 11(3) (Aug. 15, 1937), 87–97, and Levy Tron, *Colonia Iris en sus primeros 25 años, 1901–1926* (Jacinto Arauz, 1926). See also George B. Watts, *The Waldenses in the New World* (Durham, N.C., 1941), on Waldensian settlements in the United States and Latin America. For a history of one Waldensian colony and of the homeland society of the Italian immigrants who settled there, see Kristin Ruggiero, "Italians in Argentina" (Ph.D. diss., Indiana University, 1979), a study based on Waldensian as well as other sources. Another colony study for this area is by Joel Cogo et al., entitled "Estudio realizado por la Agencia de Extensión Agropecuaria La Paz en la Colonia Oficial no. 14" (La Paz, 1966?; in mimeo, available from author).

2. Large-scale Italian emigration, including that of the Waldenses, began in the last quarter of the nineteenth century. In Northern Italy, Piedmont was an especially important region of this emigration. Piedmont lost to emigration 10.3 inhabitants out of every 1,000 between 1881 and 1885, 9.6 between 1886 and 1890, and 11.3 in 1889. See Valerio Castronovo, *Economia e società in Piemonte dall'Unità al 1914* (Milan, 1969), p. 102. In Argentina during this period, the majority of Italian immigrants came

from northern Italy, and the Piedmontese outnumbered immigrants from any other region of Italy. See Vivente Vázquez-Presedo, *Estadísticas históricas argentinas, (comparadas), primera parte 1875-1914* (Buenos Aires, 1971), pp. 33-34.

Among the causes of Italian emigration were agricultural crises such as poor harvests and crop diseases. There were also more general problems under which the lower classes labored: the lack of arable land, the inequities of latifundia, overpopulation, and the failure of nascent industries. Further difficulties beset mountain people like the Waldenses, who were mainly small farmers and day laborers. Their landholdings were particularly small and became increasingly subdivided during the nineteenth century. A peasant farmer would often need several plots just to make a subsistence living; these were frequently located far apart, so that he lost time walking between them and could not work the land to maximum profit. Because of the rocky soil, steep slopes, and rapid erosion, Alpine farmers also had to transport new soil each year from the lower valleys to their plots. In addition, because the snow came earlier and stayed later in the mountains, they had to take advantage of pastureland at various elevations for their animals, often moving them to as many as three different locations during the year.

Transhumance was only one form of migration in which these farmers took part before the mass movements began. The unproductive winter months had long since necessitated temporary migration to nearby French centers such as Nice and Marseilles, and to Geneva and Ticino in Switzerland. By the later nineteenth century large numbers of seasonal migrants, the so-called "swallows" (Ital. *rondini,* Sp. *golondrinas*) had established a route between Piedmont and Argentina, taking advantage of the harvest seasons in both hemispheres. Seasonal migration was in fact the most important supplement to a farmer's income. Much of the seasonal migration to the Americas eventually became of longer duration or permanent. It was from this environment that the Waldenses came.

For more on the socioeconomic background of the Waldenses and the area they inhabited, see Ruggiero, "Italians in Argentina," pp. 10-27; Raimondo Luraghi, *Agricoltura, industria e commercio in Piemonte dal 1848 al 1861 (Comitato torinese dell'Istituto per la Storia del Risorgimento* n.s. 5, Turin, 1967); Castronovo, *Economia e società;* Giuseppe Melano, *La popolazione di Torino e del Piemonte nel secolo xix* (Turin, 1961); Francesco Adamo et al., eds., *Ricerche sulla regione metropolitana di Torino: Il Pinerolese* (Turin, 1971), vol. 1; Arnaldo Pittavino, *Storia di Pinerolo e del Pinerolese,* 2d ed. (Milan, 1964), vol. 1; and Giunta per l'inchiesta agraria e sulle condizioni della classe agricola, *Atti della Giunta . . .* (Rome, 1883), vol. 8, tomo 1, fasc. 1. The *inchiesta agraria* was commissioned by the government in 1877; its findings were published in Rome between 1879 and 1884 in fifteen volumes. Arranged by regions, it breaks down information by provinces, districts, and even communes and is one of the most informative sources on mid-nineteenth-century Italian agriculture and the agricultural population.

Studies of the economic and social background of Waldensian emigration, both nineteenth and twentieth century, include Pierluigi Jalla, *Le Valli Valdesi, problemi economici e di emigrazione* (Torre Pellice, 1966?); Augusto Armand-Hugon, *Torre Pellice, dieci secoli di storia e di vicende* (Torre Pellice, 1958); Teofilo G. Pons, *Cento anni fa alle Valli: Il problema dell'emigrazione* (Torre Pellice, 1956); and Alice Nariton Monnet, "Il problema della montagna nella Val Pellice" (Diss., Scuola Assistenti Sociali, Turin, 1953–54).

A more individualized picture of emigration from the Waldensian Valleys is revealed through the applications for passports made by prospective emigrants, the *nulla-osta*. The municipal archives of Torre Pellice and Bobbio Pellice in the Pellice Valley have good collections of these applications. For Torre Pellice: Municipal Archives, Busta-Archivio, Categoria 13ª, Esteri, Classe 1-2-3, Cartella 1, Scaffale 4, Casella 1; Folder 7–Registro–Certificati spediti dal sindaco dal 1865 al 1893; the remainder of this volume contains the nulla-osta for 1889 through 1900. Also Busta-Archivio, Categoria 13ª, Esteri, Classe 3, Cartella 1, Scaffale 4–Registri delle domande di nulla osta per ottenere passaporti per l'estero dal 1901 al 1922; 1935–47. For Bobbio Pellice: Municipal Archives, Registro dei certificati di buona condotta per girare nell'interno, ottenere libretti da operai, ottenere passaporti all'estero aperto 13 febbraio 1868.

To obtain permission to emigrate, a person had to apply to the mayor, or *sindaco*, of his commune, who would grant a nulla-osta indicating that there were no legal obstacles to his departure. Each person who intended to emigrate was supposed to complete this form, and to include family members who were to accompany him. It essentially served as an application for a passport, which was eventually procured from the prefect or sub-prefect of the province. The form specified, with some variation, paternity, date and place of birth, residence, profession, livelihood, military status, destination, port of embarkation, whether the applicant was called by relatives or friends already abroad, whether the applicant was assured of work in the country of destination, the length of time to be spent abroad, the name and age of people accompanying the applicant, and the applicant's physical characteristics. A difficulty with these documents is that not everyone who applied for a passport necessarily emigrated, and not everyone who emigrated bothered to obtain a passport, since a passport was not required before 1901 and cost 2.40 lire, not an insignificant sum for the time.

In spite of their limitations, nulla-osta are excellent sources of socioeconomic information about the portion of the population that intended to emigrate. The nulla-osta did not ask for a person's religion, but then most people were Catholic, and other groups like the Waldenses stood out anyway because of their distinctive surnames. The Waldensian community is quite inbred, even today, and a person visiting any group of Waldenses would notice a repetition of names. For an interesting catalogue and discussion of these names, see Osvaldo Coïsson, *I nomi di famiglia delle Valli Valdesi* (*Collana della Società di Studi Valdesi*, no. 8, Torre Pellice, 1975). The nulla-osta for the Pellice reveal that a large percentage of the emigrating population was Waldensian, that the most common destinations for permanent emigration were Argentina and Uruguay (whereas most temporary emigration was to France), and that the average age of emigrants was between twenty and forty years. Another interesting phenomenon is observable in these nulla-osta. As small industries were established in the Pellice, outsiders, mainly Catholics, moved into the valley in search of work, especially in the 1870's through the 1890's. Within ten to twenty years they begin to appear in the nulla-osta as prospective emigrants. Waldenses seem not to have become employed in industry, on the other hand, and to have been committed to farming, even emigrating if necessary to preserve this way of life. See Ruggiero, "Italians in Argentina," pp. 81–86, for a fuller discussion of this, and also Jean Coïsson, *Monographie sur le développement intellectuel dans nos Vallées pendant les 50 dernières années—Instruction primaire—Population légale des Vallées Vaudoises au 31 déc. 1897 comparée à celle de mai 1844* (Torre Pellice, 1898).

3. The Tavola Valdese, the Waldensian Church's governing body, kept a fairly close record of the movements of its members and their settlement in foreign countries. In Argentina and Uruguay there are some 15,000 Waldenses, the largest group outside Italy. The information appears in the Tavola's annual reports and in reports of pastors' visits and correspondence. These materials are housed in the Archivio Tavola Valdese in Torre Pellice. For the nineteenth-century Waldensian population of Colonia San Sebastiano, for example, see the section on Argentina in the Tavola's report for 1899. The increase in the Waldensian population of San Sebastiano can be followed from about 1930 from the records of the local Waldensian church, whose headquarters are now in La Paz.

The Tavola Valdese had a very practical reason for keeping track of Waldenses. First, the church was concerned that Catholics were replacing Waldensian emigrants in the valleys, and tried to encourage people to remain in their villages by suggesting alternative occupations. Second, the Tavola felt that if Waldenses had to emigrate, their place of destination should be one favored by the church. Thus they sought to control the emigration movement from the valleys. For the public debate on this, see Ruggiero, "Italians in Argentina," pp. 198–216.

4. Colonists found a very different cuisine from that of Southern Eu-

rope. In a nearby immigrant colony, San José, ten pounds of meat and three pounds of flour a day was allotted to each family of five persons ten years and older. See Filiberto Reula, *Historia de Entre Ríos; política, étnica, económica, social, cultural y moral*, vol. 2 (Santa Fe, Argentina, 1969), p. 54. One reason for the large meat allowance was that meat contained a good deal of waste, but more important was its ready availability. Esteban Prochet recalled that during the harvest, field workers received an allotment of two pounds of meat a day for their noon meal.

Argentines still eat large quantities of beef, especially in the countryside. Beef is often eaten twice a day, children snack on chorizo sausages, and greens and chicken are rarities. The most common vegetables are potatoes, pumpkin squash, and corn. The beef is quite fatty, and the fat used in other dishes tends to be animal lard. Some people who appear in this book suffer, or have died, from protein-related heart disease, and there is a growing recognition that the consumption of beef is too high. Supposedly, the tea maté helps make the beef more digestible.

As to Italo's choice of clothing, cravats and kerchiefs are much more common in the countryside than neckties, and are part of the distinction between the more Western world of the cities and the world of the campo.

5. Sweets are simple concoctions often made of milk and sugar (*dulce de leche*), pumpkin, or quinces. The shallow round *dulce de membrillo* tin is a common household item and serves a multitude of uses, as a dishpan for example.

6. At the height of Argentina's immigration and colonization period, the 1895 manuscript census reported that Colonia San Sebastiano's population included 61 Russians, 41 French, 28 Germans, and only 25 Italians. The Waldenses only began to arrive in the colony at about this time; thus they do not appear in this census. (Archivo General de la Nación, Buenos Aires, 1895 manuscript census for the department of La Paz in the province of Entre Ríos, carpetas 1057, 1058, and 1060.)

7. I will refer to these values elsewhere in the book, especially in Chapter 3; see also Kristin Ruggiero, "Gringo and Creole: Foreign and Native Values in a Rural Argentine Community," *Journal of Interamerican Studies and World Affairs* 24(2) (May 1982), 163–82. In this article I argue that Catholic as well as Protestant immigrants held such values as hard work and progress. My work indicates that these values are linked more to the position of being an immigrant than to a particular religious culture. I have been concerned with the complex of attitudes and values of emigrating peoples in several papers, including "Social and Psychological Factors in Migration from Italy to Argentina," published in Ira Glazier and Luigi De Rosa, eds., *Migration Across Time and Nations: Population Mobility in Historical Contexts* (New York, 1986). For a different analysis see Glen Caudill Dealy, *The Public Man: An Interpretation of Latin American and*

Other Catholic Countries (Amherst, Mass., 1977), which argues that different sets of values characterize Protestant and Catholic cultures. Other works that look at emigrant values and motivations for emigration include John W. Briggs, *An Italian Passage: Immigrants to Three American Cities, 1890–1930* (New Haven, Conn., 1978); Sune Åkerman, "Towards an Understanding of Emigrational Processes," and Peter A. Morrison and Judith P. Wheeler, "The Image of 'Elsewhere' in the American Tradition of Migration," both in William H. McNeill and Ruth S. Adams, eds., *Human Migration: Patterns and Policies* (Bloomington, Ind., 1978); Ercole Sori, *L'emigrazione italiana dall'Unità alla seconda guerra mondiale* (Bologna, 1979); Dino Cinel, *From Italy to San Francisco: The Immigrant Experience* (Stanford, Calif., 1982); and Gary R. Mormino and George E. Pozzetta, *The Immigrant World of Ybor City: Italians and Their Latin Neighbors in Tampa, 1885–1985* (Urbana, Ill., 1987).

8. The original San Sebastiano colonists began by renting land according to the following contract terms, here summarized from Cayetano R. Ripoll, *La Provincia de Entre Ríos bajo sus diversos aspectos* (Paraná, 1888), vol. 1, pp. 393–96. (1) Each colonist rented an area of 168 hectares (415 acres) from Eduardo Schiele, the first administrator of San Sebastiano (and sailing companion and employer of Eduardo Howard's father), for the period through the completion of the fifth harvest. (2) The colonists paid a rent of 10 percent (in kind) of each harvest, which Schiele collected after the threshing at the colonists' houses, furnishing empty sacks. (3) Colonists made the first rent payment at the conclusion of the harvest and threshing of 1889–90 for the land cultivated to that date, promising that the second payment would be made on the total area of the concession with the exception of about 32 hectares (80 acres) that was to serve them as pasture. (4) The colonists had the option of buying their concession at any time, paying Schiele 2,000 gold pesos as the purchase price, the surveying expenses being the responsibility of the colonists. (5) Schiele assumed the expenses that the colonists incurred to begin work. (6) Schiele gave the colonists the oxen necessary to cultivate 168 hectares until the end of the first harvest, with the option of buying the animals at the price of 20 gold pesos each, to be paid to him at the end of the harvest. (7) The colonists were responsible for acquiring all farm tools, although Schiele advanced them if needed, their value to be paid to him at the end of the first harvest. (8) All the advances Schiele made to the colonists were repaid to him within two years at an interest rate not to exceed 6 percent annually. (9) If others wished to move into San Sebastiano as colonists, Schiele was obliged to admit them under these same conditions.

The Waldenses' financial success was fairly rapid, especially compared with what they might have achieved in Italy. In the early 1880's the yearly earnings of a Piedmontese farmer in Italy might have been 550 lire, the equivalent of about 104 pesos (Archivio Tavola Valdese, *Rapport . . . 1897*, Torre Pellice, 1897). A farmer who bought 50 hectares of land in Entre Ríos in 1890, working 30 hectares of it, would have earned 540 pesos. These two sets of figures are ten years apart, and the cost of living was higher in Argentina, but the farmer would probably still have earned more in Argentina. His yearly earnings of 540 pesos would have been spent on rent for the land (190), maintenance (250), and animals, tools, and seeds (100). Occasional expenses might have included a rancho (80), fencing (200), 8 draft horses (100), 4 milk cows (80), a plow (20), or a cart (180). One harvester for each group of three families was needed, an added expense of 140 pesos per family. The figures are from *Boletín de la Oficina Central de Colonización de Entre Ríos*, año 2, no. 17 (July 15, 1890), p. 121.

Waldenses now own much of the land in the colony, as well as nearby land in Campo Oroño, Arroyo Hondo, Pantanoso, Ciento Uno, Colonia Oficial Numero 3, and Estación Estacas. (Censo Nacional Económico, 1974, provincia 290, carpeta 89, departamento 299; and cadastral map of Colonia San Sebastiano and surrounding area, 1972, Archivo de la Dirección General del Catastro de la Provincia de Entre Ríos, Ministerio de Hacienda, Economía y Obras Públicas, Departamento de Topografía.)

9. The struggle between "civilization" and "barbarism," which marked the nineteenth century and some would say has continued to influence the twentieth, is an important theme in Argentine and Latin American history in general. In the nineteenth century, Latin American elites accepted the tenets of European economic and political liberalism. Many Latin American governments promoted European immigration in order to increase the labor force and introduce new skills, but also to "whiten" the population and promote European values. The governments of the Southern Cone were quite successful, those of northern countries like Mexico much less so. Such programs were intended to civilize and modernize the more barbarian elements of native Latin American populations. The preferred immigrants were Northern Europeans, but Southerners came in the greatest numbers. In 1914, 40 percent of the foreigners living in Argentina were from Italy, and 35 percent from Spain. Russians ranked a distant third (4.1 percent), followed by Uruguayans and Frenchmen (3.7 and 3.4 percent), Lebanese and other immigrants from the Ottoman Empire (2.7 percent), and Austro-Hungarians, Brazilians, Chileans, Paraguayans, Britons, and Germans (between 1 and 2 percent each). The figures are from Carl E. Solberg, *Immigration and Nationalism: Argentina and Chile, 1890–1914* (Austin, Tex., 1970), p. 38. For an understanding of what was considered "civilized" Argentina, see James R. Scobie, *Buenos Aires: Plaza to Suburb, 1870–1910* (New York, 1974), and Stanley R. Ross and Thomas F. McGann, eds., *Buenos Aires: 400 Years* (Austin, Tex., 1982).

10. This evaluation of the native Argentine's lack of desire to work hard

is a frequently heard stereotype. I heard it from gringos in Argentina and in conversations with repatriated Italo-Argentines in Italy.

11. Carlos Baridon-Charbonier recounted that in the early days of the colony, Waldenses traded farm machinery, but that they stopped this practice because some colonists lost their harvest waiting for the machines. The early Waldenses did not have any formal associations, such as mutual aid societies, beyond their church groups—they did not need them. And they belonged to none outside their community. Though they were Protestant, they might have associated with the Italian Society of Mutual Aid, established in 1877 in La Paz, but they visited La Paz no more than once or twice a year.

Although Waldenses did not mix to any great extent with other immigrants, except for some English and German Protestants who eventually joined the church, they seem to have enjoyed good working relations with them. Some of the stores in the village of San Sebastiano were owned by Italian Catholics, and the old-timer Waldenses (Bruno Bouissa and Carlos Baridon) recall having received help from them—advances of money and food, for example, in years of poor harvests. Of course, it was in the store owner's interest that his clientele survive.

12. La Paz is small, but it has several barrios, among them the old center of town around the square, the barrio with the new apartment building, the barrio with the new duplexes, the barrio of rancho huts along the river (Barrio La Costa), another barrio of ranchos, and the port area (El Puerto).

Chapter 2

1. I have tried in this chapter to convey the effect of Argentina's contemporary economic crisis on individuals. For an analysis of Argentina's contemporary economic problems and their development on a broader scale, see Albert O. Hirschman, "The Turn to Authoritarianism in Latin America and the Search for Its Economic Determinants," and Robert R. Kaufman, "Industrial Change and Authoritarian Rule in Latin America: A Concrete Review of the Bureaucratic-Authoritarian Model" (esp. pp. 224–34 and 239–44), as well as other essays, in David Collier, ed., *The New Authoritarianism in Latin America* (Princeton, N.J., 1979). See also a special issue of the *Journal of Interamerican Studies and World Affairs* 25(4) (Nov. 1983), "Economic Experiments in the Southern Cone, 1974–1982," edited by Jan Peter Wogart. For the nineteenth-century background see James R. Scobie, *Revolution on the Pampas: A Social History of Argentine Wheat, 1860–1910* (Austin, Tex., 1964), and *A City and a Nation*. For background in a widely comparative context, see Donald Denoon, *Settler Capitalism: The Dynamics of Dependent Development in the Southern Hemisphere* (New York, 1983).

2. Carl E. Solberg, "Peopling the Prairies and the Pampas: The Impact

of Immigration on Argentine and Canadian Agrarian Development, 1870–1930," *Journal of Interamerican Studies and World Affairs* 24(2) (May 1982), 132.

3. Actually, attempts to attract immigrants to Argentina were made even in the first half of the nineteenth century, especially by Bernardino Rivadavia, an Argentine president and statesman in the 1820's. Generally, however, the chaotic character of the early Republic discouraged immigration. It was a time of caudillo-style leadership, in which Entre Ríos played an important part. When Juan Manuel de Rosas was overthrown in 1852, Justo José de Urquiza established a new government at Paraná, capital of Entre Ríos, and it remained one of the capitals of Argentina for almost a decade. The existence of two governments reflected the deep-set antagonism between the provincials and the *porteños*, the residents of Buenos Aires. The struggle between the two prevented Argentina from becoming truly unified until the 1880's, and it can be argued that a significant conflict still exists between city and countryside. The struggle occupied much of the Argentines' energy in the 1850's, but in the decades following, immigration and land colonization programs went ahead. In 1861 the Republic was reunited (though Buenos Aires was not federalized until the 1880's), though revolts in Entre Ríos continued under the caudillo Ricardo López Jordán throughout the 1870's. In the last quarter of the nineteenth century, the government and private companies were very active in promoting immigration and colonization programs, and Italians in particular responded. Besides being attracted by the prospect of owning land and bettering their situation, some immigrants, and Italian government officials as well, viewed Argentina (or, as it was often called, the Plata region) as a potential Italian colony. Argentina's reputation as unsettled with the absence of real national unity contributed to this perception.

For the general history of Entre Ríos, see Filiberto Reula, *Historia de Entre Ríos: política, étnica, económica, social, cultural y moral*, 3 vols. (Santa Fe, Argentina, 1963–71); Cayetano R. Ripoll, *La Provincia de Entre Ríos bajo sus diversos aspectos*, 3 vols. (Paraná, 1888); and María del Carmen Ríos et al., "Entre Ríos, fronteras naturales e historia (1883–1903)" (1974; typed manuscript available at Museo Histórico, La Paz). On La Paz see Estanislao Nestor Córdoba, *Apuntes históricos sobre la ciudad de La Paz y su Departamento* (Paraná, 1976). Many people visited the immigrant colonies in Entre Ríos and wrote about them. Among the more valuable accounts are Alejo Peyret, *Una visita a las colonias de la República Argentina* (Buenos Aires, 1889), and Arturo Reynal O'Connor, *Por las colonias* (Buenos Aires, 1921). On life in the campo see Richard Arthur Seymour, *Pioneering in the Pampas* (London, 1869); Mark Jefferson, *Peopling the Argentine Pampa* (New York, 1926); and Walter Larden, *Estancia Life* (London, 1911; repr. Detroit, 1974).

Much has been written specifically about Italian colonies and Italians in Argentina. On Italians in Entre Ríos see Giovanni María Favoino and Antonio Bufardeci, *Gli Italiani nella Provincia di Entre Ríos* (Paraná, 1914). Material on Italians in Argentina is voluminous. A good place to begin is two bibliographical sources: Grazia Dore, *Bibliografia per la storia dell'emigrazione italiana in America* (Rome, 1956), and Vittorio Briani, *Emigrazione e lavoro italiano all'estero, elementi per un repertorio bibliografico generale* (Rome, 1967). Briani's work has appeared with a new introduction and supplemental bibliography by Francesco Cordasco as *Italian Immigrants Abroad: A Bibliography on the Italian Experience Outside Italy in Europe, the Americas, Australia, and Africa* (Detroit, 1979). For more recent emigration see Centro Studi Emigrazione, *Emigrazione italiana negli anni 70* (Rome, 1975). Two indispensable statistical sources for Argentine immigration are Dirección General de Inmigración, *Resumen estadístico del movimiento migratorio en la República Argentina, años 1857–1924* (Buenos Aires, 1925), and Zulma L. Recchini de Lattes et al., *Migraciónes en la Argentina: estudio de las migraciónes internas e internacionales, basado en datos censales, 1869–1960* (Buenos Aires, 1969). For Italy see Istituto Centrale di Statistica, *Annali di Statistica*, anno 94, ser. 8, vol. 17, *Sviluppo della popolazione italiana dal 1861 al 1961* (Rome, 1965). On Argentine immigration in general, see José Panettieri, *Inmigración en la Argentina* (Buenos Aires, 1970), and Magnus Mörner, *Adventurers and Proletarians: The Story of Migrants in Latin America* (Pittsburgh, 1985). The classic early work on Italian emigration is Robert F. Foerster's *The Italian Emigration of Our Times* (Cambridge, Mass., 1919). More recent work on Italians in Argentina includes the following studies by Samuel L. Baily: "The Italians and the Development of Organized Labor in Argentina, Brazil, and the United States: 1880–1914," *Journal of Social History* 3(2) (1969), 123–34; "The Role of Two Newspapers and the Assimilation of the Italians in Buenos Aires and São Paulo, 1893–1913," *International Migration Review* 12(3) (1978), 321–40; "The Adjustment of Italian Immigrants in Buenos Aires and New York, 1870–1914," *American Historical Review* 88(2) (1983), 281–305; and "Chain Migration of Italians to Argentina: Case Studies of the Agnonesi and the Sirolesi," *Studi Emigrazione* 19(65) (Mar. 1982), 73–91. See also Carl E. Solberg, *Immigration and Nationalism: Argentina and Chile, 1890–1914* (Austin, Tex., 1970).

4. Ernesto Bunge was the Argentine representative of the Sociedad Anónima Estancia Verein based in Antwerp. In 1882 Bunge charged Eduardo Schiele, his attorney—and incidentally a Protestant—with finding land in Argentina for an agricultural colony. Schiele selected about twenty-two square leagues belonging to an Englishman, Guillermo Haycroft. Haycroft had bought the land from a creole, Urbano Iriondo, in 1863. In Buenos

Aires in March 1883, Bunge purchased Haycroft's land (Archivo Histórico de la Provincia de Entre Ríos, Paraná, División Gobierno, Registro de títulos de propiedad, vol. 1868–69, pp. 93, 162). Soon after the sale Schiele, who had become the colony's first administrator, began subdividing the land for colonization and mapping out the colony and village lands; the colony actually took its name from the surveyor's name saint. In March 1888 the provincial government approved the plans. The total area designated as fields, or campo, comprised about 16,488 hectares (40,700 acres); the land set aside for the village comprised about 684 hectares (1,689 acres). The section of the colony destined to be the village was bordered on the north and west by the fields, on the south by the Arroyo Jacinto, and on the east by the Arroyo Gringo. Each concession consisted of about 42 hectares (105 acres), but concessions were groups of four totaling 168 hectares (Archivo de la Dirección General del Catastro de la Provincia de Entre Ríos, Ministerio de Hacienda, Economía y Obras Públicas, Departamento de Topografía, legajo no. 16/4, Duplicado de la diligencia de mensura de la subdivisión en concesiónes y grupos de la Colonia San Sebastiano y traza de la Villa San Sebastiano . . .). Schiele contracted with an agent to populate the colony, and in 1888 brought in the first colonists, sixty European immigrants who had been living in Baradero in Buenos Aires province. See Ríos et al., "Entre Ríos."

5. This information is from the La Paz office of the Instituto Nacional de Tecnología Agropecuaria (INTA).

6. The classic nineteenth-century gaucho poem by José Hernández, *The Gaucho Martín Fierro* (1872; trans. Albany, N.Y., 1974), conveys well the native attitude toward the land and toward the changes that occurred during immigration and colonization in the nineteenth century. For a recent work on the gaucho, see Richard W. Slatta, *Gauchos and the Vanishing Frontier* (Lincoln, Nebr., 1983).

7. People tend to move to town for reasons of work, health, and education. There is a type of hospital cum home for the elderly in the colony, but it does not have a resident medical staff. There is no secondary school in the colony, so that if children want to attend classes beyond the seventh grade, they must go to La Paz.

8. INTA office, La Paz; statistics taken from the Empadronamiento Nacional Agropecuario y Censo Ganadero by district for the Department of La Paz, June 30, 1974.

9. Ibid.

10. Cattle must be taken through the government's tick bath about every twenty days. The fee is nominal, but there is also a cost in the time and effort it takes to round up cattle and drive them to the bath. Large ranchers can afford to install a bath on their own property, avoiding much of the cattle transportation problem.

11. The Paraná Medio project, being currently undertaken to increase the nation's electric power supply, will directly affect sections of La Paz and its department. For an anthropological analysis of the dam's influence on the population, see Instituto Nacional de Antropología, *Cultura tradicional del área del Paraná Medio* (Buenos Aires, 1984).

12. On the Triple A see Richard Gillespie, *Soldiers of Perón: Argentina's Montoneros* (Oxford, 1982), pp. 153–59. The Montoneros are an urban guerrilla group of leftist Peronists who were active in the 1970's.

13. This information is from INTA, La Paz.

14. It should be emphasized that the province of Santa Fe is in a better position to be economically prosperous than Entre Ríos. On immigration and colonization in Santa Fe see Ezequiel Gallo, *La pampa gringa: la colonización agrícola en Santa Fé (1870–1895)* (Buenos Aires, 1983) and *Farmers in Revolt: The Revolutions of 1893 in the Province of Santa Fé, Argentina* (London, 1976).

15. Comparative crop yields for La Paz and Paraná departments in 1980 were as follows (the yields, in kilos per hectare, were recorded by INTA, La Paz):

	La Paz		Paraná	
Crop	Avg.	Max.	Avg.	Max.
Wheat	800	1,200	1,200	1,500
Flax	700	1,300	900	1,500
Corn	1,600	2,500	2,000	4,000
Sorghum	2,000	3,500	2,500	5,000

16. José Alfredo Martínez de Hoz's performance as Minister of the Economy (1976–81) angered many Argentines. His economic policies, endorsed by the International Monetary Fund, not only were unpopular, but by their very nature required political repression and thus had profound effects on civil liberties. Basically "his policies benefited foreign capital, landed interests, and big financiers" and hurt local industry. "Major deindustrialization" [occurred] "as a result of gross over-valuation of the peso (which stymied exports while attracting imports). . . . The purchasing power of workers' wages dropped drastically; by the end of September 1976, real wages were down to 50 percent of their 1974 level and only had a minor recovery after 1978. When factory workers protested wage cuts, lay-offs, and shortened work weeks, the military occupied factories and made it illegal to strike, arresting hundreds of workers." Even among his peers, Martínez de Hoz was deemed to have been a failure when he left office in March 1981. (Gillespie, *Soldiers of Perón*, pp. 228–32.)

17. On Juan Perón's economic policies see Robert J. Alexander, *Juan Domingo Perón: A History* (Boulder, Colo., 1979), pp. 63–68. Alexander explains that Perón's plan was to use the revenues from agriculture to

stimulate the industrialization of Argentina. Industry did begin to benefit from the plan, but the profits from agriculture were also wasted in buying military equipment, and were deposited in private bank accounts in Switzerland as well. In addition, the prices the government paid farmers for agricultural products were so low that the rural economy suffered severe setbacks.

18. *Clarín* (one of Argentina's national newspapers, published in Buenos Aires), June 5, 1981.

19. Ibid.

20. Many studies of European towns and villages have concentrated on the way rural areas change as a result of migration and experiences in a more urban world, even if only the urban world of a nearby town. These studies provide interesting comparative material for San Sebastiano and La Paz. On Spanish villages see Joseph B. Aceves, *Social Change in a Spanish Village* (Cambridge, Mass., 1971), and Stanley H. Brandes, *Migration, Kinship and Community: Tradition and Transition in a Spanish Village* (New York, 1975). On Italy see Rudolph M. Bell, *Fate and Honor, Family and Village, Demographic and Cultural Change in Rural Italy Since 1800* (Chicago, 1979); Charlotte Chapman, *Milocca, a Sicilian Village* (Cambridge, Mass., 1971); Johan Galtung, *Members of Two Worlds: Development Study of Three Villages in Western Sicily* (New York, 1971); Feliks Gross, *Il Paese: Values and Social Change in an Italian Village* (New York, 1973); Joseph Lopreato, *Peasants No More: Social Class and Social Change in an Underdeveloped Society* (San Francisco, Calif., 1967); and Sydel Silverman, *Three Bells of Civilization: The Life of an Italian Hill Town* (New York, 1975). For France see Laurence William Wylie, *Village in the Vaucluse* (Cambridge, Mass., 1957), and Evelyn Bernette Ackerman, *Village on the Seine: Tradition and Change in Bonnières, 1815–1914* (Ithaca, N.Y., 1978). For Mexico, Oscar Lewis's works are very evocative in showing the effects of migration from villages to towns and cities. See especially *Five Families: Mexican Case Studies in the Culture of Poverty* (New York, 1959).

Chapter 3

1. Many scholars have portrayed Argentina as a true melting pot of ethnic groups. The historian José Luis Romero, for example, labeled Argentina a hybrid society (*Argentina: imágenes y perspectivas*; Buenos Aires, 1956), and the sociologist Gino Germani referred to the fusion and amalgamation of populations (*Política y sociedad en una época de transición de la sociedad tradicional a la sociedad de las masas*; Buenos Aires, 1962). Certainly the opportunities for assimilation existed. Spanish and even Italian immigrants found a language similar to their own. Many immigrants shared a similar Catholic culture with the native Argentines, and others found a policy of religious toleration. There seemed to be little open ani-

mosity between nationalities, and observers assumed that intermarriage was taking place, especially in the cities. Recent research, however, and especially the work done on marriage patterns in urban areas, makes the melting pot theory somewhat questionable. Argentina's massive immigration has been cited as responsible for a lack of national consensus. It has been shown that many immigrant groups remained apart, intermarrying neither with other nationalities nor with "natives." From the beginning, the government exerted no pressure on foreigners to become Argentine citizens, and many did not. Moreover, since the Argentine elites often preferred European manners and values, immigrants in Argentina encountered less pressure than, for example, their counterparts in the United States to conform to the host society and to assimilate. In addition, immigrants in Argentina, though fewer than in the United States, represented a much larger percentage of the total population.

On immigrant assimilation see Samuel L. Baily, "Marriage Patterns and Immigrant Assimilation in Buenos Aires, 1882–1923," *Hispanic American Historical Review* 60 (Feb. 1980), 32–48, and Mark D. Szuchman, "The Limits of the Melting Pot in Urban Argentina: Marriage and Integration in Córdoba, 1869–1909," *Hispanic American Historical Review* 57 (Feb. 1977), 24–40, and *Mobility and Integration in Urban Argentina, Córdoba in the Liberal Era* (Austin, Tex., 1980). On value differences between immigrants and natives, see Kristin Ruggiero, "Gringo and Creole: Foreign and Native Values in a Rural Argentine Community," *Journal of Interamerican Studies and World Affairs* 24(2) (May 1982), 163–82. See also note 3 of Chapter 5 below, on intermarriage in San Sebastiano.

Much Argentine fiction reflects the importance of immigration in Argentina and the confrontation of cultures there. Analyses of this literature can be found in Gladys S. Onega, *La inmigración en la literatura argentina, 1880–1910* (Buenos Aires, 1968); Germán García, *El inmigrante en la novela argentina* (Buenos Aires, 1970); Luciano Rusich, *El inmigrante italiano en la novela del 80* (Madrid, 1974); Myron I. Lichtblau, *The Argentine Novel in the Nineteenth Century* (New York, 1959); and Evelyn Fishburn, *The Portrayal of Immigration in Nineteenth-Century Argentine Fiction (1845–1902)* (Berlin, 1981). For interesting and careful analyses of Argentine society that contribute to an understanding of gringos and creoles and of the influences on each, see Gino Germani, *Estructura social de la Argentina* (Buenos Aires, 1955), and *Política y sociedad en una época de transición de la sociedad de las masas* (Buenos Aires, 1962); Julio Mafud, *Psicología de la viveza criolla* (Buenos Aires, 1965); A. J. Pérez Amuchástegui, *Mentalidades argentinas: 1860–1930*, 3d ed. (Buenos Aires, 1972); and Ezequiel Martínez Estrada, *X-Ray of the Pampa* (English trans., Austin, Tex., 1971; original Spanish ed., Buenos Aires, 1933).

2. Argentina has undergone two "deperonizations," both accompanied

by a full-scale, ruthless destruction of all materials that referred to the Peróns—posters, signs, books. Newspaper collections such as the Prochets' were therefore a source of proscribed literature. Juan Domingo Perón, first elected president in 1946, is perhaps best known to people in the United States for his all-too-obvious support of the Axis powers in World War II, and through his wife and political ally Evita, Eva Duarte de Perón. Perón's career is treated in Richard Gillespie, *Soldiers of Perón: Argentina's Montoneros* (Oxford, 1982); Frederick C. Turner and José Enrique Miguens, eds., *Juan Perón and the Reshaping of Argentina* (Pittsburgh, Penn., 1983); and Robert J. Alexander, *Juan Domingo Perón: A History* (Boulder, Colo., 1979). On Perón's popularity see note 3 below.

The first "deperonization" occurred after Perón's overthrow by the military in 1955. During his eighteen-year exile, a succession of presidents, mainly military, tried to destroy the popularity of the Peronist movement. Cities and provinces that had been renamed after the Peróns had their original names restored, and monuments were torn down. Some aspects of the Peróns' lives, such as Eva's lavish wardrobe and Juan's collection of cars and motorcycles, were preserved and put on public exhibit in order to discredit Peronism. To little avail, however. Perón was called back to Argentina and elected president again in 1973; he died soon after, in 1974, and his third wife, Isabel (Eva had died in 1952), who was vice president, became president. Isabel did not have Eva's charisma or political savvy—moreover, the 1970's were very different times from the late 1940's and early 1950's—and she was overthrown by a military coup in March 1976. Thus began the second "deperonization"; almost overnight all traces of the three Peróns disappeared.

3. The attempts by the Peróns' enemies to wipe out the memory of Peronism are understandable when one considers the movement's popularity. Under Perón, workers who formerly had had little role in an oligarchic political system became closely courted, Perón's "descamisados" or "shirtless ones." Perón's government in the 1940's and 1950's may not have been democratic, but it seemed, at least initially, to offer workers benefits and rights they had not had before. On Perón's relationship to labor see David Collier, "Overview of the Bureaucratic-Authoritarian Model," in Collier, ed., *The New Authoritarianism in Latin America* (Princeton, N.J., 1979), pp. 23–25, and Samuel L. Baily, *Labor, Nationalism, and Politics in Argentina* (New Brunswick, N.J., 1967).

In the countryside, peons employed full-time benefited to an extent from laws establishing a minimum wage, a paid vacation, one day of rest a week, and other benefits. Other laws improved conditions for day laborers and established minimum conditions for renters. Ten specific workers' rights were guaranteed by the Peronist constitution of 1949, which replaced Argentina's 1853 constitution. (The country returned to the 1853 constitution after Perón's exile in 1955.) However, economic crises and Perón's attempts to destroy the autonomy of the labor movement brought reversals for workers in the 1950's. See Alexander, *Perón: A History*, pp. 68–69. Eva Perón's popularity with the masses did a great deal to solidify Juan's position with the working class, and many of them regarded her as a saint. Other sectors of society, however, saw her as Juan's evil accomplice. On the controversy surrounding Evita see Julie M. Taylor, *Eva Perón: The Myths of a Woman* (Chicago, 1979). For a good analysis of her life see Nicholas Fraser and Marysa Navarro, *Eva Perón* (New York, 1980). For an overview of the literature see Alberto Ciria, "Flesh and Fantasy: The Many Faces of Evita (and Juan Perón)," *Latin American Research Review* 18(2) (1983), 150–65.

Peronism has survived the attempts to eliminate it; in the 1983 election the two major contending parties were the Peronists and the Radicals (Unión Cívica Radical), and it was a surprise to many that Raúl Alfonsín of the Radicals won. The Peronist party is still strong, and exerts a good deal of pressure on the Alfonsín government.

4. Anonymous denunciations have had a part in Argentine life since the days of Perón and before. Under the military junta that ruled between 1976 and 1983, requests were made regularly on the radio for denunciations of anyone acting suspiciously, even neighbors, friends, and family. It is quite possible that during Perón's time peons may have denounced their employers. It was probably not a common occurrence, however, and hardly qualifies as an adequate excuse for feeding and housing all peons poorly. Much more likely reasons are the economic crisis, the desire to save money, and the traditional disregard for peon laborers.

5. Detailed information on the characteristics of the main types of housing in San Sebastiano is given in the accompanying tables. I compiled the information from the manuscript census for 1980, which was kindly given to me by an official in the national census office in Buenos Aires, without the names of the censused population. There are three main categories of housing: casas, viviendas precarias, and ranchos. Viviendas precarias share some features of both casas and ranchos: for example, they generally have walls of masonry and metal plate roofs like casas, but half have earth floors like ranchos. "Vivienda precaria" is a category used by the census office, however, and in everyday speech people describe all lower-class dwellings, ranchos and viviendas precarias alike, simply as "ranchos." Thus, in the text I have grouped together the 98 ranchos and 47 viviendas precarias in San Sebastiano, a total of 145 lower-class dwellings.

Some of the differences between lower-class dwellings and middle- and upper-class dwellings are touched on later in the text: though the dwellings share certain disadvantages (from the perspective of a city dweller at least), the differences are quite marked, especially in terms of crowding (see table A) and building materials and facilities (see table D). In addition, a correlation

A. *Living Arrangements in San Sebastiano, by House Type, 1980*

| | | Vivienda | Casa | | |
Category	Rancho	precaria	Village	Colony	Total
Number of dwellings	98	47	73	28	101
Number of residents	469	229	356	127	483
Persons per dwelling	4.8	4.9	4.9	4.5	4.8
Rooms per dwelling	1.6	2.1	3.2	4.2	3.5
Persons per room	3.0	2.4	1.5	1.1	1.4

B. *Population of San Sebastiano, by Age Group and House Type, 1980*

| | Age group | | | |
Inhabitants	0–13	14–24	25–49	50±
In ranchos				
Number	209	69	107	84
As percent of rancho				
population	44.5%	14.7%	22.8%	17.9%
As percent of total				
population	17.7%	5.8%	9.1%	7.1%
In viviendas precarias				
Number	92	40	63	34
As percent of viv. prec.				
population	40.2%	17.5%	27.5%	14.8%
As percent of total				
population	7.8%	3.4%	5.3%	2.9%
In casas				
Number	146	102	120	115
As percent of casa				
population	30.2%	21.1%	24.8%	23.8%
As percent of total				
population	12.4%	8.6%	10.2%	9.7%

C. *Population Aged 0–13 in San Sebastiano,*
by Sex and House Type, 1980

| | Population aged 0–13 | | | | |
| | | | Total | | Percent of total |
Dwelling	Male	Female	Number	Percent	population
Rancho	106	103	209	46.6%	17.7%
Vivienda precaria	44	48	92	20.4%	7.8%
Casa	85	61	146	32.4%	12.4%
Other	1	2	3	0.7%	0.3%
TOTAL	236	214	450	100.0%	38.2%

NOTE: The figures in tables A–D are from the Dirección Nacional Estadística y Censo, "Censo nacional de población y vivienda" (Buenos Aires, 1980); see my note 5. Five dwellings that did not fit any of the three main categories have been omitted from all but table C.

D. Characteristics of Dwellings in San Sebastiano, 1980

Category	Rancho (N = 98)	Vivienda precaria (N = 47)	Casa (N = 101)
	BUILDING MATERIALS		
Walls			
Adobe	62	3	3
Masonry	8	42	91
Wood	2	0	2
Other/unknown	26	2	5
Roofs			
Straw	80	0	0
Metal plate	13	31	89
Cement	1	1	5
Other/unknown	4	15	7
Floors			
Earth	87	22	6
Cement or brick	4	21	52
Mosaic	0	2	39
Other/unknown	7	2	4
	AGE		
Years			
0–5	35	21	17
6–10	17	9	12
11–20	26	8	16
21–50	12	4	28
>50	3	4	24
Unknown	5	1	4
	OCCUPANCY		
Residence is:			
Owned	47	25	72
Free	39	17	18
Rented	2	2	5
Other/unknown	10	3	6
	FACILITIES		
Toilet			
Indoor	0	0	53
Outhouse	59	34	38
None	32	9	4
Other/unknown	7	4	6
Bathing			
Hot and cold water	0	2	23
Cold water only	0	0	30
None	87	41	44
Other/unknown	11	4	4
Drinking water			
Inside dwelling	1	3	60
Private well outside dwelling	45	20	18
Public pump	43	15	5
Other/unknown	9	9	18
Cooking			
Bottled gas	12	13	59
Public gas	0	1	1
Wood fire	82	0	0
Other/unknown	4	33	41
Electricity			
Public	8	15	72
None	86	30	25
Other/unknown	4	2	4

of age group and house type in tables B and C shows a greater number of children aged 13 and under in lower-class housing.

The rancho was the standard type of housing for colonists and peons alike in the early days of the colony. The 1895 census described ranchos as huts built with inclined roofs of tile or straw and walls of saplings or cane filled in with mud and straw (Argentine Republic, Comisión Directiva del Censo, *Segundo censo de la República Argentina, mayo 10 de 1895*; Buenos Aires, 1898, vol. 3, p. x). Waldenses knew even before they left Italy that this was the type of housing they could expect to have in Argentina. According to an advertisement in a local Piedmontese newspaper (*Avvisatore Alpino*, Sept. 11, 1891, in reference to Concordia), ranchos could be built quickly and inexpensively. Argentina's Rural Society estimated the cost of a rancho to be 80 pesos in 1890; it stated that on small rural properties the cost of a house represented one-quarter to one-third of a colonist's total expenses, and that the cost of farm buildings was two-thirds to three-quarters of the total (Sociedad Rural, *Argentina, Buenos Aires, Anales . . . 1890*; Buenos Aires, 1891, pp. 421–23).

In 1895, housing in San Sebastiano consisted of 88 ranchos, 3 viviendas precarias, and 13 casas of brick. The rest of the rural area of the Department of La Paz resembled San Sebastiano: there were 2,061 ranchos, 44 viviendas precarias, and 87 casas of brick. The housing for the town of La Paz was considerably better: 23 ranchos, 87 viviendas precarias, and 118 casas of brick. (Archivo General de la Nación, Buenos Aires, 1895 manuscript census for the department of La Paz in the province of Entre Ríos, carpetas 1057, 1058, 1060.)

6. José Hernández's poem, published in 1872, is available in translation as *The Gaucho Martín Fierro* (Albany, N.Y., 1974). There is ample evidence that prejudice toward peons and creoles is widespread in Argentina. Particularly intriguing is George Reid Andrews's account, *The Afro-Argentines of Buenos Aires, 1800–1900* (Madison, Wisc., 1980). Andrews analyzes the Argentine elite's attitude toward the so-called inferior races. For example, Domingo Sarmiento (Argentine president, 1868–74) believed that European immigration "would correct the indigenous blood with new ideas ending [Argentina's] medievalism," and Juan Bautista Alberdi (nineteenth-century political philosopher and diplomat) was convinced that though you might "put the bum, the gaucho, the peasant, the basic element of our population, through all the transformations of the best systems of education, in one hundred years you won't make of him an English worker" (Andrews, pp. 103–4). Andrews also discusses the prejudice against the "cabecitas negras" (literally little black heads), migrants to Buenos Aires from the interior of Argentina who were of racially mixed ancestry (pp. 209–10). Especially interesting for our purposes are Andrews's discussions of current racial prejudice in Argentina (pp. 214–15) and the country's continued pride in being a European, "white" nation (p. 107).

A. J. Pérez Amuchástegui discusses Argentine attitudes toward the "inferior classes" in his *Mentalidades argentinas, 1860–1930*, 3d ed. (Buenos Aires, 1970). He documents at length the disrespect shown the gaucho, the creole, and the peon, adding that it was still observable in 1964, "especially in the provinces where the relationship between patron and employee is that of important person to insignificant individual" (p. 16). For related material from the colonial period, see Emiliano Endrek, *El mestizaje en Córdoba: siglo XVIII y principios del XIX* (Córdoba, 1966).

7. On Jewish settlement in Argentina, see Judith Laikin Elkin, *Jews of the Latin American Republics* (Chapel Hill, N.C., 1980); Eugene Sofer, *From Pale to Pampa: A Social History of the Jews of Buenos Aires* (New York, 1982); and Morton D. Winsberg, *Colonia Baron Hirsch: A Jewish Agricultural Colony in Argentina* (Gainesville, Fla., 1964).

8. The Waldenses have had a long history of challenging authorities they deem unjust, beginning in the twelfth century when they held to the belief that laymen should be able to read the Bible and preach. In defiance of the Catholic church, they questioned the importance of priests as intermediaries between man and God, and even the sacraments and saints and concepts like purgatory. They joined the Protestant movement during the Reformation. In World War II, Waldenses were an important part of the Italian Resistance in Piedmont against the Italian Fascists and the German Nazis. On Waldenses as heretics see Euan Cameron, *The Reformation of the Bible Heretics: The Waldenses of the Alps, 1480–1580* (Oxford, 1984), and on their Resistance activities see Donatella Gay Rochat, *La Resistenza nelle Valli Valdesi (1943–44)* (Turin, 1969).

In Argentina and Uruguay, Waldenses took a pro-human-rights (thus an anti-military) stance, and though they were not actively revolutionary, their social welfare activities made them suspect in the eyes of the military.

9. The anti-Semitic aspects of the military regime have attracted particular attention thanks to Jacobo Timerman's *Prisoner Without a Name, Cell Without a Number* (New York, 1981). Timerman's experiences were confirmed for me by Jews I knew in Buenos Aires, people who did not have the visibility Timerman had as a newspaper editor, and thus may have been less vulnerable, but who nevertheless were afraid that their Jewishness alone was reason enough for them to be picked up by the police.

10. The period of military rule in the late 1970's and early 1980's saw an interruption of important changes that had been developing within the Argentine church for over a decade. Since the 1960's a growing number of clergy and laymen in Argentina, and in Latin America in general, have come to view the church's concerns as going beyond personal sin and reform to encompass the sins and reform of society as a whole. Two events within the church during the papacies of John XXIII and Paul VI in the 1960's both reflected this new orientation and helped stimulate it: the Second Vatican Council (1963–65) and the Latin American Bishops' Conference at Medellín (1968). Progressive-thinking worker-priests were active in Argentina

even before the Conference and officially launched the Third World Priests Movement in 1967.

The 1960's were therefore a time of change for the church, a time when many espoused the belief that good Christians must become actively involved in righting the wrongs in society. Since the 1960's class struggle has become a concern of many clergymen preaching "liberation theology," that is, liberation of people from poverty, oppression, illiteracy, injustice, and exploitation. Catholic *comunidades de base*, grass-roots communities, have been organized in many towns, villages, and urban barrios where people are encouraged to read and interpret the Bible for themselves and to apply its principles toward improving their situation in life. Current development ideologies, capitalism, and domination of the Third World by the West have come under strong attack from these sectors, and it is pointed out that institutionalized violence against the people by the powerful is as bad as or even worse than the violence of the oppressed. The progressive arm of the Catholic church continues to be a dynamic force, but there was a counter-movement against it in the 1970's, due in no small part to the growing importance and conservatism of authoritarian military regimes in Latin America. On the subject of the church and the state in Latin America, see José Comblin, *The Church and the National Security State* (Maryknoll, N.Y., 1979); Daniel H. Levine, ed., *Churches and Politics in Latin America* (Beverly Hills, Calif., 1979); Brian H. Smith, *The Church and Politics in Chile: Challenges to Modern Catholicism* (Princeton, N.J., 1982); Thomas C. Bruneau, *The Church in Brazil: The Politics of Religion* (Austin, Tex., 1982); and Scott Mainwaring, *The Catholic Church and Politics in Brazil, 1916–1985* (Stanford, Calif., 1986).

11. High school textbooks reflected an authoritarian military and conservative Catholic hierarchy, which to a great extent is opposed to the new progressive segment of the church. The military junta aligned itself to the Catholic church for reasons of political strategy: by doing so, it hoped to legitimate its regime and make its ideology acceptable to the people. The military, in textbooks and elsewhere, strove to link people's beliefs in Catholicism and the family to the principles of national-security ideology, stressing that support of the military government was necessary for the survival of traditional values. Textbooks therefore reflected traditional Catholic views on relations between the sexes, marriage, birth control, and abortion, as well as the military's opposition to the questioning of authority, subversion, and Marxism. The non-traditional, "new" church, described in the previous note, was of course anathema to military regimes, whose interests were scarcely served by the development of a public consciousness of society's ills.

12. The promotion of the cult of the Virgin Mary also reflects the more conservative views of the Church toward women, reinforcing woman's traditional role as mother and wife whose honor must be upheld, and the role of the family as the basis of society. These are also the values of the military.

In "Women in Contemporary Argentina," *Latin American Perspectives*, issue 15, 4(4) (Fall 1977), 114–20, Ana María Marini talks of the government's "ideological campaign to redefine the role of women in Argentine society." She describes the campaign as part of a broad ideological attack on Marxism, intended to undermine Marxism's appeal to workers by stressing its consequences for the family. An altogether different version of motherhood and family from that of the military was displayed during the regime by the Mothers of the Plaza de Mayo, who marched each week in front of the presidential palace in Buenos Aires to protest on behalf of the "desaparecidos" (the disappeared).

13. The place of honor in society has been well analyzed in two works on Europe: Rudolph M. Bell, *Fate and Honor, Family and Village: Demographic and Cultural Change in Rural Italy Since 1800* (Chicago, 1979), and Jean G. Peristiany, ed., *Honor and Shame: The Values of Mediterranean Society* (Chicago, 1966).

14. See Glen Caudill Dealy, *The Public Man: An Interpretation of Latin American and Other Catholic Countries* (Amherst, Mass., 1977), for an instructive comparison of the methods people use to achieve honor in "public man" society and in capitalist society.

15. For an interesting essay on this phenomenon of informal adoption of children in Brazil, see Ruth C. L. Cardoso, "Creating Kinship: The Fostering of Children in *Favela* Families in Brazil," in Raymond T. Smith, ed., *Kinship Ideology and Practice in Latin America* (Chapel Hill, N.C., 1984), pp. 196–203. See also Hugo G. Nutini and Betty Bell, *Ritual Kinship: The Structure and Historical Development of the Compadrazgo System in Rural Tlaxcala*, 2 vols. (Princeton, N.J., 1980). On the importance of kinship for the more elite entrepreneurial and political level of society, see Diana Balmori et al., *Notable Family Networks in Latin America* (Chicago, 1984), and Linda Lewin, "Some Historical Implications of Kinship Organization for Family-Based Politics in the Brazilian Northeast," *Comparative Studies in Society and History* 21 (1979), 262–92. Much of Oscar Lewis's work shows the daily workings of kinship systems; see, for example, *Five Families: Mexican Case Studies in the Culture of Poverty* (New York, 1959).

16. The following tabulation indicates the civil status of the 1980 San Sebastiano population aged 14 and older, and the types of unions that couples had chosen (the data are from Dirección Nacional Estadística y Censo, "Censo nacional de población y vivienda"; Buenos Aires, 1980):

Status	Male	Female	Total	Percent
Married	133	128	261	34.7%
Common law	58	64	122	16.2
Separated	5	5	10	1.3
Widowed	8	30	38	5.1
Single	182	139	321	42.7
TOTAL	386	366	752	100.0%

Common-law unions are found mainly among the lower-class creole population. Since divorce is allowed in Argentina only in unusual cases such as non-consummation of the marriage, separation is effectively the only option; thus the very few divorced people fall within the category of "separated." For a discussion of consensual unions in Peru, see Susan Bourque and Kay Warren, *Women of the Andes: Patriarchy and Social Change in Two Peruvian Towns* (Ann Arbor, Mich., 1981), especially pp. 98–103.

Chapter 4

1. General Juan Carlos Onganía became president of Argentina in 1966 after military intervention. He initiated what he called the Argentine Revolution, a program designed to revive Argentina economically and socially and then return it to the electoral system. Economically, it meant favoring large industry and finance associated with foreign capital. Socially and politically, it meant dissolving congress, provincial legislatures, and political parties, imposing censorship, and crushing the autonomy of the major universities—many student protestors were beaten and killed, and faculty fled the country. The result was widespread disaffection and radicalization, manifested for example in the activities of the Montoneros guerrilla group. The situation approached crisis proportions in May 1969 when a protest by a united student and worker body turned into near insurrection in Córdoba. The incident became known as the Cordobazo. Onganía was removed by the military and replaced by Roberto M. Levingston in 1970. See Richard Gillespie, *Soldiers of Perón: Argentina's Montoneros* (Oxford, 1982), pp. 60–66, and James R. Scobie, *Argentina: A City and a Nation*, 2d ed. (New York, 1971), pp. 227–30.

2. The Federal Police had an infamous reputation under the military regimes of the 1970's and 1980's. See Jacobo Timerman, *Prisoner Without a Name, Cell Without a Number* (New York, 1981), and Andrew Graham-Yooll, *A Matter of Fear: Portrait of an Argentinian Exile* (Westport, Conn., 1982). See also Elvira Orphée, *El Angel's Last Conquest* (New York, 1985), an Argentine's fictional account of a torturer.

3. The military has been reasserting its power in Latin America since the 1960's; the number of military governments has increased, and many have had cruel reputations for ignoring human rights on a massive scale. Onganía's regime of 1966–70 is only one example; the Argentine military again controlled the government from 1976 until elections were finally held in 1983 and Raúl Alfonsín, refreshingly a lawyer by profession, was elected president. In Brazil, the elected government of João Goulart was overturned by the military in 1964. The Chilean government of Salvador Allende Gossens suffered the same fate in 1973, and the country was still laboring under the oppression of Augusto Pinochet Ugarte's regime in 1987. Brazil, however, began moving toward constitutional government in 1984–85, and Uruguay, after eleven years of military rule, held elections in the fall of 1984.

In Argentina, the war against the "subversives," known as the Dirty War, was a systematic, wholesale attempt to wipe out all opposition to the military junta running the country. Groups like the Montoneros were essentially eliminated—victims of the military and the police or exile. The military government continued its campaign, however, against people like Annina Pascal, whose experience is recounted later in this chapter—against innocent acquaintances of people under suspicion, people whose names might have appeared in someone's address book, or people who might have once been seen talking with a person suspected by the police or military. The contrast between the number of actual active "subversives," as perceived by the military when they took over the government in 1976, and the number of ordinary citizens who suffered imprisonment, torture, and often death is frightening. At its peak in the mid-1970's, Montonero armed opposition to the government, for example, numbered only 5,000 to 10,000 persons (the range of figures is explained by Gillespie, *Soldiers of Perón*, p. 178, n. 46). It is estimated that the Montoneros, together with the other important opposition group, the Ejército Revolucionario del Pueblo (ERP) or People's Revolutionary Army, killed perhaps 2,000 people between the late 1960's and mid-1978. However, as a result of the government's response, the Dirty War, some 20,000 to 30,000 persons "disappeared" in Argentina: children and pregnant women, clergy, workers, students, professionals, teachers, journalists, abducted and tortured in secret detention centers, many then killed and buried in unmarked graves or dropped from planes over the La Plata River. A government campaign that was begun supposedly to wipe out subversion became a sadistic war against its citizens. (See *Nunca Más, the Report of the Argentine Commission on the Disappeared*; New York, 1986.)

As the economic crisis of the early 1980's intensified, the junta entered into a war with Britain in the spring of 1982 over sovereignty of the Malvinas (Falkland) Islands. The war was fought to regain prestige for the military and to distract the population from the economic crisis. The Malvinas issue is one of the few that unite Argentines, and a victory would have given them reason to feel proud of their country, to have faith that the military was capable of something other than warfare against its own citizens, and to forget about their personal financial situation.

Argentina was defeated, however, and the military junta had to succumb to pressure for a civilian government. Quite simply, the military had failed in the civilian duties it assumed and had failed in its own area of military expertise. The transfer of power was a delicate operation because the military feared prosecution for its actions during the Dirty War. It issued reports justifying its use of repression and torture, and voted itself amnesty. But under the Alfonsín government, the amnesty was cancelled and junta leaders did in fact come to trial—and were sentenced, two of them to life imprisonment (see n. 5 below).

Military governments such as Argentina's are a new breed in Latin America, especially in the Southern Cone; they have been termed "bureaucratic-authoritarian" governments by social scientists. They are non-democratic and, unlike Perón's populist government, which sought to include labor and other sectors of society, they are exclusive. The dominant forces in these governments are high-level technocrats, military and civilian, whose policies are geared toward industrialization and toward eliminating all political competition. These governments operate from the conviction that civilian politicians, political parties, labor unions, and liberal democratic institutions in general are responsible for Latin America's underdevelopment, and that the only means of achieving modernization, economic development, and political stability is long-term military rule; thus they are openly anti-political. Such military regimes should be distinguished from earlier military regimes, in which a single individual (rather than the military as an institution) took control, or in which the military staged a coup with the intention of retiring to the barracks once a new government was installed. In contrast, bureaucratic-authoritarian governments are run by a junta representing the military as an institution and foresee a long tenure in office until dissent, both violent and non-violent, is eliminated and economic stability is reached.

These governments subscribe to a doctrine of "national security" that justifies the waging of constant warfare against their own citizens. This doctrine necessarily curtails or eliminates people's most basic human rights, allowing illegal searches, arrests, detainment without charges, and censorship and prosecution of any criticism. Governments subscribing to the doctrine encourage people to be apathetic, uninvolved, and conservative; they institute policies that make it difficult or impossible for people to mobilize; and they demand that people be loyal to the state, that is, the military, above all else. Anti-military sentiment is considered unpatriotic and thus subversive.

When Argentina's military handed the government over to civilians in 1983, a return to democracy was heralded. A return it was, but many scholars agree that the pattern that has emerged for the Southern Cone is one of continuous cycles of military governments followed by civilian ones.

On military regimes in the Southern Cone see César Caviedes, *The Southern Cone: Realities of the Authoritarian State in South America* (Totowa, N.J., 1984). On the new bureaucratic-authoritarian governments see David Collier, ed., *The New Authoritarianism in Latin America* (Princeton, N.J., 1979), and José Comblin, *The Church and the National Security State* (Maryknoll, N.Y., 1979). On the antipolitical nature of the military see Brian Loveman and Thomas M. Davies, Jr., eds., *The Politics of Antipolitics: The Military in Latin America* (Lincoln, Nebr., 1978). On human rights under these governments see *Nunca Más*; Amnesty International's reports; and "Argentina Today: A Reign of Terror" (from a report made to the

Latin American Studies Association), *Latin American Perspectives,* issue 8, 3(1) (Winter 1976), 157–68.

   4. Had there been any political arrests in San Sebastiano, they would not have been included in Hernán García's crime report, since most of the time the military was careful to leave no trace of its arrests and actions. But in fact there were no such arrests in San Sebastiano, and they would in any case have been difficult to conceal from the community.

   The peace-keeping tasks of Hernán García recall the early colony, when thefts and brawls, and sometimes more violent physical acts, were the most common crimes. In a case in 1895, a farmer was reluctant to comply with a request from the La Paz Commission on Bridges and Roads to widen the gates onto his land. He pointed out that doing so would only encourage thieves from Yeso to invade his land and steal his cattle and sheep. (Archivo Histórico de la Provincia de Entre Ríos, Paraná, División Gobierno, serie XV, carpeta 8, legajo Dec. 1895, letter to the president of the Comisión de Puentes y Caminos in La Paz.)

   Other crimes were of a more violent nature. Few runs of crime statistics have been preserved for the Department of La Paz, but one list is available for the period February 1, 1889, to May 22, 1890. Of the seven crimes reported there, all were murders (ibid., serie XII, letra "I," carpeta 2, legajo 13, La Paz, May 22, 1890). At least one of them involved a potential San Sebastiano colonist. He was one of four colonists traveling to San Sebastiano together from Baradero, part of the first group to settle in the colony. On the day of his arrival he disappeared and the police could find no trace of him. Ten days later his body was found in a stream. Officials assumed that the motive for the murder was robbery since he had been carrying 240 pesos, about a year's salary for a peon. (Ibid., legajo 12, letter from La Paz, July 15, 1889, to Ministro General de Gobierno, Paraná.)

   5. President Roberto Viola headed Argentina's military junta from March to December 1981. In 1985 he was sentenced to seventeen years imprisonment for his part in the Dirty War. His predecessors, Jorge Rafael Videla (1976–81) and Eduardo Emilio Massera (1976–79) were sentenced to life imprisonment. Viola was succeeded as head of the junta by Leopoldo Fortunato Galtieri (Dec. 1981–June 1982), whose successor was Reynaldo Benito Antonio Bignone (1982–83).

   6. Several of the agents used to induce abortions in San Sebastiano have long histories stretching back at least as far as the Middle Ages. See, for example, B. F. Musallam, *Sex and Society in Islam: Birth Control Before the Nineteenth Century* (Cambridge, 1983), which discusses the use of savin, rue, and parsley.

   7. The passage in question was from the textbook *Formación moral y cívica 3,* by Angela E. Luchenio (Buenos Aires, 1981), pp. 55–56.

   8. The statistics are from the provincial Public Health Office in Paraná.

9. The statistics are from the 9 de Julio Hospital files.

10. People describe the death of a baby in this way—as a sacrifice to God—perhaps because it gives meaning to something that seems to have no meaning. See Richard W. Slatta, *Gauchos and the Vanishing Frontier* (Lincoln, Nebr., 1983), pp. 80–81.

11. According to the provincial Public Health Office in Paraná, there were 1,325 live births in the department of La Paz in 1970 and 1,818 in 1980. The infant mortality rates per 1,000 live births were as follows:

	1970	1980
0–28 days	26.4	11.0
28–365 days	41.6	22.0
0–365 days	68.8	33.0

Infant mortality has declined as a result of the expanded services of the 9 de Julio Hospital, and public health campaigns that have increased people's awareness about health and sanitation. The decline may seem more dramatic than it really is, however, since many births and deaths, like that of Pedro and Filipa's child, go unreported.

According to the 9 de Julio Hospital files, the most common children's diseases in 1980 were (1) diarrhea, with 1,045 cases, (2) grippe, with 817 cases, (3) respiratory diseases, with 680 cases, (4) intestinal parasites, with 282 cases, (5) whooping cough, with 87 cases, (6) pneumonia, with 69 cases, and (7) scabies, with 60 cases. The hospital considered the leading adult diseases to be cardiovascular disease, cancer (uterine in women and gastrointestinal in men), and tuberculosis (a distant third). The three main causes of death in Entre Ríos and in the nation are cardiovascular disease, cancer, and accidents.

12. Chagas-Mazza disease, also known as Chagas' disease, a form of trypanosomiasis, is widespread in Central and South America, and is caused by the Trypanosoma cruzi, a microscopic parasite. It was named after two doctors, Carlos Chagas, a Brazilian, and Salvador Mazza, an Argentine. It is transmitted by various types of biting bug: one type establishes itself in henhouses, corrals, and so forth, and feeds on domestic animals; another lives with humans and feeds on their blood. The disease occurs in an acute and a chronic form. The acute form, which is most common in children, almost always affects the heart, and the prognosis is poor. The chronic form is most common in adolescents and young adults, and the prognosis depends on the extent to which the heart is involved. There is no effective drug treatment. The acute disease is characterized by fever, edema, skin eruptions, lymph node enlargement, and occasionally inflammation of the brain and its membranes. The chronic disease manifests itself in cardiomyopatry with heart failure, an enlarged esophagus, and megacolon. This description is based on "Enfermedad de Chagas-Mazza," *Educación para la salud*, series 2, no. 9 (1977), issued by the National Public Health Office

in Buenos Aires, Ministerio de Bienestar Social, Secretaría de Estado de Salud Pública.

13. Project EMER (Expansion and Improvement of Rural Education), report, Paraná 1977.

14. Again, the textbook is Luchenio, *Formación moral*; chapter 13 treats morality and the family. General Videla defined a terrorist as "not just someone with a gun or a bomb but also someone who spreads ideas that are contrary to Western and Christian civilization" (Gillespie, *Soldiers of Perón*, p. 229).

15. The military attached great importance to "correct thinking" in high schools and universities. According to General Acdel Eduardo Vilas, a member of the military junta, "It is necessary to destroy the sources which feed, form, and indoctrinate the subversive delinquent, and this source is in the universities and the secondary schools themselves" (quoted in Amnesty International, *Report of an Amnesty International Mission to Argentina, 6–15 November 1976*; London, 1977, p. 65). Universities were particularly subject to repressive measures under the military government. Students and faculty were beaten, imprisoned, killed, or forced into exile. In the area of the social sciences, the disciplines of psychology, sociology, anthropology, and political science were seriously restricted. The research and activities of these social scientists was seen as dangerous by the military, as was the social work of the Waldenses. In addition, a more general cultural repression of society as a whole resulted from the strict censorship of reading materials and ideas.

16. A European textbook might justifiably turn this around, since the Red Brigades, for example, one of Italy's terrorist organizations, reportedly used the Argentine Montoneros and Uruguayan Tupamaros as models. See Roberto P. Guimarães, "Understanding Support for Terrorism Through Survey Data: The Case of Argentina, 1973," in Frederick C. Turner and José Enrique Miguens, eds., *Juan Perón and the Reshaping of Argentina* (Pittsburgh, Penn., 1983), pp. 190, 201, 220 n35.

17. The Dirección Nacional Estadística y Censo, "Censo nacional de población y vivienda" (Buenos Aires, 1980), gives the following breakdown of San Sebastiano residents who had dropped out of primary school. The percentages are percentages of the total population in each age group (potentially making up a total censused population of 752 respondents aged 14 and older) who actually responded to the education questions on the census form.

Age group	14–24	25–34	35–44	45–54	55±
Percent drop-outs	41%	57%	55%	61%	61%

Seven percent of the people aged fourteen and older who had dropped out of primary school had not even completed the first grade. The census figures for the total group who dropped out, by last grade completed, are as follows:

grade 0	7%	grade 3	27%	grade 6	9%
grade 1	6%	grade 4	20%	TOTAL	100%
grade 2	17%	grade 5	14%		

A total of 150 people aged fourteen and older were illiterate. The census figures for the total group who were illiterate, by age group and by sex, are as follows:

Age group	14–24	25–34	35–44	45–54	55±	14±
Male	8%	13%	25%	24%	36%	100%
Female	7%	14%	18%	23%	38%	100%
Both sexes	8%	13%	21%	23%	37%	100%

The Waldenses have traditionally been a very literate, education-conscious people, and they carried this concern from Italy to their South American colonies. The colony of San Gustavo, for example, procured a teacher almost immediately and attempted to hold at least informal classes continuously. In 1916 a member of the Garnier family there provided land for a school building; see Elio Maggi-Pasquet, "La colonia San Gustavo," *Boletín de la Sociedad Sudamericana de Historia Valdense* 11(3) (Aug. 15, 1937), 87–97. Statistical reports in the Archivio Tavola Valdese (Torre Pellice, province of Turin) show that Waldenses in Uruguayan colonies, and presumably the other South American colonies as well, continued to subscribe to libraries and newspapers. Colonia Valdense in Uruguay, for example, listed 34 library subscriptions and 18 newspapers in circulation in 1883, and similar numbers for subsequent years.

In their high level of literacy, foreigners contrasted sharply with the native population. Of the population surveyed in the 1895 census for the department of La Paz (Archivo General de la Nación, Buenos Aires), 61 percent of foreigners aged ten and older were literate, compared with only 19 percent of the natives. But the census figures also suggest that literacy among immigrants was on the decline, since many literate immigrant adults in the department had illiterate children who did not attend school—whether because schools were lacking or because the children were needed for farm work in the campo. Of the immigrant families surveyed in the colony of San Sebastiano, however, of the 60 cases in which the literacy level of both immigrant parents and children is recorded, only 12 contained literate parents with illiterate children. The colony was atypical of the department as a whole in this respect. In 28 of the families, both parents and children were literate; in 13, both parents and children were illiterate; and in 7, the parents were illiterate and the children literate. I was unable to compare Waldensian children directly in any of these statistics since the 1895 La Paz census lists only one Waldensian family. Neither can a comparison be made using the 1914 census, because the manuscript copy of the census was not available.

18. Under Perón, universities were open to anyone with a secondary education. There remained, of course, the expenses of maintaining a residence away from home, transportation, books and supplies, and clothes, not to mention the loss of a potential income.

19. These telegrams are from a collection of telegrams given to the author by Radio La Paz.

Chapter 5

1. For an overview of the family and the household in Latin America, see Man Singh Das and Clinton J. Jesser, eds., *The Family in Latin America* (New Delhi, 1980). Donna J. Guy analyzes *patria potestad* in Argentina in "Lower-Class Families, Women, and the Law in Nineteenth-Century Argentina," *Journal of Family History* 10(3) (Fall 1985), 318–31. The work of Oscar Lewis shows in vivid and human fashion the nature of households and the working out of family relationships. For his work on Mexico see especially *Five Families: Mexican Case Studies in the Culture of Poverty* (New York, 1959); *The Children of Sánchez: Autobiography of a Mexican Family* (New York, 1961); *Pedro Martínez: A Mexican Peasant and His Family* (New York, 1964); and *A Death in the Sánchez Family* (New York, 1969). For Cuba see Oscar Lewis et al., *Living the Revolution: An Oral History of Contemporary Cuba*, 3 vols. (Urbana, Ill., 1977–78). June Nash supplies us with interesting information on behavior in family life for Bolivia in *We Eat the Mines and the Mines Eat Us: Dependency and Exploitation in Bolivian Tin Mines* (New York, 1979); see especially Chapter 3.

2. The manuscript census figures, from Dirección Nacional Estadística y Censo, "Censo nacional de población y vivienda" (Buenos Aires, 1980), are as follows:

Household	Number	Percent
Nuclear	106	47.5%
Multi-generational	75	33.6
Non-family	42	18.8

As defined by the census, nuclear family households contain a head, spouse, and children; a head, spouse, and no children; or a head, no spouse, and children. Multi-generational households contain three or more direct generations; two direct generations; or one generation plus other family members. Non-family households contain a head and non-family; a nuclear family and non-family; or an extended family and non-family. These figures exclude single-person households, the local hospital, and unoccupied houses.

Aggregated by house type, the households break down as follows:

Household	Rancho	Vivienda precaria	Casa
Nuclear	40	19	45
Multi-generational	34	18	23
Non-family	11	7	24

(In this case the nuclear households total 104 rather than 106 because an identification of house type was omitted from two of the relevant census responses.) The 42 "non-family" households contained a total of 64 non-family members, mostly males and of all age groups:

Age group	Male	Female	Total
0–13	14	4	18
14–24	17	5	22
25–49	17	1	18
50±	6	0	6

3. These household groupings might well have seemed unstable and impermanent to early Waldensian colonists. Judging from the 1895 census, it was not uncommon for native households to contain married men without their wives, with and without children; unmarried men and women, some with children; and numerous orphans or children in their early teens without parents. Such households contrasted markedly with the typical nuclear and extended family households of the immigrants. Moreover, all the reported illegitimate births in San Sebastiano occurred in the native population. Perhaps Waldenses judged native society immoral or at least perceived it as unstable and therefore unattractive. In any case, the infrequency of intermarriage between creoles and gringos is an established fact in San Sebastiano. The 1895 manuscript census for the department of La Paz (Archivo General de la Nación, Buenos Aires) recorded 38 marriages in San Sebastiano between persons of the same nationality; 4 between different nationalities (other than Argentine); and 2 foreign and native mixed. In 35 cases, the nationality of one marriage partner is not given. An early case of intermarriage between a Waldense (Luigi Baridon) and a creole in 1930 still causes talk in the community. The number of intermarriages has been increasing since the 1970's and seems to be eliciting less comment; Domenico and Lucia Antonini's marriage is one of these.

4. The figures are from the 1980 manuscript census. The rate of 28.0 per thousand total population breaks down by housing type as follows:

Birth rate per 1,000:	Rancho	Vivienda precaria	Casa
Within housing type	38.4	31.0	17.0
In total population	15.1	6.0	7.0

5. The 1980 manuscript census gives the following breakdown of adults living with their parents. The percentages are percentages of the total men or women in each age group:

Age group	Male	Female	Age group	Male	Female
20–24	70%	43%	30–34	28%	33%
25–29	23	27	35–39	26	11

6. Much of the television programming in Argentina in 1981 consisted of older U.S. films and U.S. television series; series on the American West such as "Bonanza," situation comedies and dramas, and police programs were especially popular. Argentine programming included news, cultural series, and films.

7. As for the elderly, of the 61 persons aged seventy and older in San Sebastiano, 11 lived alone, 12 in nuclear households, 26 in multi-generational households, and 12 in households containing non-family members. Again, the figures are from the 1980 manuscript census.

8. See table A on p. 189 above.

9. The emphasis on family over the individual has a long tradition in Latin America. For a discussion of this phenomenon see Glen Caudill Dealy, *The Public Man: An Interpretation of Latin American and Other Catholic Countries* (Amherst, Mass., 1977), and Claudio Veliz, *The Centralist Tradition of Latin America* (Princeton, N.J., 1980).

10. On women in Latin America in general, a good place to begin for an overview is Meri Knaster, *Women in Spanish America: An Annotated Bibliography from Pre-Conquest to Contemporary Times* (Boston, 1977). The items mentioned in note 1 of this chapter are also of interest for the subject of women.

Since the publication of Knaster's book, the field has expanded and the significant work that has appeared is too voluminous to detail here. Among the important works not cited elsewhere in the notes are Donna J. Guy, "Women, Peonage, and Industrialization: Argentina, 1810–1914," *Latin American Research Review* 16(3) (1981), 65–89; Sandra F. McGee, "The Visible and Invisible Liga Patriotica Argentina, 1919–1928: Gender Roles and the Right Wing," *Hispanic American Historical Review* 64(2) (May 1984), 233–58; and Susan Migden Socolow, "Women and Crime: Buenos Aires, 1757–1797," *Journal of Latin American Studies* 12 (1980), 39–54.

11. The concepts of "public" and "private," used to describe women's particular place in Latin American society, are discussed in several works. For an analysis of Argentine women's place in the work force, both in the public and private spheres, see Catalina H. Wainerman et al., "The Participation of Women in Economic Activity in Argentina, Bolivia, and Paraguay: A Comparative Study," *Latin American Research Review* 15(2) (1980), 143–51, and in the same issue, Ruth Santu, "The Female Labor Force in Argentina, Bolivia, and Paraguay," pp. 152–61. Ximena Bunster and Elsa M. Chaney, in *Sellers and Servants, Working Women in Lima, Peru* (New York, 1985), discuss working women, mothers, and children. Elsa M. Chaney, *Supermadre: Women in Politics in Latin America* (Austin,

Tex., 1979), discusses the image and reality of women's role in public life, particularly in political life.

Eva Perón, the politically powerful wife of Juan Perón, offered an example to Argentine women of a woman who transcended the traditional female sphere of activity, the private world of home and family, and entered the world of men, the public sphere. In essential ways, she dominated the public sphere, calling the nation her home, and its citizens her "children." Women's suffrage became part of the Peronist constitution of 1949, and Eva began a specifically female branch of the Peronist Party. Ana María Marini ("Women in Contemporary Argentina," *Latin American Perspectives*, issue 5, 4(4); Fall 1977, p. 116) raised an interesting point about the change in women's role under the military dictatorship in the 1970's. "Under Eva," she says, "women felt they could do anything. Now [in 1977] they are getting a different message," that women should be mothers and housewives and not aspire to careers. "Moreover, Isabel Perón's overthrow by the military in 1976 tended to be explained," says Marini, "as a female failure."

For an interesting essay on the public and private spheres of men and women in a small village in France, see Rayna R. Reiter, "Men and Women in the South of France: Public and Private Domains," in Rayna R. Reiter, ed., *Toward an Anthropology of Women* (New York, 1975), pp. 252–82.

12. See, in addition to Bell's and Peristiany's works on the concept of honor, cited in note 14 of Chapter 3, Reiter's *Toward an Anthropology of Women*.

13. According to the manuscript census of 1980, 30 San Sebastiano

TABLE FOR NOTE 13
Legitimate and Illegitimate Children in San Sebastiano,
by Mothers' Age Group, 1980

Mothers' age group	Legitimate children		Illegitimate children	
	Number of mothers	Avg. number of children	Number of mothers	Avg. number of children
14–19	4	2.0	6	1.2
20–24	14	3.3	2	2.2
25–29	23	3.3	6	3.0
30–34	15	5.0	4	4.0
35–39	29	5.0	2	6.0
40–44	11	6.0	3	5.0
45–49	20	6.0	2	4.0
50–54	19	7.0	1	3.0
55–59	17	6.0	2	5.0
60–64	21	7.0	0	0.0
65–69	17	7.0	0	0.0
70±	18	6.0	2	2.0

SOURCE: Dirección Nacional Estadística y Censo, "Censo nacional de población y vivienda" (Buenos Aires, 1980).

women were mothers of illegitimate children, compared with a total of 208 who were mothers of legitimate children. See the accompanying table for the average number of legitimate and illegitimate children per mother in the manuscript census's five-year age groups. These figures depend very much on the perception of legitimacy of the census taker and of the person being censused. In a solid, enduring common-law union, the children of that union would probably be considered legitimate. In less stable relationships or in single parent families, the children might be more likely to be considered illegitimate.

Glossary of Names

Women are listed under their husband's names for the sake of convenience and clarity. On the treatment of women's names in the text, see the note on p. 8. Unless otherwise indicated, all the persons listed here live or work in San Sebastiano.

Angelini, Teresa, postmistress.
Antonini, Domenico, estanciero.
 Lucia Prochet, his wife.
 Two daughters, one named Michela.
 Irene, his sister (girlfriend of Stefano Gilly).
 Juan, his peon.
Barea, Miriam de, woman from peon family.
Baridon, Alessandra, secretary in Howard and Guzmán's law office in La Paz.
Baridon, Carlos, old-timer.
Baridon, Claudia, high school student in La Paz and boarder at Elsa Martínez de Prochet's house, daughter of Fita Gilly de Baridon in San Sebastiano.
Baridon, Daniele, relative of Elsa Martínez de Prochet's.
Baridon, Edgar, and his wife María Cesan, members of the Hermanos Libres sect. They live in La Paz and have traveled in Europe.
Baridon, Enrique, old-timer, first Waldensian settler in San Sebastiano.
 Inés Charbonier, his wife.
 Carlos Baridon-Charbonier, his son.
 Luis, Tomás, and Felipe, his brothers.
Baridon, Fita Gilly de, owner of a dispensary.
 Claudia, her high-school-age daughter.
Baridon, Luigi, old-timer.
 Three children.
Baridon, Marco, employee of the electric company in La Paz.
 Rosa Collet, his wife, school administrator and teacher.
 Nicolás (his "adopted" son) and four daughters.
Baridon, Oscar, owner of the Girasol appliance store in La Paz.
 Alicia, his wife.
 Two children, one "adopted."

Baridon, Renato, Junta de Gobierno president.

Baridon-Charbonier, Carlos, old-timer.

Enrique Baridon and Inés Charbonier, his parents.

Lidia, his daughter (one of fifteen children).

Benabou, Pierre, head of the INTA (National Institute for Agricultural Technology) office in La Paz.

Bert, María Baridon de, resident of La Paz who is married to a Catholic and has traveled outside the community.

Bouissa, Bruno, old-timer.

Bounous, Adolfo, owner of small advertising firm in Buenos Aires.

Eside, his wife, sister of Dora de Micol.

Marisa, his daughter.

Fabio, his son.

Albertina Bounous, his sister in Paraná.

Bounous, Albertina, employee in provincial office and schoolteacher in Paraná, separated from her husband.

Angelina and Benita, her "adopted" daughters.

Two sons, one named Manuel.

One daughter.

Adolfo Bounous, her brother.

Cagliero, Franco, Catholic priest in La Paz.

Carolina (Doña), neighbor of Ernestina Prochet in La Paz.

Cerutti family, owners of a general store and bar, who also rent land to Miguel Moreno.

Coisson, Juan, Animal Health Office inspector.

Hilda Costantino, his wife.

Two sons.

De Pereda, Laura, gynecologist and obstetrician in La Paz, divorced.

One daughter.

Eckstein, Umberto, retired estanciero now living in La Paz.

His wife.

Two granddaughters.

Guillermo, his peon.

Emilia, high school student in La Paz and boarder at Elsa de Prochet's house, lives in San Sebastiano.

Galdós (Sra.), head of a women's charity group in La Paz.

García, Hernán, policeman.

His wife and four children.

García, María Carmen, daughter of a peon family in Barrio La Costa in La Paz.

Five brothers and sisters.

Gilly, Alberto, estanciero, newlywed.

Elvira Musset, his bride.

Gilly, Italo, owner of the Gillys' general store.

Inés, his wife.

Stefano, his son.

Tullio, his brother.

Fita, his sister.

Gilly, Tullio, secretary of the Junta de Gobierno.
Iolanda Avondet, his wife.
Two sons, one "adopted" doing military service.
Two daughters, both married to the owners of a shop in La Paz.
Italo, his brother.
Fita, his sister.
González, Gabriel, peon in San Sebastiano.
Teresa, his wife.
Two sons and three daughters.
Guzmán, Rodolfo, lawyer in La Paz.
His wife and two daughters.
Antonio (Toni) Howard, his partner.
Hernández, former member of the Junta de Gobierno.
Hernández, Joaquín, local historian of San Sebastiano and La Paz and writer for the local newspaper.
Howard, Antonio (Toni), lawyer in La Paz.
Marina Merati, his wife, pediatrician in La Paz.
Jaime and Fernando, his adopted sons.
Eduardo and Lora Howard, his parents.
Rodolfo Guzmán, his partner.
Juana, his live-in babysitter.
Rosa, his part-time babysitter.
His brother and sister and his uncle.
Howard, Eduardo, old-timer, estanciero in San Sebastiano who lives in La Paz.
Lora Muir, his wife.
Antonio (Toni), his son.
One other son and one daughter.
Jorge, streetcleaner in La Paz.
José, churros vendor in La Paz.
José and Julio, peons Aldo Prochet usually hires.
Koenig, Baltasar, estanciero.
López, Juan, in charge of water sanitation.
López, Zurita, employee in the statistics office at the 9 de Julio Hospital in La Paz.
Lorenzo, Rosa, social worker at the Social Services Office in La Paz.
Losada, Isidora Saavedra de, clerk in municipal office in La Paz.
Her husband and four children.
Luna, Raquel de, old woman with no family who lives at the San Sebastiano Home for the Elderly. In the narrative, a passenger of officer García.
Malvasio, Filipa de, wife of a peon.
Pedro, her husband.
One son and one daughter.
Martinelli, Cesare, landowner, lawyer, and politician in La Paz.
Micol, Oscar, Waldensian pastor in La Paz and San Sebastiano.
Dora Cabrera, his wife, schoolteacher in La Paz.

Zully, Claudia, and Vera, their daughters.
Mirta, their "adopted" daughter.
Tango, their collie dog.
Montañes, Diego, radio announcer at Radio La Paz.
Morales, Luis, employee in Prefect's Office in La Paz.
His wife, employee in public telephone phone office in San Sebastiano.
Moreno, Miguel, peon in San Sebastiano.
His wife, twelve children, and two grandchildren.
Orlando, member of the Junta de Gobierno.
Orlando, Lucio, customer at the butcher shop.
Orlando, Xavier, student at village school, from peon family.
Pascal, Annina, secretary for Howard and Guzmán's law firm, and former
    university student in Córdoba.
Prochet, Aldo, estanciero.
Elsa Martínez, his wife, keeps house and boarders in La Paz.
Antonio, his son, high school student in La Paz.
Miguel, his son, university student in Rosario.
Lucia, his daughter, wife of Domenico Antonini.
Amalia, his sister.
Attilio, his brother.
Prochet, Ernestina, housekeeper and seamstress in La Paz.
Liliana, her sister.
Esteban, her brother.
Italo, her brother.
Andrés, her brother.
Prochet, Esteban, old-timer.
Prochet, Piero, estanciero.
Pujol, Luis, employee of INTA (National Institute for Agricultural Technol-
    ogy) and producer of a radio program.
His wife and one daughter.
Rodriguez, Pablo, of the Education Office for Department of La Paz.
Saavedra (Dr.), dentist in La Paz and San Sebastiano, helped set up the
    Junta de Gobierno.
Sabelli brothers, former members of Junta de Gobierno and now employees
    of the Gillys' store.
Salas, Neli Rivera de, principal at the village school.
Vicente, her husband, from the San Sebastiano Hospital and Home for
    the Elderly.
Sánchez family, wealthy creole estancieros.
Sánchez, Alicia, museum employee in La Paz.
Sánchez, Pío, retired peon.
His wife, fifteen children, and two children of relatives.
Santos, Jaime, son of a peon family.
Santucho, Felipe, owner of auto body shop.
Roberto, his cousin.
Sotos, neighbors of Dora de Micol's parents in Paraná.
Stringat, Hugo, head of dairy cooperative.

Vilas, Juana Inés, midwife.
  Her son.
Von Bergers, relatives of Toni Howard's.
Von Ruden, (Sra.), estanciera.
Weber, Olga de, museum employee in Paraná.
  Her husband and four children.

Bibliography

Primary Sources

Buenos Aires

Archivo General de la Nación. 1895 manuscript census for the department of La Paz in the province of Entre Ríos, carpetas 1057, 1058, 1060.
Dirección Nacional Estadística y Censo. "Censo nacional de población y vivienda," 1980, for San Sebastiano.
Offices of the Departamento General de Inmigración; Dirección General de Tierras, Inmigración, y Agricultura; Ministerio de Agricultura y Ganaderia; and Ministerio de Relaciónes Exteriores y Culto.

Paraná

Archivo de la Dirección General del Catastro de la Provincia de Entre Ríos, Ministerio de Hacienda, Economía y Obras Públicas: Departamento de Topografía.
Archivo Histórico de la Provincia de Entre Ríos: División Gobierno.
Public Health Office, Province of Entre Ríos.

La Paz and San Sebastiano

La Paz: Museo Histórico; Oficina de Registro Civil; Registro de Propiedad; Radio La Paz; Instituto Nacional de Tecnología Agropecuaria; Howard and Guzmán law firm; 9 de Julio Hospital; and Waldensian Church.
San Sebastiano: Comisaría; San Sebastiano elementary school; and private collections.

Italy

Archivio Tavola Valdese, Torre Pellice, province of Turin.
Municipal Archives of Torre Pellice and Bobbio Pellice, province of Turin.
 Esteri archives (including *nulla osta*, or passport applications).
———. Municipal censuses, 1858–1911.
———. Cadastral records.

Selected Secondary Sources

Adamo, Francesco, et al., eds. *Ricerche sulla regione metropolitana di Torino: Il Pinerolese.* 2 vols. Turin, 1971.

Alexander, Robert J. *Juan Domingo Perón: A History.* Boulder, Colo., 1979.

Amnesty International. *Report of an Amnesty International Mission to Argentina, 6–15 November 1976.* London, 1977.

Andrews, George Reid. *The Afro-Argentines of Buenos Aires, 1800–1900.* Madison, Wisc., 1980.

Argentine Republic, Comisión Directiva del Censo. *Segundo censo de la República Argentina, mayo 10 de 1895.* 3 vols. Buenos Aires, 1898.

Argentine Republic, Ministerio de Bienestar Social, Secretaría de Estado de Salud Pública. "Enfermedad de Chagas-Mazza," *Educación para la Salud,* series 2, no. 9 (Buenos Aires, 1977).

Armand-Hugon, Augusto. *Torre Pellice: Dieci secoli di storia e di vicende.* Torre Pellice, 1958.

Baily, Samuel L. "The Adjustment of Italian Immigrants in Buenos Aires and New York, 1870–1914," *American Historical Review* 88(2) (1983), 281–305.

————. "Chain Migration of Italians to Argentina: Case Studies of the Agnonesi and the Sirolesi," *Studi Emigrazione,* anno 19, no. 65 (Mar. 1982), 73–91.

————. "Marriage Patterns and Immigrant Assimilation in Buenos Aires, 1882–1923," *Hispanic American Historical Review* 60 (Feb. 1980), 32–48.

————. "The Role of Two Newspapers and the Assimilation of the Italians in Buenos Aires and São Paulo, 1893–1913," *International Migration Review* 12(3) (1978), 321–40.

Boletín de la Oficina Central de Colonización de Entre Ríos.

Briani, Vittorio. *Emigrazione e lavoro italiano all'estero: Elementi per un repertorio bibliografico generale.* Rome, 1967. This work has appeared with a new introduction and supplemental bibliography by Francesco Cordasco as *Italian Immigrants Abroad: A Bibliography on the Italian Experience Outside Italy in Europe, the Americas, Australia, and Africa.* Detroit, 1979.

Castronovo, Valerio. *Economia e società in Piemonte dall'Unità al 1914.* Milan, 1969.

Cogo, Joel, et al. "Estudio realizado por la Agencia de Extensión Agropecuaria La Paz en la Colonia Oficial no. 14" (La Paz, 1966?; in mimeo).

Coïsson, Jean. *Monographie sur le développement intellectuel dans nos Vallées pendant les 50 dernières années—Instruction primaire—Population légale des Vallées Vaudoises au 31 déc. 1897 comparée à celle de mai 1844* (Torre Pellice, Besson, 1898).

Collier, David, ed. *The New Authoritarianism in Latin America.* Princeton, N.J., 1979.

Córdoba, Estanislao Nestor. *Apuntes históricos sobre la ciudad de La Paz y su Departamento*. Paraná, 1976.

Dealy, Glen Caudill. *The Public Man: An Interpretation of Latin American and Other Catholic Countries*. Amherst, Mass., 1977.

Dirección General de Inmigración. *Resumen estadístico del movimiento migratorio en la República Argentina, años 1857–1924*. Buenos Aires, 1925.

Dore, Grazia. *Bibliografia per la storia dell'emigrazione italiana in America*. Rome, 1956.

Favoino, Giovanni María, and Antonio Bufardeci. *Gli Italiani nella Provincia di Entre Ríos*. Paraná, 1914.

Ganz-Bert, Emilio, and E. Rostan. *Il centenario della colonizzazione valdese nel Río de la Plata*. Torre Pellice, 1959.

Germani, Gino. *Estructura social de la Argentina*. Buenos Aires, 1955.

————. *Política y sociedad en una época de transición de la sociedad tradicional a la sociedad de las masas*. Buenos Aires, 1962.

Gillespie, Richard. *Soldiers of Perón: Argentina's Montoneros*. Oxford, 1982.

Giunta per l'inchiesta agraria e sulle condizioni della classe agricola. *Atti della Giunta* . . . . 15 vols. Rome, 1879–1884.

Gori, Gaston. *La pampa sin gaucho*. Buenos Aires, 1952.

Guimarães, Roberto P. "Understanding Support for Terrorism Through Survey Data: The Case of Argentina, 1973." In Frederick C. Turner and José Enrique Miguens, eds., *Juan Perón and the Reshaping of Argentina*. Pittsburgh, 1983.

Hernández, José. *The Gaucho Martín Fierro*. English trans., Albany, N.Y., 1974; original Spanish ed., 1972.

Instituto Nacional de Antropología. *Cultura tradicional del área del Paraná Medio*. Buenos Aires, 1984.

Istituto Centrale di Statistica. *Annali di statistica*, anno 94, series 8, vol. 17 (Rome, 1965): *Sviluppo della popolazione italiana dal 1861 al 1961*.

Jalla, Pierluigi. *Le Valli Valdesi: Problemi economici e di emigrazione*. Torre Pellice, 1966?

Jefferson, Mark. *Peopling the Argentine Pampa*. New York, 1926.

Larden, Walter. *Estancia Life*. Detroit, 1974; original ed., London, 1911.

Lewis, Oscar. *Five Families: Mexican Case Studies in the Culture of Poverty*. New York, 1959.

Luchenio, Angela E. *Formación moral y cívica 3*. Buenos Aires, 1981.

Luraghi, Raimondo. *Agricoltura, industria e commercio in Piemonte dal 1848 al 1861 (Comitato torinese dell'Istituto per la Storia del Risorgimento*, n.s. 5, Turin, 1967).

Mafud, Julio. *Psicología de la viveza criolla*. Buenos Aires, 1965.

Maggi-Pasquet, Elio. "La colonia San Gustavo," *Boletín de la Sociedad Sudamericana de Historia Valdese* 11(3) (Aug. 15, 1937), 87–97.

Marini, Ana María. "Women in Contemporary Argentina," *Latin American Perspectives*, issue 15, 4(4) (Fall 1977), 114–20.

Martínez Estrada, Ezequiel. *X-Ray of the Pampa.* English trans., Austin, Tex., 1971; original Spanish ed., Buenos Aires, 1933.

Melano, Giuseppe. *La popolazione di Torino e del Piemonte nel secolo xix.* Turin, 1961.

Nariton Monnet, Alice. "Il problema della montagna nella Val Pellice." Diss., Scuola Assistenti Sociali, Turin, 1953–54.

Nunca Más, the Report of the Argentine National Commission on the Disappeared. New York, 1986.

Panettieri, José. *Inmigración en la Argentina.* Buenos Aires, 1970.

Pérez Amuchástegui, A. J. *Mentalidades argentinas, 1860–1930.* 3d ed. Buenos Aires, 1972.

Peyret, Alejo. *Una visita a las colonias de la República Argentina.* Buenos Aires, 1889.

Pittavino, Arnaldo. *Storia di Pinerolo e del Pinerolese.* 2 vols. Milan, 1963–66.

Pons, Teofilo G. *Cento anni fa alle Valli: Il problema dell'emigrazione.* Torre Pellice, 1956.

Recchini de Lattes, Zulma L., et al. *Migraciónes en la Argentina: Estudio de las migraciónes internas e internacionales, basado en datos censales, 1869–1960.* Buenos Aires, 1969.

Reula, Filiberto. *Historia de Entre Ríos: Política, étnica, económica, social, cultural y moral.* 3 vols. Santa Fe, Argentina, 1963–71.

Reynal O'Connor, Arturo. *Por las colonias.* Buenos Aires, 1921.

Ríos, María del Carmen, et al. "Entre Ríos, fronteras naturales e historia (1883–1903)" (typed manuscript, 1974).

Romero, José Luis. *Argentina: Imágenes y perspectivas.* Buenos Aires, 1956.

Ruggiero, Kristin. "Gringo and Creole: Foreign and Native Values in a Rural Argentine Community," *Journal of Interamerican Studies and World Affairs* 24(2) (May 1982), 163–82.

———. "Italians in Argentina." Ph.D. diss., Indiana University, 1979.

———. "Social and Psychological Factors in Migration from Italy to Argentina." In Ira Glazier and Luigi De Rosa, eds., *Migration Across Time and Nations: Population Mobility in Historical Contexts.* New York, 1986.

Scobie, James R. *Argentina: A City and a Nation.* 2d ed. New York, 1971.

———. *Buenos Aires: Plaza to Suburb, 1870–1910.* New York, 1974.

———. *Revolution on the Pampas: A Social History of Argentine Wheat, 1860–1910.* Austin, Tex., 1964.

Seymour, Richard Arthur. *Pioneering in the Pampas.* London, 1869.

Slatta, Richard W. *Gauchos and the Vanishing Frontier.* Lincoln, Nebr., 1983.

Sociedad Rural. Argentina, Buenos Aires, *Anales . . . , 1890.* Buenos Aires, 1891.

Solberg, Carl E. *Immigration and Nationalism: Argentina and Chile, 1890–1914.* Austin, Tex., 1970.

———. "Mass Migrations in Argentina, 1870–1970." In William H. Mc-

Neill and Ruth S. Adams, eds., *Human Migration, Patterns and Policies.* Bloomington, Ind., 1978.

——. "Peopling the Prairies and the Pampas: The Impact of Immigration on Argentine and Canadian Agrarian Development, 1870–1930," *Journal of Interamerican Studies and World Affairs* 24(2) (May 1982), 131–61.

Szuchman, Mark D. "The Limits of the Melting Pot in Urban Argentina: Marriage and Integration in Córdoba, 1869–1909," *Hispanic American Historical Review* 57 (Feb. 1977), 24–40.

——. *Mobility and Integration in Urban Argentina: Córdoba in the Liberal Era.* Austin, Tex., 1980.

Timerman, Jacobo. *Prisoner Without a Name, Cell Without a Number.* New York, 1981.

Tourn, N. *I Valdesi in America.* Turin, 1906; published by the Comitato "I Valdesi all'Estero" for the Exposition of Milan of 1906.

Tron, Ernesto. *Historia de los Valdenses.* Colonia Valdense, Uruguay, 1952.

Tron, Ernesto, and Emilio H. Ganz. *Historia de las colonias valdenses sudamericanas en su primer centenario (1858–1958).* Colonia Valdense, Uruguay, 1958.

Tron, Levy. *Colonia Iris en sus primeros 25 anos, 1901–1926.* Jacinto Arauz, 1926.

Turner, Frederick C., and José Enrique Miguens, eds. *Juan Perón and the Reshaping of Argentina.* Pittsburgh, 1983.

Vázquez-Presedo, Vicente. *Estadísticas históricas argentinas (comparadas), primera parte 1875–1914.* Buenos Aires, 1971.

Watts, George B. *The Waldenses in the New World.* Durham, N.C., 1941.

Newspapers

Argentina

Clarín (Buenos Aires).
Buenos Aires Herald (Buenos Aires).
La Opinión de Entre Ríos (Paraná).

Italy

L'Avvisatore Alpino (Torre Pellice).
La Buona Novella (Turin).
L'Écho des Vallées (Torre Pellice/Pinerolo).
L'Eco delle Alpi Cozie (Pinerolo).

Index

Library of Congress Cataloging-in-Publication Data

Ruggiero, Kristin Hoffman.
   And here the world ends: the life of an Argentine village /
Kristin Hoffman Ruggiero.
      p.   cm.
   Bibliography: p.
   Includes index.
   ISBN 0-8047-1379-0 (alk. paper)
   1. Colonia San Sebastiano (Argentina)—History.   2. Colonia San
Sebastiano (Argentina)—Social life and customs.   3. Waldenses—
Argentina—Colonia San Sebastiano—History.   I. Title.
F3011.C653R83   1988
982'.76—dc19   87-20311
                                                        CIP